CALIFORNIA CIVIL TRIALBOOK

RICHARD J. WHARTON
Associate Clinical Professor of Law
University of San Diego School of Law
Member, California Bar
U.S. Court of Appeals for the District of Columbia
U.S. District Court for the Southern District of California

ROGER S. HAYDOCK
Professor of Law
William Mitchell College of Law
Former Visiting Professor
University of San Diego School of Law

JOHN O. SONSTENG
Professor of Law
William Mitchell College of Law
Faculty, National Institute for Trial Advocacy

LAW SCHOOL AND CLE EDITION

WEST PUBLISHING COMPANY
St. Paul, Minnesota, 1990

COPYRIGHT © 1990
By
WEST PUBLISHING CO.

ISBN 0-314-77290-1

*To
Joyce (A.L.J.)*

INTRODUCTION

The California Civil TRIALBOOK provides an innovative system and a comprehensive approach to the preparation and presentation of a case for trial. This notebook is designed to be a case construction guide, a trial primer and advocacy refresher, and a resource manual of trial theories, tactics, and techniques. This strategic system provides you with a structure and analytical approach to trial advocacy that will both improve your trial performance and increase the chances of obtaining a favorable decision for your client.

This TRIALBOOK has been designed to be used in all California civil jury and court trials. Each major facet of preparation and trial practice appears in a separate chapter. A presentation of the applicable rules, procedures, and law and an explanation of recognized strategies, tactics, and techniques follow in a summary format. An analysis of ethical guidelines and standards is included to provide depth and balance. Each chapter also includes a set of worksheets that are helpful in preparing each portion of the pre-trial and trial proceedings.

This integrated system attempts to present a simplified and thorough approach to the preparation and presentation of the trial of a case. The tactics and theories have been selected for inclusion based upon their success during trial, our litigation and teaching experience, the advice of experienced trial lawyers, the usable empirical research available, and common sense. The approaches and strategies listed in this book detail the factors that need to be considered in trial advocacy and provide an orderly system for implementing trial tactics and techniques.

The format of this TRIALBOOK has been designed to be flexible. It is also designed to be read in one or two sittings so that one can get the full picture of how each area of pre-trial preparation and trial practice fit together. After the first read-through, one may go back over each section and work on specific areas using the forms and worksheets. Space is available in each chapter for ideas and insights that you have as you use and apply the materials. This space may also be used to include notes regarding local practice, procedure, and case law which affect trial advocacy. Forms have been provided which provide a guide to the planning and organization of a case. The ring binder allows you to three-hole punch copies of rules, statutes, cases, and other materials and create one source for all your trial information. You may create one general trial notebook or a specific notebook for an individual trial, or a combination of the two.

We view this book as a starting point and a guide. No one system serves all purposes for all trial lawyers. We encourage you to adapt it for your own use and make it a part of every trial preparation and presentation. You may revise, add or delete any of the sections, outlines, checklists, or forms to suit your practice. This book, which adds a new dimension to the California trial literature, will be most useful when used by you in a way that meets your specific needs and individual preferences. It may be used in conjunction with other publications which may give more in-depth treatment of specific areas.

No one book can claim to be an all-inclusive source on why, how and when to do it. The presentation of a case depends upon many variables including the available legal theories, the facts, the witnesses, and the individual lawyer's abilities. A book which aspires to be a thorough coverage of all the available alternative approaches would be enormous. This book does, however, address all major facets of trial practice in a systemized format.

Lawyers at all levels of experience will find this TRIALBOOK very useful. Novice lawyers will learn what they need to know to plan and try a case competently. Attorneys with some experience will find valuable suggestions and approaches to effective trial practice. Experienced lawyers will read about new ideas and insights about trial advocacy. With all the demands placed on the limited time of practitioners it is impossible to do all of the preparation we would like to or believe we should do to plan for trial properly. *The California Civil TRIALBOOK* will assist you in using your time more efficiently and economically.

We view trial practice as exciting and fun as well as stressful and frustrating. We hope and believe *The California Civil TRIALBOOK* will make your practice more enjoyable, rewarding, and successful.

ACKNOWLEDGEMENTS

This California Civil TRIALBOOK represents a joint effort by many individuals who suggested ideas, made revisions, prodded us on, and assisted us in a variety of ways.

We thank, again, all those individuals acknowledged in the first edition of *Trialbook*. Their contributions and assistance have made this book a reality. We would also like to acknowledge and thank the people who helped bring *The California Civil TRIALBOOK* to fruition.

Lisa Zember, then a student at the University of San Diego School of Law and now an attorney in private practice, provided valuable assistance by organizing materials and helping with the first stage of editing.

A special acknowledgement goes to Rosemary Getty, who did the word processing of the many drafts of the book. Her invaluable assistance is greatly appreciated. Leah Holzman provided valuable assistance by helping to design and prepare many of the forms and assisted with word processing.

Our editors at West Publishing Company provided invaluable assistance with the format and publication of this book.

Our clients afforded us the opportunities to develop our approach to trial practice.

Our colleagues provided their ideas and suggestions regarding this venture.

Our families, who provided much more than support and to whom we owe the most, deserve much more than we can ever acknowledge.

*

ABOUT THE AUTHORS

Richard J. Wharton is Associate Clinical Professor of Law at the University of San Diego School of Law. He has taught and practiced civil litigation for over seventeen years. Professor Wharton has developed and taught a comprehensive pre-trial and trial advocacy course to over 2,000 students at the University of San Diego where he also directs the Environmental Law Clinic. He has successfully litigated numerous civil jury trials and as director of the Environmental Law Clinic he supervised law students in litigating major environmental cases.

Roger S. Haydock is a Professor of Law at William Mitchell College of Law in Minnesota. He has over twenty years of teaching and practice experience in civil litigation and trial practice, including practicing and counseling with the national law firm of Robins, Kaplan, Miller and Ciresi, with offices in San Francisco and Newport Beach. Professor Haydock has taught continuing legal education and National Institute for Trial Advocacy courses in numerous states including California. He has authored and co-authored several national practice books, including *Fundamentals of Pretrial Litigation* (West), *Discovery Practice* (Little, Brown), *Motion Practice* (Little, Brown), and *Negotiation Practice* (John Wiley).

John O. Sonsteng is a Professor of Law at William Mitchell College of Law. He has over twenty-two years of teaching and practice experience in trial advocacy, including many years of criminal law prosecution and defense practice in Minnesota. Professor Sonsteng is a Regional Director of the National Institute for Trial Advocacy and has taught NITA and CLE courses in California and throughout the country. He has co-authored, with Roger Haydock, *Trial: Theories, Tactics, Techniques* (West), *Trialbook* (West) and *Trial Advocacy Exercise Cases and Materials* (NITA).

*

TABLE OF CONTENTS

		Page
CHAPTER 1 CASE ANALYSIS AND PLANNING		1–1

Sec.
1.1	Client Interview	1–2
1.2	Attorney Fees	1–2
1.3	Referral Fees	1–2
1.4	Evaluating Facts and the Law	1–2
1.5	Procedural Posture	1–2
1.6	Proof	1–3
1.7	Theories	1–3
1.8	The Theme	1–3
1.9	Legal Research	1–4
1.10	Fact Gathering	1–4
1.11	Pleadings	1–4
	A. Traditional Typed Pleadings	1–4
	B. Form Pleading	1–5
1.12	Support Staff	1–5
1.13	Systemized Approach	1–5
1.14	Evidence	1–5
1.15	Planning the Case Around Jury Instructions	1–5
1.16	Planning the Case Around the Closing Argument	1–5
1.17	Settlement Considerations	1–5
1.18	Court or Jury Trial	1–6
1.19	Preparation and Presentation of Court Trial	1–6
	A. Opening	1–6
	B. Evidentiary Rulings	1–6
	C. Introduction of Evidence	1–6
	D. No Side Bar Conference	1–7
	E. Closing Argument	1–7
	F. Overall Approach	1–7
	Client Information General	Form 1–1
	Case Construction and Evaluation Worksheet	Form 1–2
	Tentative Trial Schedule	Form 1–3
	Proof of Facts Worksheet	Form 1–4
	Legal Theories Worksheet	Form 1–5
	Theme Selection Worksheet	Form 1–6
	Legal Research Worksheet	Form 1–7
	Summons and Complaint Worksheet	Form 1–8
	Pleading Ultimate Facts Constituting a Cause of Action	Form 1–9
	Prayer for Relief	Form 1–10
	Answer and Response Worksheet	Form 1–11
	Closing Argument Planning Worksheet	Form 1–12
	Negotiation Worksheet	Form 1–13

CHAPTER 2 DISCOVERY		2–1
2.1	Purposes and Scope	2–2
2.2	Planning Discovery	2–3
	A. Available Discovery Devices	2–3
	B. Typical Sequence of Formal Discovery in a Personal Injury Case	2–3

xi

Sec.			Page
2.3	Informal Investigation		2–4
	A.	Information From the Client	2–4
	B.	Information From Documents	2–4
	C.	Information From Witnesses	2–4
2.4	Interrogatories C.C.P. § 2030		2–5
	A.	Timing	2–5
	B.	Subject Matter	2–5
	C.	Number of Interrogatories C.C.P. § 2030(1)	2–6
	D.	Form and Format C.C.P. § 2030(5)	2–6
	E.	Service of Interrogatories	2–6
	F.	Answers to Interrogatories	2–6
	G.	Grounds for Objections	2–6
	H.	Failure to Respond and Motion to Compel	2–7
	I.	Use of Interrogatories at Trial C.C.P. § 2030(n)	2–7
2.5	Deposition Practice		2–7
	A.	Why Should a Deposition be Taken?	2–7
	B.	Planning a Deposition	2–8
	C.	Preparing to Take a Deposition	2–9
	D.	Beginning the Deposition	2–10
	E.	What Instructions Should Be Given to Deponent?	2–10
	F.	How Should Objections Be Handled?	2–10
	G.	Questioning Tactics and Strategies	2–11
	H.	Representing the Deponent	2–12
2.6	Written Depositions C.C.P. § 2028		2–13
	A.	Procedure for Use	2–13
	B.	Advantages of Written Depositions	2–13
	C.	Disadvantages of Written Depositions	2–13
2.7	Production of Documents, Things and Places C.C.P. § 2031		2–13
	A.	Manner of Request and Demand	2–14
	B.	Responses C.C.P. § 2031(f)	2–14
2.8	Requests for Admissions		2–14
	A.	Subject Matter	2–14
	B.	Number of Requests	2–15
	C.	Form and Format	2–15
	D.	Responses to Request	2–15
	E.	Failure to Respond	2–15
	F.	Grounds for Objections	2–15
	G.	Use of Admission at Trial C.C.P. § 2033(n)	2–16
2.9	Physical or Mental Examination C.C.P. § 2032		2–16
	A.	Who May Be Examined	2–16
	B.	When Appropriate	2–16
	C.	Procedure to Be Followed	2–16
	D.	Response to Demand for Physical Examination	2–16
2.10	Limiting Discovery		2–16
	A.	Privileged Matters Not Discoverable	2–17
	B.	Attorney Trial Preparation Materials (Attorney Work Product) Not Discoverable	2–17
	C.	Protective Orders	2–17
2.11	Enforcing Discovery Requests		2–17
	A.	Initial Failure to Respond	2–17
	B.	Continued Failure to Respond	2–18
	C.	Seeking Sanctions	2–18
2.12	Avoiding Monetary Sanction and Terminating Sanction		2–19
	A.	Respond Promptly to All Requests for Discovery	2–19
	B.	Meet and Confer Whenever Possible	2–19

Table of Contents   **xiii**

Sec.   Page
2.12 Avoiding Monetary Sanction and Terminating Sanction—Continued
    C. Do Not Withhold Evidence 2–19
    D. Comply With Court Orders 2–19
    Discovery Worksheet .... Form 2–1
    Discovery Plan .... Form 2–2
    Factual Investigation Worksheet .... Form 2–3
    Interrogatories Worksheet .... Form 2–4
    Deposition Worksheet .... Form 2–5
    Production of Documents/Things Worksheet .... Form 2–6
    Request for Admission Worksheet .... Form 2–7
    Physical Examination Worksheet for Plaintiff Seeking Personal Injury Damages C.C.P. Section 2032 .... Form 2–8

CHAPTER 3 TRIAL FRAMEWORK 3–1
3.1 Analysis of Self 3–1
    A. Verbal Analysis 3–1
    B. Mental Analysis 3–1
    C. Physical Analysis 3–2
    D. Coping With Stress 3–2
3.2 Analysis of Opponent 3–2
3.3 Analysis of the Judge 3–3
3.4 Analysis of Courtroom 3–3
3.5 Analysis of Court Personnel 3–3
3.6 Trial Brief 3–3
    A. Need for a Trial Brief 3–3
    B. Contents of Trial Brief 3–4
3.7 Arriving in the Assigned Court and Chambers Conference 3–4
    A. Court Personnel 3–4
    B. Conduct in Chambers Conference 3–5
3.8 Attorney's Trial Conduct 3–6
    A. Avoiding Familiarity 3–6
    B. Names 3–6
    C. Interruptions 3–6
    D. Approaching the Witness/Bench 3–6
    E. To Stand or Sit 3–6
    F. "Off the Record" 3–7
    G. Demeanor 3–7
    H. Dress 3–7
    I. Drama 3–7
    Opposing Lawyer Log .... Form 3–1
    Judge Log .... Form 3–2
    Courtroom Log .... Form 3–3
    Clerk Log .... Form 3–4
    Bailiff Log .... Form 3–5
    Trial Brief Worksheet .... Form 3–6

CHAPTER 4 MOTIONS 4–1
4.1 Scheduling a Case 4–1
    A. Superior Court Trial Settings: Basic Steps 4–2
    B. Setting Cases in Municipal and Justice Court 4–2
    C. Assignment to Trial Department 4–2
4.2 Judge Removal 4–3
    A. Be Prepared for a Peremptory Challenge 4–3
    B. Challenge With Caution 4–3
4.3 Motion in Limine 4–3
4.4 Motion to Amend Pleadings at Trial 4–4

Sec.		Page
4.5	Motion for Continuance	4-4
4.6	Motion to Strike	4-4
4.7	Motion to Admonish the Jury to Disregard the Testimony	4-5
4.8	Motion for Non-suit	4-5
4.9	Motion for Directed Verdict	4-5
4.10	Motion Argument Preparation	4-5
	A. Time	4-5
	B. Court Proceedings	4-6
	C. Memoranda	4-6
	D. Written Order	4-6
	E. Time and Manner of Making Motions	4-6
4.11	Motion Argument Presentation	4-6
	A. The Facts	4-6
4.12	Motion Argument Techniques	4-6
	A. Conversational Approach	4-6
	B. Preface	4-7
	C. Structure	4-7
	D. Substance of Argument	4-7
	E. The Law	4-7
	F. Factual Descriptions	4-7
	G. Notes	4-7
	H. Visual Aids	4-7
	I. Interruptions	4-8
	J. Candor and Compromise	4-8
	K. Questions by the Judge	4-8
	L. Involving the Judge	4-8
	Motion In Limine Worksheet	Form 4-1
	Trial Motion Worksheet	Form 4-2

CHAPTER 5 PREPARING FOR AND PRESENTATION OF EVIDENCE ... 5-1

Sec.		Page
5.1	Witness Logistics	5-3
	A. Excluding Witnesses at Trial	5-3
	B. Use of Interpreters	5-3
	C. Compelling Attendance for Testimony at Trial	5-3
5.2	Court Intervention	5-3
	A. Court Appointed Experts	5-3
	B. Court Witnesses	5-3
5.3	Expert Witnesses	5-4
	A. When to Use an Expert	5-4
	B. Who Is an Expert?	5-4
	C. Qualifying the Expert	5-4
	D. Knowing the Subject Area	5-4
	E. Preparing the Expert on the Law of the Case	5-4
	F. Preparing the Expert on the Facts of the Case	5-4
	G. Opinion Testimony	5-4
	H. Sources of Information	5-4
	I. Hypothetical Questions	5-4
	J. Questions and Answers	5-5
	K. Opinions	5-5
	L. Explaining Technical Terms	5-5
5.4	Preparation of Witnesses	5-5
	A. Meeting the Witness	5-5
	B. Gathering Information	5-5
	C. Witness Satisfaction and Effectiveness	5-5
	D. Preparation for Direct and Cross-Examination	5-6
	E. Providing the Witness With Guidelines for Testifying	5-6

Sec.			Page
5.4	Preparation of Witnesses—Continued		
	F.	Witness' Dress	5–7
	G.	Rehearsal	5–7
	H.	Ensure Attendance	5–7
	I.	Client Guidelines	5–7
5.5	Problems With Foundation		5–7
	A.	Foundation Questions	5–7
	B.	Foundation Checklist	5–8
5.6	Types of Exhibits		5–9
	A.	Real Evidence	5–9
	B.	Demonstrative Evidence	5–9
	C.	Visual Aids	5–9
5.7	Purposes		5–9
5.8	Relevancy Considerations		5–9
	A.	Threshold Test—Is the Exhibit Logically Relevant?	5–9
	B.	Is the Exhibit Legally Relevant?	5–9
5.9	Selecting Exhibits		5–10
5.10	Foundation for Exhibits		5–10
5.11	Legal Foundation		5–10
	A.	Tangible Objects and Properties (Including Products, Clothing, Appliances, and Weapons)	5–10
	B.	Chain of Custody	5–11
	C.	Documents	5–11
	D.	Business Correspondence (Including Letters, Memos, and Notes)	5–11
	E.	Business Records (Including any Memorandum, Report, Writing, or Data Compilation)	5–11
	F.	Copies	5–12
	G.	Electronic Recordings (Including Audio and Video Recordings)	5–12
	H.	Test Results (Including X-ray Films and Laboratory Analysis)	5–12
	I.	Photographs (Including Prints, Slides, and Movies)	5–12
	J.	Diagrams (Including Charts, Models, Drawings, Overhead Transparencies and Similar Illustrative Aids)	5–13
	K.	Past Recollection Record	5–13
	L.	Stipulations	5–13
	M.	Statements of Admissions in Judicial Proceedings	5–13
	N.	Discovery Information	5–13
	O.	Self-Authenticating Documents	5–13
5.12	Persuasive Foundation		5–14
5.13	Stipulating to Foundation		5–14
5.14	Exhibit Systems		5–14
5.15	Planning Introductions		5–14
	A.	Preparing the Witness	5–14
	B.	Preparing for Possible Objections	5–14
	C.	Supplementing Exhibits	5–15
5.16	Presentation and Delivery		5–15
	A.	Professional Presentation	5–15
	B.	Practical Problems	5–15
	C.	The Steps to Introduction of Exhibits	5–16
	D.	Variation in Word Usage	5–16
	E.	Leading Questions	5–17
	F.	Finessing the Foundation	5–17
	G.	Location	5–17
	H.	Voir Dire Examination	5–17
5.17	Offer and Use of Requests for Admissions		5–17
5.18	Offer and Use of Stipulations		5–17

Sec.		Page
5.19	Evidence Summaries	5–18
5.20	Judicial Notice	5–18
5.21	Matters to Be Heard Outside the Presence of the Jury	5–18
	Professional/Expert Witness Log	Form 5–1
	Expert Testimony Planning Worksheet	Form 5–2
	Witness Preparation Worksheet	Form 5–3
	Exhibit Selection Worksheet	Form 5–4
	Exhibit Foundation Worksheet	Form 5–5
	Trial Exhibits Chart	Form 5–6
	Exhibit Introduction Checklist	Form 5–7
	Trial Proof Worksheet	Form 5–8

CHAPTER 6 OBJECTIONS ... 6–1

6.1	Purposes	6–2
6.2	Preparation and Organization	6–2
	A. When to Object	6–2
	B. Examining Attorney	6–3
	C. Anticipating Evidentiary Problems	6–3
6.3	Objections Under California Evidence Code	6–3
6.4	Objections Made to Exclude Evidence	6–3
	A. Relevance Evid.C. §§ 210, 350–351	6–3
	B. Legal Relevance Evid.C. § 352	6–3
	C. Evidence Which Is Inadmissible Under the California Rules of Evidence	6–4
	D. Privileges Evid.C. §§ 930–1060	6–4
	E. Competence C.C.P. Section 701	6–6
	F. Lack of Foundation Evid.C. §§ 400–406	6–6
	G. Questioning by the Court Evid.C. § 775	6–6
	H. Opinion Testimony Evid.C. §§ 800–805	6–7
	I. Speculation Evid.C. §§ 702, 801	6–7
	J. Best Evidence Rule Evid.C. §§ 1500–1511	6–7
	K. Lack of Authentication Evid.C. §§ 1400–1454	6–7
	L. Hearsay Evid.C. § 1200	6–8
6.5	Objections to the Form of the Questions	6–10
	A. Leading Evid.C. §§ 764, 767	6–10
	B. Narrative Evid.C. § 765	6–11
	C. Asked and Answered Evid.C. § 774	6–11
	D. Cumulative Evid.C. § 352	6–11
	E. Vague, Ambiguous, Misleading, Confusing or Unintelligible Evid.C. § 765	6–11
	F. Multiple or Compound Questions Evid.C. § 765	6–11
	G. Assuming Facts Not in Evidence Evid.C. § 765	6–11
	H. Misstatement or Mischaracterization of Testimony or Evidence Evid.C. §§ 765, 774	6–11
	I. Argumentative Evid.C. § 765	6–11
	J. Improper Impeachment Evid.C. §§ 780, 785	6–11
	K. Beyond the Scope Evid.C. §§ 761, 773	6–11
6.6	Objections to Demonstrative Evidence	6–12
	A. Misleading, Inaccurate or Distorting Evid.C. § 352	6–12
	B. Lack of Foundation Evid.C. §§ 403–405	6–12
	C. Waste of Court's Time/Undue Delay Evid.C. § 352	6–12
	D. Evidence Does Not Aid or Assist Jury Evid.C. § 352	6–12
6.7	Objections During Jury Selection	6–12
	A. Mentioning Insurance Evid.C. § 1155	6–12
	B. Arguing or Indoctrinating Jurors About the Law	6–12
	C. Arguing Facts	6–12

Sec.		Page
6.8	Objections During Opening Statement	6–12
	A. Explaining the Law or Instructions	6–12
	B. Argumentative	6–12
	C. Mentioning Inadmissible Evidence	6–12
	D. Mentioning Unprovable Evidence	6–12
	E. Personal Opinions	6–13
	F. Misstating the Law	6–13
	G. Referring to Insurance Coverage	6–13
6.9	Objections During Closing Arguments	6–13
	A. Misstating Evidence	6–13
	B. Misstating Law and Quoting Instructions	6–13
	C. Personal Opinions	6–13
	D. Appealing to Jury's Bias or Prejudice	6–13
	E. Appealing to Jury's Pecuniary Interests	6–13
	F. Reference to Judgments Awarded in Similar Cases	6–13
	G. Personal Attacks on Parties and Counsel	6–13
	H. Prejudicial Arguments	6–13
6.10	Presentation and Delivery	6–13
	A. How to Object	6–13
	B. Motion to Strike	6–14
	C. Admonition to Disregard the Evidence	6–14
	D. Offers of Proof	6–14
	E. When an Offer of Proof Is Not Required	6–14
Appendix.	Common Legal Objections	A–1
	Objection Planning Worksheet	Form 6–1

CHAPTER 7 THE JURY SELECTION PROCESS ... 7–1

Sec.		Page
7.1	Description	7–2
7.2	Purposes	7–2
	A. Obtaining Information About the Jurors	7–2
	B. Determining Attitudes	7–2
	C. Disqualifying a Juror	7–2
	D. Establishing Rapport	7–2
	E. Other Uses of Jury Voir Dire	7–2
7.3	Procedure for Obtaining a Jury Trial	7–2
7.4	Preparation and Investigation	7–2
	A. Advance Investigation	7–2
	B. Develop a Theory for Selection	7–3
	C. Selection Considerations	7–3
7.5	Jury Selection Procedures	7–4
	A. Overview	7–4
	B. Voir Dire Procedures	7–4
	C. Jury Selection Topics to Be Discussed in Pre-trial Conference	7–4
	D. Voir Dire by Judge	7–4
	E. Voir Dire by Attorney	7–4
	F. Preliminary Instructions	7–5
7.6	Selection Process	7–5
	A. Generally	7–5
	B. Notes	7–5
	C. Addressing the Jurors	7–6
	D. Areas of Questioning	7–6
	E. Selection of Question Areas	7–6
	F. Types and Forms of Questions	7–6
	G. Conduct of Voir Dire	7–8
	H. Rehabilitation	7–8

Sec.		Page
7.7	Objecting to Improper Voir Dire Questions	7–8
	A. Improper Voir Dire	7–9
7.8	The Final Selection Process	7–9
	A. Challenge for Cause C.C.P. § 225(a)	7–9
	B. Peremptory Challenges	7–10
	C. Use of Client	7–11
	D. Alternative Jurors	7–11
	E. Making the Challenge	7–11
	F. Keeping Track of Challenges	7–11
	Jury Selection Worksheet	Form 7–1
	Jury Seating Chart	Form 7–2
	Jury Selection Chart	Form 7–3
	Jury Challenge Worksheet	Form 7–4

CHAPTER 8 OPENING STATEMENT 8–1

Sec.		Page
8.1	Purposes	8–2
8.2	What Can Be Presented	8–2
	A. Facts	8–2
	B. Argument	8–2
	C. Law	8–2
	D. A Fact Test	8–2
8.3	Preparation and Organization	8–3
	A. Knowing the Case	8–3
	B. Developing Issues and Themes	8–3
	C. Opening Statement Based on Closing Argument	8–3
	D. Anticipating Opposition's Positions	8–3
	E. Pretrial Rulings	8–3
	F. Selecting Visual Aids	8–3
	G. Order of Presentation	8–3
	H. When to Present or Reserve Opening Statement	8–4
	I. Written Outline or Detailed Script	8–4
	J. Practice	8–4
	K. Local Requirements	8–4
8.4	Structure of an Opening Statement	8–5
	A. Introduction	8–5
	B. Personalizing the Client	8–5
	C. Preliminary Remarks	8–5
	D. The Story	8–5
	E. The Scene and the Characters	8–5
	F. Conclusion	8–6
	G. Length	8–6
	H. An Opening Statement Test	8–6
8.5	Content of Opening Statement	8–6
	A. Detailed Information	8–6
	B. The Use of Exhibits	8–6
	C. References to the Law	8–6
	D. Case Weaknesses	8–7
	E. Qualifying Remarks	8–7
	F. Request for Verdict	8–7
	G. Understatement	8–7
	H. Overstatement	8–7
	I. Promises	8–7
	J. Improper Comments	8–8
8.6	Presentation and Delivery	8–8
	A. Manner	8–8
	B. Word Choice	8–9

Sec.		Page
8.6	Presentation and Delivery—Continued	
	C. Drama	8–9
	D. A Positive, Assertive Position	8–9
	E. Developing Style	8–9
	F. Observing the Jurors' Reaction	8–9
8.7	Objections and Motions	8–9
	A. Objections	8–9
	B. Motions on the Opening Statement	8–10
	Opening Statement Worksheet	Form 8–1

CHAPTER 9 DIRECT EXAMINATION 9–1

Sec.		Page
9.1	Purpose	9–2
9.2	The Order of Direct Examination	9–2
9.3	Preparation and Organization	9–2
	A. Considerations in Preparation	9–2
	B. Witness Selection and Preparation	9–2
	C. Order of Questions	9–3
	D. Exhibit Management	9–3
9.4	Presentation and Delivery	9–3
	A. Portraying a Story	9–3
	B. Parts of Direct Examination	9–4
	C. Conduct of the Attorney	9–4
	D. Enhancing the Credibility of the Witness	9–4
	E. The Questions	9–5
	F. Questions to Avoid	9–6
	G. Order of Witnesses	9–7
9.5	Types of Direct Examination	9–8
	A. Adverse Examinations and Hostile Witnesses	9–8
	B. Deposition Transcripts or Videotaped Depositions	9–8
9.6	Redirect Examination	9–8
	A. Question Format	9–8
	B. Limited Scope	9–8
	C. Reserving the Introduction of Evidence	9–8
	D. Refreshing the Witness' Recollection	9–9
	E. Foregoing Redirect	9–9
9.7	Avoiding Mistrials and Reversals	9–9
	A. Never Facilitate the Presentation of Perjured Testimony	9–9
	B. Do Not Willfully Conceal Evidence	9–9
	C. Prepare the Witness	9–9
	D. Instruct Witnesses to Avoid Contact With Jurors	9–9
	E. Do Not Allow Any Witness Under Your Control to Knowingly Testify Falsely	9–9
	F. Do Not Intentionally Mis-state or Cite the Law	9–9
	G. Do Not Assert Personal Knowledge of the Facts at Issue Unless Called as Witness	9–9
	Witness List	Form 9–1
	Direct Examination Outline	Form 9–2

CHAPTER 10 CROSS–EXAMINATION 10–1

Sec.		Page
10.1	Purposes	10–1
10.2	Preparation and Organization	10–2
	A. Background	10–2
	B. Anticipation	10–2
	C. Scope of Cross–Examination	10–2
	D. Credibility	10–2
	E. Should There Be a Cross–Examination?	10–2
	F. Prepare Written Questions in Advance	10–3

Sec.		Page
10.2	Preparation and Organization—Continued	
	G. Structure	10–3
	H. Attention	10–3
10.3	Presentation and Delivery	10–3
	A. Be Confident	10–3
	B. Do Not Repeat Direct Examination	10–3
	C. Lead the Witness	10–3
	D. Ask Simple, Short Questions	10–3
	E. Ask Factual Questions	10–3
	F. Control the Witness	10–3
	G. Maintain Composure	10–3
	H. Adopt an Appropriate Approach	10–3
	I. Stop When Finished	10–4
10.4	Expert Witnesses	10–4
10.5	Impeachment	10–4
	A. Sources of Impeachment	10–4
	B. Extrinsic Evidence of Prior Inconsistent Statement	10–5
	C. Cross-Examination of Character Witness	10–5
10.6	The Ten Commandments	10–5
10.7	Avoiding Mistrials and Reversals	10–6
	A. Do Not Ask Insinuating Questions or Use Innuendo	10–6
	B. Do Not Make Derogatory Remarks to the Witness	10–6
	Cross-Examination Outline	Form 10–1
	Cross-Examination Planning Worksheet	Form 10–2
	Impeachment by Prior Inconsistent Statement Worksheet	Form 10–3

CHAPTER 11 JURY INSTRUCTION AND CLOSING ARGUMENT — 11–1

Sec.		Page
11.1	Jury Instructions	11–2
	A. Understandable Jury Instructions	11–2
	B. Party's Right to Instructions	11–2
	C. Necessity to Submit Instructions	11–2
	D. Time for Submission	11–2
	E. Formal Requirements	11–2
	F. How to Prepare and Submit Jury Instructions	11–3
	G. Selection of Jury Instructions	11–3
11.2	Closing Argument	11–4
	A. Purposes	11–4
	B. Right to Closing Argument and Order of Argument	11–4
	C. What Can Be Argued	11–5
11.3	Preparation and Organization of Closing Argument	11–5
	A. Early Preparation	11–5
	B. Refining the Issues and Theme for the Case	11–5
	C. Jury Instructions	11–5
	D. Anticipate the Opponent's Position	11–6
	E. Select Visual Aids and Exhibits	11–6
	F. Written Outline or Detailed Script	11–6
	G. Practice	11–6
	H. Local Requirements	11–6
11.4	Structure of a Closing Argument	11–6
	A. Introduction	11–7
	B. Explanation of Purpose	11–7
	C. Argument	11–7
	D. Explanation of the Evidence	11–7
	E. Explanation of Law	11–8
	F. Conclusion	11–8
	G. Jury Participation	11–8

Sec.		Page
11.4	Structure of a Closing Argument—Continued	
	H. Length	11–8
	I. A Final Argument Test	11–9
11.5	Content of Closing Argument	11–9
	A. Analogies/Anecdotes	11–9
	B. Credibility of Witnesses	11–9
	C. Contradictions	11–9
	D. The Use of Exhibits and Visual Aids	11–9
	E. Burden of Proof	11–9
	F. Liability and Damages—Which to Argue First	11–10
	G. Case Weaknesses	11–10
	H. Attacking Opposition's Positions	11–10
	I. Broken Promises	11–10
	J. Non-facts	11–10
	K. Lie v. Mistake	11–10
	L. Rhetorical Questions	11–10
	M. Emotion v. Logic	11–10
	N. Avoiding Improper Comments	11–11
	O. Rebuttal	11–11
	P. Request for Verdict and Damages	11–11
11.6	Presentation and Delivery	11–11
11.7	Objections	11–12
	Request for Jury Instructions	Form 11–1
	Jury Instruction Worksheet	Form 11–2
	Closing Argument Worksheet	Form 11–3

CHAPTER 12 VERDICT AND POST VERDICT MOTIONS 12–1

Sec.		Page
12.1	Jury Deliberation Procedures	12–1
12.2	The Verdict	12–1
	A. General Verdict	12–1
	B. Special Verdict	12–2
	C. Reading of Verdict	12–2
	D. Entry of Verdict	12–2
12.3	Post Trial Motions	12–2
	A. Motion for Judgment Notwithstanding the Verdict	12–2
	B. Motion for a New Trial	12–2
	C. Motion to Vacate Judgment	12–3
	Post Trial Motion Worksheet	Form 12–1

*

Chapter 1
CASE ANALYSIS AND PLANNING

Table of Sections

Sec.
1.1 Client Interview.
1.2 Attorney Fees.
1.3 Referral Fees.
1.4 Evaluating Facts and the Law.
1.5 Procedural Posture.
1.6 Proof.
1.7 Theories.
1.8 The Theme.
1.9 Legal Research.
1.10 Fact Gathering.
1.11 Pleadings.
    A. Traditional Typed Pleadings.
    B. Form Pleading.
1.12 Support Staff.
1.13 Systemized Approach.
1.14 Evidence.
1.15 Planning the Case Around Jury Instructions.
1.16 Planning the Case Around the Closing Argument.
1.17 Settlement Considerations.
1.18 Court or Jury Trial.
1.19 Preparation and Presentation of Court Trial.
    A. Opening.
    B. Evidentiary Rulings.
    C. Introduction of Evidence.
    D. No Side Bar Conference.
    E. Closing Argument.
    F. Overall Approach.

Forms
1-1 Client Information General.
1-2 Case Construction and Evaluation Worksheet.
1-3 Tentative Trial Schedule.
1-4 Proof of Facts Worksheet.
1-5 Legal Theories Worksheet.
1-6 Theme Selection Worksheet.
1-7 Legal Research Worksheet.
1-8 Summon and Complaint Worksheet.
1-9 Pleading Ultimate Facts Constituting a Cause of Action.
1-10 Prayer for Relief.
1-11 Answer and Response Worksheet.
1-12 Closing Argument Planning Worksheet.
1-13 Negotiation Worksheet.

1.1 CLIENT INTERVIEW

The client interview provides the first source of facts and legal theories to initiate analysis of the case. The attorney needs to begin a systemized approach to trial preparation with the first client contact. See Form 1-1 Client Information.

1.2 ATTORNEY FEES

A written contract for attorney fees is now required in almost all cases. Contingency fee contracts must be in writing and must include a statement disclosing the contingent fee rate and a statement as to how disbursements and costs will affect the fee and the client's recovery. Bus. & Prof. C. § 6147.

1.3 REFERRAL FEES

Fee splitting agreements are permitted only if: (1) the client consents in writing to employment of the other attorney after a full written disclosure of the proposed division of fees and (2) the total fee charged by all attorneys is not increased solely by reason of the division of fees, and does not exceed reasonable compensation for all services they render to the client. Cal.Rules of Professional Conduct 2-108.

1.4 EVALUATING FACTS AND THE LAW

The theories supporting recovery or defenses need to be tested against the facts and law of the case. Arguments for and against the various positions should be reviewed to determine their strengths and weaknesses. Theories lacking factual or legal support will need to be revised or abandoned depending on the circumstances of that case. See Form 1-2 Case Construction and Evaluation Worksheet. This process should continue throughout the preparation of your case. From the beginning you need to:

1. Determine what facts you know to be true.

2. From the facts you know, determine the applicable law and possible causes of action.

3. After a preliminary review of facts and law, determine what further facts you need to know to satisfy the elements of the law.

4. Do further legal research to determine if there are any other legal theories or evidentiary considerations. You should then have a good idea of the applicable law and what facts you will have to prove and how you are going to get such evidence admitted.

5. Determine the best sources of the needed evidence.

6. Prepare a preliminary discovery plan that will provide a systematic method for obtaining all of the information you will need, and will lead to and result in access to the admissible evidence needed to prove up your case or disprove your opponent's case.

7. As soon as possible, determine if the case is subject to local "fast track" rules. If so, obtain the most recent edition of the applicable fast track rules and make a tentative calendar for the case which clearly sets forth the filing deadlines under the applicable fast track rules. Do this before you file the case.

8. Throughout this process, formulate your theme of the case. This is a continuous process. Do not jump to premature judgments.

1.5 PROCEDURAL POSTURE

The procedural posture of a case must be analyzed to determine timing and notice requirements. A tentative calendar scheduling the service of pleadings, taking of discovery, hearing of motions, and date of trial provides the initial structure for a case. See Form 1-3 Tentative Trial Schedule. The starting point for determining the procedural rules is to consult the latest edition of the California Code of Civil Procedure and Rules of the Court. In addition you *must* have the latest edition of the Local Rules of Court and any applicable Fast Track Rules for the court in which you contemplate filing your case. Do not take any procedural steps in your case without a complete review of these basic references. Make sure

Case Analysis and Planning

they are current, especially the Local Rules, which can change every few months. In preparing your tentative calendar, pay special attention to any applicable "Fast Track" rules of the court in which your case is filed.

1.6 PROOF

Outline and match the elements and requirements of proof with the facts to determine which facts support the claims or defenses and whether additional facts need to be gathered. See Form 1-4 Proof of Facts Worksheet.

Considerations include:

1. Which facts are necessary to prove the prima facie elements of a claim or defense?

2. Which facts will bolster the persuasive weight of the evidence?

3. Which facts will corroborate evidence?

4. How will a fact be proved? If a fact will be proven using testimony, who will prove it? If a fact will be proven using a document or exhibit, which document or exhibit will prove it?

5. When during the trial should a fact be proved? See Form 1-4 Proof of Facts Worksheet.

6. How will you obtain the facts necessary to prove your case? See Chapter 2 on Discovery.

1.7 THEORIES

Every case needs to be analyzed to determine the most appropriate legal theories and the most effective factual theories.

Legal Theories. Case law and statutory law will provide the elements for the available legal theories. In most cases, the appropriate legal precedent will be obvious. In other cases, the legal theories may need to be modified, analyzed, or created from analogous precedent. See Form 1-5 Legal Theories Worksheet.

Factual Theories. The facts of a case will usually be susceptible to various interpretations. One or more inferences may be drawn from direct and circumstantial evidence. Factual theories must be selected from the reasonable interpretations and favorable inferences. Factual theories must be consistent with the themes of a case, appropriate to the legal theories, and supported by the evidence.

Alternative Theories. Each case presents alternative legal and factual theories. The attorney will need to review and select the most appropriate theories. Several sequential theories may be selected. For example, in a contract case, the defense might be: There was no acceptance. If there was, the consideration was inadequate. If it was, the contract was not written. If there was a written contract, the defendant did not sign it. If the defendant did sign it, the plaintiff defrauded the defendant.

1.8 THE THEME

The theme is the central unifying concept of a case. It may be made up of one or more major concepts and several consistent sub-themes. The theme of a case brings the evidence together into a pattern the jury can easily understand. Common examples of themes for a plaintiff in a personal injury case include the payment of an obligation, the value of human life, and the importance of public safety. Every case has a critical factual issue upon which the case will turn. The theme should be used to pull the whole case together to convince the finder of fact to see the conflicting evidence your way.

The first step in developing a theme is to identify the issue upon which the case will turn and build a theme around that issue. It could be used to show that something happened a certain way, or that something happened because of malice or ill will.

An effective theme must be a concept that the jurors can identify with and believe in. A theme should motivate the jury to decide a case favorably. The more the fact finder shares the emotion espoused by a theme, the more likely the fact finder will accept the concept and render a decision consistent with the theme.

Present and reinforce the theme throughout the trial by the use of key words, phrases, images, and evidence. Present each witness' testimony and each exhibit in a manner that is consistent with the theme of the case. By using a combination of evidence, some directly supporting the themes and some subtly reinforcing the themes, lay a solid foundation for closing argument. During summation, show the jury how the theme of the case matches neatly and consistently with the facts. See Form 1-6 Theme Selection Worksheet.

The need to select the themes early in the trial preparation process should not preclude the refinement of the themes as the trial progresses. The central unifying theme may not be solidified until shortly before trial. Stay flexible and keep testing various themes for consistency with the facts. Consistent themes are important in presenting a credible case, and the attorney must retain enough flexibility to adapt to the changing circumstances of the case.

1.9 LEGAL RESEARCH

Legal research and investigation will initially help develop the legal theory of the case, uncover new theories, suggest possible theories of the opponent, and set the parameters of the case. See Form 1-7 Legal Research Worksheet. Legal research during later stages of the case will aid in discovery, assist in negotiations, and form the basis for jury instructions.

1.10 FACT GATHERING

Facts will need to be obtained from a variety of sources, including the client, witnesses, documents, public records, private records, photographs, recordings, personal property, real property, illustrations, and the scene of the event. See Chapter 2 on Discovery.

1.11 PLEADINGS

Analysis of the law and facts will form the basis for the pleadings of a case. The complaint and answer provide the framework for preparing the case for trial. See Form 1-8 Summons and Complaint Worksheet and Form 1-11 Answer and Response Worksheet.

A. Traditional Typed Pleadings. While California allows the use of Judicial Council Forms to expedite Pleadings, use of the traditional typed pleadings, in which one must state ultimate facts which constitute a cause of action, is a very valuable exercise in case construction. By drafting a formal complaint, one must confront and artfully state all the ultimate facts which must be proven in order to prevail. The same is true of affirmative defenses. In preparing a plaintiff's complaint case, for example, the pleader must:

1. Give a clear statement of ultimate facts, avoiding legal conclusion and mere evidentiary facts, which show the plaintiff's rights and the defendant's duties and state how the defendant breached his duties to plaintiff and how such breach was the legal and actual cause of damages suffered by the plaintiff.

2. In so doing, the pleader must distill the factual allegations down to their essentials, discarding the nonessential but supportive facts and stating the ultimate facts which constitute a cause of action for this particular case. In performing this task the attorney learns that which he *must* prove. If the allegations are stated too specifically, it may limit evidence which can be introduced at trial. If stated too generally, the pleading may be subject to a demurrer for uncertainty or failure to state a cause of action for which relief may be granted. In performing this task the attorney should prepare an outline of the essential facts of the case and compare the outline to a summary of each element of a proposed cause of action or affirmative defense. Forms 1-9 and 1-10 are designed to facilitate this task. Once the drafter has matched up the elements of each cause of action with the operative facts of the case it is simply a matter of discarding unessential statements of evidence and conclusions of law. What remains are the ultimate facts which state a cause of action.

B. Form Pleading. The Judicial Council "check the box" forms can be used for most cases. These forms are almost demurrer proof. The use of some Judicial Council forms is mandatory, but most pleading forms remain optional. West's Cal. Forms, Forms 982.1(1)–982.1(95).

1.12 SUPPORT STAFF

Determine which members of the support staff should become involved in the case. Legal research and fact gathering responsibilities may be delegated to paralegals, investigators, law clerks, clerical staff, or other attorneys. While the clerical staff's role is usually limited, the opportunity to gain these persons' ideas and insights should not be overlooked. The client and other third persons may also be of assistance when gathering and reviewing information.

1.13 SYSTEMIZED APPROACH

The planning of a case should occur in a logical, rational, and systematized way. Files should be arranged to maintain the pleadings, correspondence, and documents in an orderly manner. Research memos need to be maintained in a central location. Computerized law office equipment can be used to create research data banks, preventing the needless repetition of legal research in later cases.

1.14 EVIDENCE

The facts which will constitute evidence in the case need to be documented and preserved for use at trial. Potential testimony may need to be recorded. Documents may need to be authenticated, and exhibits may need to be prepared.

1.15 PLANNING THE CASE AROUND JURY INSTRUCTIONS

The starting point for final preparation for trial is to prepare the jury instructions for the case. This should be done even if it is a judge trial, because it forces the attorney to address all of the legal issues in the case and to set forth in plain language what the plaintiff must prove to prevail and what the defendant must prove to prevail on affirmative defenses. The attorney should select the appropriate standard instructions from the Book of Approved Jury Instructions Civil (BAJI) and should modify the instructions where appropriate. The most important of these is BAJI 2.60, in which the facts which must be proven by each side by a preponderance of the evidence must be spelled out in clear language. Special instructions, not found in BAJI are also to be submitted. See Chapter 7 for discussion of Jury Instructions.

Once the jury instructions are complete, the attorney should know the law of the case and what facts must be proven by a preponderance of evidence. The attorney is then ready to put facts and law into final presentation form.

1.16 PLANNING THE CASE AROUND THE CLOSING ARGUMENT

The closing argument is the destination point of the case. The content of a closing argument provides a form and structure for the presentation of the case. The closing argument contains an explanation of the facts, inferences, and arguments that will be necessary to secure a verdict for a party. The preparation of a closing argument should precede the preparation of all other facets of a case, including the opening statement. The other parts of the trial may then be planned around the content of the prepared summation. If a fact must be established to support a statement during closing argument, the attorney can plan to introduce the fact through direct or cross-examination. If a closing argument omits certain unnecessary facts, the attorney need not plan to present that evidence during trial. Form 1–12 provides a format for preparing an outline for an initial closing argument.

1.17 SETTLEMENT CONSIDERATIONS

Over 90% of all cases are settled. One of the most important factors affecting settlement and negotiation is the attorney's trial skills and reputation for winning at trial. The willingness of the attorney to try a case, the skill and experience of that attorney, and the preparation of the case for trial, all significantly influence the negotiation process. There are five fundamental steps in the negotiation and bargaining process:

1. Make your personal evaluation as to the value range of the case.

2. Discuss possible settlement options with your client and obtain authorization to settle in a general range.

3. Contact opposition and negotiate.

4. Obtain final authorization from your client to settle on specific terms.

5. Finalize the settlement with opposing attorney, including preparing and signing all paperwork.

The key to successful negotiations is to present an initial demand or offer which is reasonable and fully supported and meets all of your client's and your expectations regarding the value of the case. See Form 1-13 Negotiation Worksheet.

1.18 COURT OR JURY TRIAL

There exist many theories concerning whether a judge or jury is more desirable in a particular case. Considerations include:

1. Whether the case can be presented more effectively to a jury or a judge.

2. Whether it is the type of case that has some sympathetic or emotional aspect which might make it more advantageous if a jury considers the case.

3. Whether the case involves technical issues or other complexities that may be better understood by a judge.

4. How effective an advocate the opposing lawyer is before a jury or judge.

5. Whether the witnesses or evidence will be better perceived by a judge or jury.

6. The preferences of the client.

The attorney may want to initially demand a jury trial because the demand can be waived if it appears that a bench trial would be better. The effect of this decision on a potential appeal should be considered. Appellate courts are usually less likely to overturn the factual findings of a jury than those of a trial judge.

1.19 PREPARATION AND PRESENTATION OF COURT TRIAL

A trial before a judge will require different forms of preparation and presentation than a jury trial. These differences include the following considerations.

A. Opening. There may be no need to make an opening statement if the judge appears familiar with the case. Often the trial judge will discuss the case in chambers with the attorneys to determine the issues and attempt to mediate a settlement. This discussion may be a sufficient substitute for an opening statement. It is usually advisable to present an opening statement, even if merely a summary of the evidence to be presented. It may include explanation of the legal principles, particularly in a complex or technical case.

B. Evidentiary Rulings. The judge who must both decide the admissibility of evidence and the facts may have a difficult time avoiding the influence of inadmissible evidence. When deciding whether to admit or deny the introduction of certain evidence, a judge must understand what the evidence is and may have to accept an offer of proof. Judges may not rely on inadmissible evidence in reaching their decision, but it may be difficult for them to disregard the impact of such evidence. Judges in a court trial will be more inclined to admit, rather than exclude evidence. Trial judges realize appellate courts are more likely to overturn a decision if key evidence is omitted, rather than admitted. The exclusionary rules of evidence have been primarily designed to restrict the introduction of evidence in jury trials.

C. Introduction of Evidence. The presentation of evidence is directed to a one person audience—the judge. Strategies and tactics that present information in a persuasive and effective way should be employed. When presenting evidence, some attorneys will be less formal and less careful when a jury is not present. This should be avoided.

D. No Side Bar Conference. Objections, arguments, statements, and motions may be brought without regard to having those matters heard outside the presence of a non-existent jury.

E. Closing Argument. The attorney needs to fashion a closing argument that will have the most impact on a judge. Many parts of a closing argument that are designed for a jury will be inappropriate or ineffective if directed to a judge.

F. Overall Approach. Judges will be influenced and persuaded by some of the same tactics and techniques that affect jurors. For example, the use of demonstrative evidence may be as helpful to a judge in understanding a case as it is to a jury. Case themes and impact phrases may be equally persuasive with a judge. Most judges will be influenced by factors other than pure rationality and cold logic.

CLIENT INFORMATION
GENERAL

Date _____   Attorney of Record _____

Office File # _____   Inverviewer _____

| **Client** | **Spouse** |

Name _____   Name _____

Address _____   Address _____

_____   _____

_____   _____

Phone _____   Phone _____
    home   business   home   business

Social Security _____   Social Security _____

Occupation _____   Occupation _____

Employer _____   Employer _____

Address _____   Address _____

_____   _____

_____   _____

Age _____ Birth date _____   Age _____ Birth date _____

Marital Status _____   Marital Status _____

Income: **Gross Pay**   Income: **Gross Pay**

Annual: _____ Monthly _____   Annual: _____ Monthly _____

Weekly: _____ Hourly _____   Weekly: _____ Hourly _____

Net Pay   **Net Pay**

Annual: _____ Weekly _____   Annual: _____ Weekly _____

Hourly: _____ Pay period from   Hourly: _____ Pay period from

_____ to _____   _____ to _____

Education _____   Education _____

Military _____   Military _____

Form 1-1

Past Employment _____

_____

_____

_____

Member of business, Civic, Fraternal, Social Organizations/Clubs _____

_____

_____

_____

Criminal/Traffic Record _____

_____

_____

If Minor: Father's Name _____

        Address: _____

                  _____

                  _____

        Mother's Name _____

        Address: _____

                  _____

                  _____

        Custody with: Father _____ Mother _____ Other _____

Person to be guardian ad litem: Name _____

        Address: _____

        Relation: _____

CHILDREN – NAMES AND ADDRESSES

1. _____
2. _____
3. _____
4. _____

Form 1-1 (continued)

CLIENT INFORMATION
CLAIMS OR DEFENSES

Client Name: _____   Date: _____

Attorney: _____

1. Nature of Claim:

    If Personal Injury:

    Date of Injury: _____   Time of Day: _____

    Day of Week: _____   Location: _____

    Nature of Injury: _____

    If Breach of Contract:

    Date of Contract: _____   Place of Contract: _____

    Date of Breach: _____   Place of Breach: _____

    Amount in Controversy: $_____

    If Other:

    Nature of Claim: _____   Date Claim Made: _____

    Place Claim Arose: _____   Amount in Controversy: $_____

2. Names and Addresses of Potential Plaintiffs and/or Defendants:

Name	Address	Employer

3. Description of scene or events leading up to incident: _____

    _____

    _____

    _____

Form 1-1 (continued)

4. Description of What Happened: _____

   _____

   _____

   _____

5. Description of injury or basis of claim for damages or affirmative defenses:

   _____

   _____

   _____

6. Client Statements: To Whom: _____

   Address: _____

   Contents of Statement: _____

   _____

   _____

   Location of Written Statement: _____

7. Adverse Party Statements: To Whom: _____

   Address: _____

   Contents of Statement: _____

   _____

   _____

8. Documents: Location

   Accident Report: _____

   Copy of Contract: _____

   Other Documents:

   _____   _____

   _____   _____

   _____   _____

Form 1-1 (continued)

CLIENT INFORMATION
DAMAGES TO DATE

Medical Bills	
Doctor	
Hospital	
Ambulance	
Drugs	
Appliances	
Other	
Total	

Loss of Income	
Gross Pay From To	
Net Pay From To	
Total	
Property Damage: Market Value Before After	
Collision	
Deductible	
Misc. Other Damages – Specify	
Total	

Total Damages To Date _____

Note: Get copies of all bills, receipts, cancelled checks, estimates, appraisals, etc.

_____
_____
_____
_____
_____

INSURANCE DATA

Client's Insurance Company _____
Address _____
Phone _____ Policy Number _____ Adjuster _____
Opposing Party's Insurance Company: _____
Address _____
Phone _____ Policy Number _____ Adjuster _____

PRIOR CLAIMS

Date	Nature of Claim	Court	Outcome

Form 1–1

CLIENT INFORMATION
ADVICE

Advice Provided Client _____

_____

_____

Fee Arrangement _____

Action to Be Taken _____

Additional Information Documents to Be Provided by Client _____

_____

_____

Need client compose written summary of facts or event? _____

_____

A diary of past, present, and future damages or incidents? _____

Need client obtain documentation (bills, receipts, checks, estimates) for damages? _____

Has client executed the following:

    1. Retainer agreement: _____

    2. Medical authorization: _____

    3. Employment authorizations: _____

    4. Income tax authorization: _____

    5. Accident report authorization: _____

Next scheduled appointment: _____

Attorney's impressions of client's case:

    Liability _____

_____

_____

Form 1-1

Damages _____

_____

_____

_____

Client as a witness

    Appearance _____

    Demeanor _____

    Speech _____

    Eye contact _____

Other considerations _____

_____

_____

_____

_____

_____

Form 1–1 (continued)

CASE CONSTRUCTION AND EVALUATION WORKSHEET

Client _____   File _____

1. Summary of facts of case as given by client and other confirmed information: _____
   _____
   _____
   _____
   _____
   _____
   _____
   _____

2. Possible causes of action/defenses and applicable law: _____
   _____
   _____
   _____
   _____
   _____
   _____
   _____

3. Further information needed to confirm causes of action or affirmative defenses: _____
   _____
   _____
   _____
   _____
   _____
   _____

4. Further legal research needed to incorporate facts and law and confirm all possible causes of action or defenses: _____
   _____
   _____
   _____
   _____
   _____

Form 1-2

5. Further factual information needed: _____
   _____
   _____
   _____
   _____
   _____

6. Possible sources of information: _____
   _____
   _____
   _____

7. Analysis of liability or defenses:

   A. Strongest argument in favor: _____
      _____
      _____
      _____
      _____

   B. Strongest argument against: _____
      _____
      _____
      _____
      _____

8. Probability of establishing liability or affirmative defense on a scale of 1 to 10 (1 being poor and 10 being excellent):

   _____ rating

9. Comparative fault rating: 0 to 100%

   _____%

Form 1–2 (continued)

CASE CONSTRUCTION AND EVALUATION WORKSHEET
DAMAGE ANALYSIS

Client _____   File _____

1. Damages _____
   _____
   _____
   _____

2. Strengths & Weaknesses _____
   _____
   _____
   _____

3. Mitigating Factors _____
   _____
   _____
   _____

4. Basis of Recovery for Damages _____
   _____
   _____
   _____

5. Basis of Non–Recovery Against Damages _____
   _____
   _____
   _____

6. Analysis of Damages:

   A. Facts _____
   _____
   _____
   _____

   B. Law _____
   _____
   _____
   _____

7. Amount of Probable Damage Recovery $ _____

   Why Reasons _____
   _____
   _____

Form 1–2

CASE CONSTRUCTION AND EVALUATION WORKSHEET
ADDITIONAL FACTORS

Client _____   File _____

1. How will Plaintiff appear as a witness? _____
   _____
   _____
   _____

2. How will Defendant appear as a witness? _____
   _____
   _____
   _____

3. How will non-party witnesses appear:

   A. Plaintiff witnesses _____
   _____
   _____
   _____
   _____

   B. Defendant witnesses _____
   _____
   _____
   _____
   _____

4. What other factors affect case such as bias, sympathy, prejudice, status of parties? ___
   _____
   _____
   _____
   _____

Form 1-2

TENTATIVE TRIAL SCHEDULE

Case _____   File _____

Timing or Notice Requirement	Deadline/Calendared	Date Completed
Statute of Limitations		
Complaint		
Answer		
Discovery:		
Interrogatories		
1. _____		
2. _____		
3. _____		
4. _____		
5. _____		
Oral Depositions		
1. _____		
2. _____		
3. _____		
4. _____		
5. _____		
Written Depositions: _____		
_____		
_____		
_____		

Form 1-3

Timing or Notice Requirement	Deadline/Calendared	Date Completed
Requests for Production: _____		
_____		
_____		
_____		
Examinations: _____		
_____		
_____		
_____		
Exchange of Expert Witness Information: _____		
_____		
_____		
_____		
Motions: _____		
_____		
_____		
_____		
At Issue Memorandum		
_____		
_____		
_____		
Trial: _____		
_____		
_____		
_____		
Other: _____		
_____		
_____		
_____		

Form 1-3 (continued)

PROOF OF FACTS WORKSHEET

CASE: _____ FILE: _____

Prima Facie Facts to be Proved	Persuasive Weight Facts to be Proved	Corroboration Evidence	Proof through Testimony	Proof through Exhibits	Proof through Depositions and Declarations

Form 1–4

LEGAL THEORIES WORKSHEET

Case _____   File _____

What are the appropriate legal theories to support the client's claims or defenses? _____
_____
_____
_____
_____
_____
_____
_____

What are alternative legal theories? _____
_____
_____
_____
_____
_____
_____
_____
_____

What statutory or case precedent supports the legal theories? _____
_____
_____
_____
_____
_____
_____
_____
_____

Form 1–5

THEME SELECTION WORKSHEET

A. What is the key contested factual issue in the case?

_____
_____
_____

B. What are the possible themes that would convince the fact finder to resolve this issue in your favor?

Theme 1: _____
_____
_____
_____

Facts which support the theme: _____
_____
_____
_____

Facts which do not support the theme: _____
_____
_____
_____

Theme 2: _____
_____
_____
_____

Facts which support the theme: _____
_____
_____
_____

Form 1–6

Facts which do not support the theme: _____
_____
_____
_____

Theme 3: _____
_____
_____
_____

Facts which support the theme: _____
_____
_____
_____

Facts which do not support the theme: _____
_____
_____
_____

C. What sub-themes appear in the case:

1. _____
2. _____
3. _____

D. What is the central unifying theme of the case that combines the central issue theme and sub-themes and pulls the whole case together:

_____
_____
_____

E. What key words, phrases, images, or evidence will highlight the theme and sub-themes?

_____
_____
_____

Form 1–6 (continued)

LEGAL RESEARCH WORKSHEET

1. *Jurisdiction:*

    A. Court

Superior _____   Municipal _____   Federal _____   Other _____

   B. Basis for selection _____
   _____
   _____

   C. Authority _____
   _____
   _____

2. *Venue:*

   A. Location of Court: _____

   B. Basis for selection: _____

3. *Capacity to Sue:*

   A. Plaintiff: _____

   B. Authority: _____

4. *Capacity to be sued:*

   A. Defendant 1: _____

   B. Defendant 2: _____

5. *Government claim or exhaustion of other remedies necessary?*

   What claims or remedies: _____
   _____
   _____

   Applicable law: _____
   _____
   _____

Form 1-7

6. *Causes of Action:*

   First cause of action—Elements: _____

   _____

   _____

   Legal Authority:

   A. Statutes: _____

   _____

   _____

   B. Case Law: _____

   _____

   _____

   C. Further Research Needed for each element or Other Legal Issues: _____

   _____

   _____

   Second cause of action—Elements: _____

   _____

   _____

   Legal Authority:

   A. Statutes: _____

   _____

   _____

   B. Case Law: _____

   _____

   _____

   C. Further Research Needed for each element or Other Legal Issues: _____

   _____

   _____

Form 1–7 (continued)

Third cause of action—Elements: _____

_____

_____

Legal Authority:

  A. Statutes: _____

_____

_____

  B. Case Law: _____

_____

_____

  C. Further Research Needed for each element or Other Legal Issues: _____

_____

_____

_____

7. *Affirmative Defenses:*

  A. First Affirmative Defense—Elements: _____

_____

_____

  B. Legal Authority:

  1. Statutes: _____

_____

_____

  2. Case Law: _____

_____

  3. Further legal research needed: _____

_____

_____

Form 1-7 (continued)

8. *Evidentiary Issues:*

   First evidentiary issue: _____

   _____

   _____

   A. Applicable evidence code: _____

   _____

   B. Further research needed: _____

   _____

   _____

   Second Evidentiary Issues: _____

   _____

   _____

   A. Applicable evidence Code: _____

   _____

   B. Further research needed: _____

   _____

9. *Procedural Issues:*

   First issue: _____

   A. Applicable code of civil procedure: _____

   B. Applicable local rule: _____

   C. Applicable fast track rule: _____

   Second issue: _____

   A. Applicable code of civil procedure: _____

   B. Applicable local rule: _____

   C. Applicable fast track rule: _____

Form 1-7 (continued)

SUMMONS AND COMPLAINT WORKSHEET
PLAINTIFF

A. Identify, status and capacity to sue:

   1. Individual

      a. Name: _____

      b. Residence: _____
      _____

      c. Citizenship: _____

   2. Partnership

      a. D.B.A.: _____

      b. Name of partners: _____
      _____
      _____

      c. Fictitious Name: _____

         On file? _____

      d. Place of business: _____

      e. Nature of business: _____

   3. Unincorporated Association

      a. Name: _____

      b. Filed statement and notice under Business and Professions Code Section 17900?
      _____

   4. Domestic Corporation

      a. Corporate name: _____

      b. Date incorporated under laws of State of California: _____
      _____

      c. Present corporate status: _____

Form 1-8

5. Foreign Corporation

   a. State of incorporation: _____

   b. Conducting business in California since: _____

6. Minor or Incompetent and Status of Guardian Ad Litem

   a. Name of Minor: _____

   b. Age of Minor: _____

   c. Name of person adjudged incompetent: _____
   _____

   d. Date of Adjudication: _____

   e. Name of Guardian Ad Litem: _____

   f. Relationship of Guardian Ad Litem to minor or incompetent person: _____

   g. Date of appointment: _____

B. Jurisdiction

   1. Superior Court

      a. Basis for jurisdiction: _____
      _____

      b. Why not Municipal? _____
      _____

   2. Municipal Court

      a. Basis for jurisdiction: _____
      _____

      b. Why not Justice Court? _____
      _____

      c. Why not Small Claims? _____
      _____

Form 1-8 (continued)

        d. Why not Superior? _____

    3. Justice Court

        a. Basis for jurisdiction: _____

        b. Why not Small Claims: _____

C. Venue (which Judicial District)

    a. Location of injury: _____

    b. Location of real property: _____

    c. Location of entering into contract: _____

    d. Location of performance of contract: _____

    e. Residence of Defendant: _____

D. Defendants

    1. Defendant 1:

        Name: _____

        Legal Capacity: _____

        Address for service: _____

    2. Defendant 2:

        Name: _____

        Legal Capacity: _____

        Address for service: _____

Form 1–8 (continued)

3. Defendant 3:

   Name: _____

   Legal Capacity: _____

   Address for service: _____
   _____

4. Fictitious Named Defendants:

   a. Basis for need: _____

   b. Name of other possible Defendants: _____
      _____
      _____
      _____

Form 1-8 (continued)

PLEADING ULTIMATE FACTS CONSTITUTING A CAUSE OF ACTION
FIRST CAUSE OF ACTION

Essential Allegations	Facts Which Support	Ultimate Facts to Plead
Element: One		
Element: Two		
Element: Three		
Element: Four		
Other Elements Number ___		
Other Elements Number ___		

Form 1-9

PLEADING ULTIMATE FACTS CONSTITUTING A CAUSE OF ACTION
SECOND CAUSE OF ACTION

Essential Allegations	Facts Which Support	Ultimate Facts to Plead
Element: One		
Element: Two		
Element: Three		
Element: Four		
Other Elements Number ___		
Other Elements Number ___		

Form 1–9

PLEADING ULTIMATE FACTS CONSTITUTING A CAUSE OF ACTION
THIRD CAUSE OF ACTION

Essential Allegations	Facts Which Support	Ultimate Facts to Plead
Element: One	_____	_____
Element: Two	_____	_____
Element: Three	_____	_____
Element: Four	_____	_____
Other Elements Number ___	_____	_____
Other Elements Number ___	_____	_____

Form 1-9

PLEADING ULTIMATE FACTS CONSTITUTING A CAUSE OF ACTION
FOURTH CAUSE OF ACTION

Essential Allegations	Facts Which Support	Ultimate Facts to Plead
Element: One		
Element: Two		
Element: Three		
Element: Four		
Other Elements Number ___		
Other Elements Number ___		

Form 1–9

PRAYER FOR RELIEF

1. General damages (if allowed to state): _____
   _____

2. Special Damages: _____

3. Compensatory Damages: _____

4. Benefit of Bargain: _____

5. Punitive Damages (if allowed): _____

6. Injunctive or Declaratory Relief: _____

7. Double or Treble Damages (statutory Authority): _____
   _____

8. Interest: _____

9. Cost of Suit: _____

10. Attorney Fees: _____

11. Other: _____

Verification:

1. Verification required by statute? _____

2. Other reasons to verify: _____
   _____

3. Reasons not to verify: _____
   _____

4. Verification by attorney? _____

Judicial Council Forms:

1. Any forms required for this action? If so, list (Cal.Rules of Court 982) _____
   _____
   _____

2. List applicable Judicial Council complaint forms (Cal.Rules of Court 982.1) _____
   _____
   _____

3. Which Judicial Council Forms should be used for this action: _____
   _____

Form 1-10

ANSWER AND RESPONSE WORKSHEET

I. DEMURRER

    A. General Demurrer: Fails to state facts sufficient to constitute a cause of action. CCP Section 430.10(e).

        Grounds: _____

        _____

        _____

        _____

    B. Special Demurrer:

        1. No jurisdiction of subject matter. CCP 430.10(a).

            Grounds: _____

            _____

            _____

            _____

        2. No legal capacity to sue. CCP 430.10(b).

            Grounds: _____

            _____

            _____

            _____

        3. Another action pending on the same cause. CCP 430.10(c).

            Grounds: _____

            _____

            _____

            _____

        4. Misjoinder of parties. CCP 430.10(d).

            Grounds: _____

            _____

            _____

            _____

Form 1–11

5. Uncertainty. CCP 430.10(f).

   Grounds: _____
   _____
   _____

6. Cannot be ascertained whether contract is written or oral. CCP 430.10(g).

   Grounds: _____
   _____
   _____

II. ANSWER

   A. Admissions

      1. Specific admissions

         Paragraphs: _____

      2. Failure to deny or admit

         Paragraphs: _____

   B. Denials

      1. Generally deny paragraphs:
         _____
         _____

      2. Specifically deny paragraphs:
         _____
         _____

      3. Qualified general denial of paragraphs:
         _____
         _____

Form 1-11 (continued)

4. Deny based on information and belief paragraphs:

_____
_____

5. Deny based on lack of information and belief paragraphs:

_____
_____

C. Affirmative Defenses (most common)

1. Statute of limitations—Basis for: _____
_____

2. Comparative negligence—Grounds: _____
_____

3. Failure to mitigate damages—Basis: _____
_____

4. Estoppel—Basis for: _____
_____

5. Lack of consideration—Basis: _____
_____

6. Illegality of contract—Basis: _____
_____

7. Failure of consideration—Basis: _____
_____

8. Fraud—Basis: _____
_____

9. *Ultra Vires* Act by Corporation—Basis: _____
_____

Form 1-11 (continued)

10. Accord and Satisfaction—Basis: _____
_____

11. Good Faith Settlement—Basis: _____
_____

12. Laches—Basis: _____
_____

13. Unclean Hands—Basis: _____
_____

14. Discharge in bankruptcy—Basis: _____
_____

15. Privilege in Defamation Actions—Basis: _____
_____

16. Self Defense in Battery Actions—Basis: _____
_____

17. Res Judicata—Basis: _____
_____

18. Collateral Estoppel—Basis: _____
_____

19. Other: _____
_____

III. CROSS–COMPLAINT

   A. Against Parties:

      1. Name _____

      2. Basis for Claim: _____
_____
_____

Form 1–11 (continued)

B. Against Third Parties;

    1. Name: _____

    2. Legal Capacity: _____

    3. Address for service: _____
       _____

    4. Basis for claim: _____

(for causes of action, see Complaint Worksheet form)

CLOSING ARGUMENT PLANNING WORKSHEET

Case _____   File _____

1. Introduction: _____
   _____
   _____
   _____
   _____
   _____

2. Theme of case: _____
   _____
   _____
   _____
   _____
   _____

3. Persuasive Factual Theories: _____
   _____
   _____
   _____
   _____
   _____

4. Facts/Witnesses/Documents which directly support the theme and factual theories of the case: _____
   _____
   _____
   _____
   _____

5. Inferences and deductions from evidence which support theme and factual theories: _____
   _____
   _____
   _____

Form 1-12

6. Facts/Witnesses/Documents that rebut opponents theme and theories of case: _____

_____
_____
_____
_____
_____
_____

7. Jury Instructions: _____

_____
_____
_____
_____
_____
_____

8. Inferences and Deductions jurors should draw from facts and law: _____

_____
_____
_____
_____
_____
_____

9. Conclusion and Requested Verdict: _____

_____
_____
_____
_____
_____
_____

Form 1-12 (continued)

NEGOTIATION WORKSHEET

Case _____   File _____

1. Preliminary considerations:

   a. Anticipated litigation/trial cost equal: $_____

   b. Advantages of settling now include: _____
   _____

   c. Disadvantages of settling now include: _____
   _____

   d. Client's reason for or interest in settling now: _____
   _____
   _____

   e. Client's reason for or interest in not settling now: _____
   _____
   _____

2. Preparation

   a. What needs to be done to prepare for negotiations? _____
   _____
   _____

   b. What should be included in the negotiation agenda? What topics, issues, facts, law and positions need to be discussed? _____
   _____
   _____

   c. What information needs to be obtained from opposing lawyer? What questions need to be asked? _____
   _____
   _____

Form 1-13

d. How should the negotiation process proceed? By telephone, letter, face to face discussions? _____
_____

e. What authority has the client provided for settlement? What settlement range has the client approved? _____
_____

3. Positions

   a. What interests, needs, wants and positions of the client complement the interests, needs, wants and positions of the opponent? _____
   _____

   b. Which conflict? _____
   _____

4. Value of the case

   a. What is maximum jury verdict possible and likelihood? _____
   _____

   b. What is minimum jury verdict possible and likelihood? _____
   _____

   c. Factors to consider: (for example)

      1. Easily verifiable actual damages:

         Medical Expenses   _____

         Lost wages (present)   _____

         Property Damage   _____

         Lost Profits   _____

         Value of Contract   _____

         Benefit of Bargain   _____

         Others   _____

Form 1–13 (continued)

2. General Damages:

   Future Earnings _____

   Pain and Suffering _____

   Mental Distress _____

   Loss of Enjoyment _____

   Loss of Consortium _____

5. What reasons/explanations support negotiation positions:

   Facts _____
   _____
   _____
   _____

   Law _____
   _____
   _____
   _____

   Prior Verdicts with similar facts: Highest _____

   Average _____

   Lowest _____

   Tax Consequences _____

   Business Concerns _____

   Fairness _____

   Objective Factors _____

6. Previous Negotiations:

   Initial Offer/Demand _____ Supportive Reasons _____
   _____
   _____

   Subsequent Offers/Demands _____
   _____
   _____

Form 1–13 (continued)

7. Negotiating Strategy:

   Opening Demand/Offer: _____

   Reasons: _____

   Settlement amount you want: _____

   Limit of settlement authority ("bottom line") _____

   _____

8. Prediction of Opponent's Offers/Demands: _____

   _____

9. Settlement

   Case settled for $ _____ Client approved $ _____

   Settlement check sent _____ Received _____

   Release of claims executed _____

   Stipulation of dismissal executed _____

Form 1–13 (continued)

Chapter 2

DISCOVERY

Table of Sections

Sec.
2.1 Purposes and Scope.
2.2 Planning Discovery.
    A. Available Discovery Devices.
    B. Typical Sequence of Formal Discovery in a Personal Injury Case.
2.3 Informal Investigation.
    A. Information From the Client.
    B. Information From Documents.
    C. Information From Witnesses.
2.4 Interrogatories C.C.P. § 2030.
    A. Timing.
    B. Subject Matter.
    C. Number of Interrogatories C.C.P. § 2030(1).
    D. Form and Format C.C.P. § 2030(5).
    E. Service of Interrogatories.
    F. Answers to Interrogatories.
    G. Grounds for Objections.
    H. Failure to Respond and Motion to Compel.
    I. Use of Interrogatories at Trial C.C.P. § 2030(n).
2.5 Deposition Practice.
    A. Why Should a Deposition Be Taken?
    B. Planning a Deposition.
    C. Preparing to Take a Deposition.
    D. Beginning the Deposition.
    E. What Instructions Should Be Given to Deponent?
    F. How Should Objections Be Handled?
    G. Questioning Tactics and Strategies.
    H. Representing the Deponent.
2.6 Written Depositions C.C.P. § 2028.
    A. Procedure for Use.
    B. Advantages of Written Depositions.
    C. Disadvantages of Written Depositions.
2.7 Production of Documents, Things and Places C.C.P. § 2031.
    A. Manner of Request and Demand.
    B. Responses C.C.P. § 2031(f).
2.8 Requests for Admissions.
    A. Subject Matter.
    B. Number of Requests.
    C. Form and Format.
    D. Responses to Request.
    E. Failure to Respond.
    F. Grounds for Objections.
    G. Use of Admission at Trial C.C.P. § 2033(n).
2.9 Physical or Mental Examination C.C.P. § 2032.
    A. Who May Be Examined.
    B. When Appropriate.

Sec.
2.9 Physical or Mental Examination C.C.P. § 2032—Continued
    C. Procedure to Be Followed.
    D. Response to Demand for Physical Examination.
2.10 Limiting Discovery.
    A. Privileged Matters Not Discoverable.
    B. Attorney Trial Preparation Materials (Attorney Work Product) Not Discoverable.
    C. Protective Orders.
2.11 Enforcing Discovery Requests.
    A. Initial Failure to Respond.
    B. Continued Failure to Respond.
    C. Seeking Sanctions.
2.12 Avoiding Monetary Sanction and Terminating Sanction.
    A. Respond Promptly to All Requests for Discovery.
    B. Meet and Confer Whenever Possible.
    C. Do Not Withhold Evidence.
    D. Comply With Court Orders.

Forms
2–1 Discovery Worksheet.
2–2 Discovery Plan.
2–3 Factual Investigation Worksheet.
2–4 Interrogatories Worksheet.
2–5 Deposition Worksheet.
2–6 Production of Documents/Things Worksheet.
2–7 Request for Admission Worksheet.
2–8 Physical Examination Worksheet for Plaintiff Seeking Personal Injury Damages C.C.P. Section 2032.

2.1 PURPOSES AND SCOPE

The investigation and discovery of facts serve many purposes in the trial system. The general purposes may be summarized as follows:

1. To establish the various versions of what happened.
2. To provide for the mutual disclosure of information.
3. To explore the perceptions and approaches of the opposition.
4. To document data and preserve facts and exhibits.
5. To narrow issues and isolate disputed facts.
6. To promote settlements based upon accurate and complete information.
7. To foster verdicts based upon accurate and complete information.

"Any party may obtain discovery regarding any matter, not privileged, that is relevant to the subject matter involved in the pending action or to the determination of any motion made in that action, if the matter either is itself admissible in evidence or appears reasonably calculated to lead to the discovery of admissible evidence." C.C.P. § 2017.

California has historically taken a liberal approach to discovery. The Discovery Act of 1986 broadened that liberal approach to discovery by expanding the scope of discovery to include relevance to the subject matter of the action not just to the issues in controversy. Generally, parties have a right to disclosure "as a matter of right unless statutory or public policy considerations clearly prohibit it." Greyhound Corporation v. Superior Court, 56 Cal.2d 355, 15 Cal.Rptr. 90, 364 P.2d 266 (1961).

However, C.C.P. § 2017(c) enacted after *Greyhound* directs the court to limit the scope of discovery if "it determines that the burden, expense, or intrusiveness of that discovery clearly outweighs the likelihood that the information sought will lead to the discovery of admissable evidence." The test to determine the limits of discovery appears to hinge, not so much on relevancy, but on a weighing of the burden of discovery versus the likelihood that the discovery sought will lead to admissable evidence.

2.2 PLANNING DISCOVERY

Before discovery, do a thorough case analysis as discussed in Chapter 1 at §§ 1.4–1.11. Know the elements of each cause of action and the proof necessary to satisfy each cause of action. Have a list of all facts needed to establish a prima facie case. Include: (1) a list of the facts already established as true and the source of that information; (2) further facts needed to prove a prima facie case; and (3) the possible sources of that information. Once the attorney has a firm grasp of what facts are needed to prove the case and the best sources of the needed evidence, he is ready to prepare the discovery plan for the case. See Form 2–1 Discovery Worksheet.

When preparing your discovery plan, keep your client's objectives in mind. Discovery is expensive and should be geared to specific objectives based upon available resources and the immediate and long term objectives of the discovery. The use of informal and formal discovery and other discovery devices should be geared to the purpose of the discovery itself. The following illustrates client objectives which require the least extensive (and expensive) discovery up to the most extensive (and expensive) discovery.

1. To use discovery to merely decide how to proceed.

2. To use discovery to determine the possibilities of quick settlement.

3. To use discovery to explore a settlement after you put the opposing party on the defensive.

4. To use discovery for purposes of proceeding to trial if it can be determined through discovery that risk and cost at trial will be limited.

5. To use discovery for purposes of preparing for trial even though it may be risky and may be costly.

The above objectives should be reviewed for purposes of determining the amount of discovery, the type of discovery, the timing of discovery and the expected cost of the discovery. These objectives should also be used in preparing your discovery plan. See Form 2–2 Discovery Plan.

A. Available Discovery Devices. Each discovery device has advantages and disadvantages. Weigh the strengths and limitations of each along with its expense and burden. The following discovery devices are available in California:

1. oral and written depositions;

2. interrogatories to a party;

3. inspections of documents, things and places;

4. physical and mental examinations;

5. requests for admissions;

6. simultaneous exchanges of expert trial witness information. C.C.P. § 2019.

The formal methods of discovery may be used in any sequence. The timing and sequence of discovery varies from case to case, depending upon tactical, logistic and economic considerations. Before any formal discovery takes place, the attorney should pursue as much informal discovery as possible. Interview the client and witnesses, gather all documents that are available and go the to scene of the accident or occurrence. See § 2.3.

B. Typical Sequence of Formal Discovery in a Personal Injury Case

1. Serve interrogatories on attorney for opposing party to obtain hard data such as names and addresses of witnesses; location and availability of documents, reports, and records, and other tangible evidence that the opponent will rely on to support his or her cause of action, claims or defenses.

2. Serve request for production of documents and things that opposing party intends to rely on in support of his or her cause of action, claim or defenses.

3. Take depositions of non-party witnesses who the opponent contends support his or her cause of action, claim or defenses.

4. When the attorney believes he or she has a good grasp of the evidence which the opposing party will rely on, take the deposition of party witnesses.

5. After a thorough review and analysis of discovery to this point, serve a request for admissions of facts and of the genuineness of documents.

6. Where appropriate, require physical or mental examinations of the parties whose physical or mental condition is at issue.

7. Once the identity of expert witnesses who will testify at trial is known, notice the deposition of expert witnesses.

The discovery plan should be ordered to do the following:

a) Pin down adversary's position as soon as possible (Interrogatories + Request for admissions);

b) Obtain documents early (Request for documents);

c) Move from broad to specific;

d) Follow up with in depth probing questions (Deposition).

See Form 2–2 Discovery Plan.

2.3 INFORMAL INVESTIGATION

A. Information From the Client. Initial and subsequent client interviews will reveal information and sources of information. See Form 1–1 Client Information in Chapter 1.

B. Information From Documents. Every case will involve written materials or data which provide additional information. Form 2–3. Factual Investigation Worksheet, provides a listing of common documentary sources.

C. Information From Witnesses. Witnesses will have vital knowledge and information. See Form 2–3 Factual Investigation Worksheet. These individuals may have firsthand or hearsay information. Several considerations affect the fact gathering process:

1. *Who Should Be Contacted?* All persons with information need to be contacted. This includes persons who can confirm, add to, fill in, corroborate as well as contradict and challenge the client's version.

2. *When Should They Be Contacted?* Contact witnesses as soon as possible after the event. You will usually obtain more accurate and worthwhile responses at this time. It may be advisable to contact witnesses before the opposition in an attempt to gain untainted or even favorable responses from the witnesses.

3. *How Should the Witnesses Be Contacted?* Friendly witnesses will usually cooperate. Neutral witnesses may need a reason to tell what they know. Unfriendly witnesses may disclose little or no information unless deposed. Most witnesses will cooperate if they understand why they are being questioned. Reasons investigators use to persuade a witness to cooperate include:

a) The client's crucial need for the information;

b) The importance of the witness and the information to the case;

c) The cooperation of the witness now may prevent further involvement in the future;

d) The witness' responsibility as a citizen to cooperate;

e) A sense of fairness and justice on the part of the witness;

f) The witness need only listen to the investigator relate what happened and then correct the story; and

g) A threat to subpoena the witness later.

4. *What Approach Should Be Taken?* The two extremes of witness interviewing are (a) the narrative, open-ended approach where the witness tells the story, and (b) the leading question, controlled approach where the witness corrects or confirms a story told by the investigator. Most interviews will involve a series of narrative questions followed by specific, clarifying, and probing questions. This method usually provides a complete and accurate account of the witness' perceptions.

5. *How Should the Information Be Preserved?* Preserve the information through a statement, memo, or tape recording. The need to make a record, the concerns about discoverability of such information, and the potential use of a record at trial are factors to be considered.

6. *Types of Witness Statements.* Witnesses may provide information in a variety of ways:
   a) Handwritten statements;
   b) Investigator handwritten or typed statements signed, initialed, or approved by the witness;
   c) Court reporter transcripts of the interview; and
   d) Contemporaneous tape recording of the person-to-person or telephone interview.

7. *What Should the Statement Include?* The contents of a statement should include:
   a) Name, address, home phone, business phone of witness;
   b) Witness' occupation and employer's name;
   c) Brief background of the witness;
   d) Date, time, location of event from the perspective of the witness;
   e) Description of the event, including all details and documents;
   f) Presence of any other witness; and
   g) Agreement of witness to sign, initial, or affirm statement.

2.4 INTERROGATORIES C.C.P. § 2030

Interrogatories are written questions posed by one party to another party to be answered in writing under oath. C.C.P. § 2030. See Form 2–4 Interrogatories Worksheet.

A. Timing. A defendant may propound interrogatories to a party to the action without leave of court at any time after service of the summons. The plaintiff may propound interrogatories to a party without leave of court at any time 10 days after service of the summons.

B. Subject Matter. Interrogatories are usually used to ascertain a party's contentions and the factual basis for them. In practice, since interrogatories are usually answered by the opposing attorney after consultation with his client, the answers to the interrogatories will usually contain the opposing attorney's view of the contentions and the factual basis for them.

Interrogatories can effectively obtain the following type of information:

1. Identity of persons who know facts, who have witnessed an event, or who have hearsay information.

2. The existence, identity and location of documents and things discoverable.

3. Specific information such as dates, times, amounts, distance, speed, measurements, location, dimensions, contracts, data, statistics, test results and other types of objective hard data information.

4. Relevant financial information including location and custodian of such relevant financial records.

5. Information about the business entity involved in the case such as corporate status or partnership arrangements.

6. Liability insurance coverage.

7. Government licenses.

8. Similar events, incidents or transactions involving third persons.
9. Identity of trial experts, employee experts, and specially retained experts.
10. Opinions and supporting data of trial and employee experts.
11. More definite explanations of allegations contained in pleadings.
12. Specific amounts of alleged damages, with supporting documentation.
13. Opinions and contentions that relate the law to the facts.
14. Relevant medical history.
15. Relevant employment history.
16. Relevant educational or vocational background.

C. Number of Interrogatories C.C.P. § 2030(1). The party may propound to another party 35 specially prepared interrogatories, in addition to any number of official form interrogatories as described in C.C.P. § 2033.5. An attorney may make a special request for additional interrogatories following the procedure and requirements set forth in C.C.P. § 2030(a).

To maximize the use of interrogatories, first consult the official Judicial Council Form Interrogatories. See West Cal.Forms F120, F129. Under C.C.P. § 2033.5 an attorney may propound as many of these official form interrogatories as desired. The attorney should decide which points of the particular case are covered by the Judicial Council Form interrogatories and which points are not covered and then prepare the specially prepared interrogatories to supplement the official Judicial Council form interrogatories.

D. Form and Format C.C.P. § 2030(5). Each interrogatory must be full and complete in and of itself. No preface or instructions shall be included in a set of interrogatories unless it has been approved under C.C.P. § 2030(5). "A party propounding interrogatories shall number each set of interrogatories consecutively. In the first paragraph immediately below the title of the case, there shall appear the identity of the propounding party, the set number and the identity of the responding party. Each interrogatory in a set shall be separately set forth and identified by number or letter." C.C.P. § 2030(4).

E. Service of Interrogatories. The parties propounding the interrogatories should serve a copy of them on the party to whom they are directed and all other parties who appear in the action. Within 30 days after a service of interrogatories, the party on whom the interrogatories are served shall serve the original of the response on the propounding party, and a copy to all other parties to the case. Any agreement to extend time for answering interrogatories must be in writing. C.C.P. § 2030(d)(h)(i).

F. Answers to Interrogatories. Questions must be interpreted and answered in good faith by the answering parties. Answers to interrogatories must be in writing, under oath, truthful, and complete. The responding party must make a reasonable and good faith effort to obtain information not readily available by inquiry to other natural persons or organizations. The responding party has a duty to investigate in order to answer the questions as completely as possible. C.C.P. § 2030(i).

The answering party may answer all or part of the interrogatories. The parts that are not answered may be objected to with the specific ground for the objection clearly stated. If an objection is based on privilege, the privilege invoked shall be clearly stated. If an objection is based on a claim that the information sought is protected work product, that claim shall be expressly asserted. C.C.P. § 2030(f)(3). The answering party may also apply for a protective order under C.C.P. § 2030(e).

G. Grounds for Objections. Common objections to interrogatories include:

1. *Irrelevant to the Subject Matter of the Action.* C.C.P. § 2017A.

However, because the standard of relevancy in discovery is quite broad, courts do not generally favor objections on grounds of irrelevancy (see Sec. 2.1 herein.)

2. *More Than 35 Specially Prepared Interrogatories.* The party may object to more than 35 specially prepared interrogatories unless they are accompanied by supporting declaration

which sets forth the reason for more than 35. The declaration is also subject to challenge. C.C.P. §§ 2030(c)(1), 2030(f)(3).

3. *Undue Burden.* The standard for an undue burden objection is that the burden of discovery clearly outweighs the likelihood that the information sought will lead to discovery of admissible evidence. C.C.P. § 2017(c).

4. *Information Equally Available to Both Parties.* This objection applies in cases where the information sought is available in public records that are available to the party requesting the information. C.C.P. §§ 2030(f)(1), 2019(b)(1).

5. *Attorney Work Product* see page 2–17, sec. 2.10B herein for discussion of attorney work product.

6. *Privilege* see page 6–5 herein.

7. *Uncertain, Ambiguous or Unintelligible Interrogatories.* These objections can be made when the questions simply cannot be answered because it is not clear what information is requested. Cembrook v. Superior Court, 56 Cal.2d 423, 15 Cal.Rptr. 127, 364 P.2d 303 (1961).

8. *Continuing Interrogatories.* A party has no duty to supplement an answer that is still correct and complete. C.C.P. § 2030(c)(7).

H. Failure to Respond and Motion to Compel. The party who fails to make a timely response to a written interrogatory waives any objections to the interrogatories including any based on privilege or work product protection. The party propounding the interrogatories may move for an order compelling response to the interrogatory and the court shall impose a monetary sanction against any party, person or attorney who unsuccessfully makes or opposes a motion to compel a response to interrogatories unless it finds that the party acted with substantial justification. If the party further refuses to answer the interrogatories, the court may dismiss the action. C.C.P. § 2030(k).

If the propounding party determines that an answer to a particular interrogatory is evasive or incomplete or an objection to the interrogatory is without merit or too general, the party may move for an order compelling further response. This motion shall be accompanied by a declaration which states facts showing a reasonable and good faith attempt at informal resolution of each issue presented by the motion. The objecting party has the burden of establishing the legitimacy of the objection. The court, after hearing, can order further responses and may impose a monetary sanction against any party, person or attorney who unsuccessfully makes or opposes a motion to compel further responses to interrogatories.

I. Use of Interrogatories at Trial C.C.P. § 2030(n). Interrogatory responses, so far as admissible under the rules of evidence, may be used by any party against the responding party only for purposes of establishing affirmative facts or admissions and for purposes of impeachment. C.C.P. § 2030(n) does not require that the responding party be available to testify, has testified, or will testify at the trial or hearing. It leaves open the option to use answers to interrogatories for any purposes that the attorney deems fit. The answering party may rebut or explain by introducing new evidence.

To use interrogatories at trial one should first lodge the original of the interrogatories and answers. Before reading the Interrogatories counsel should first identify the question and answer and, in a jury trial, make an offer of proof at sidebar. The court has discretion to determine whether the question and answers are admitted and/or read to the jury.

2.5 DEPOSITION PRACTICE

See Form 2–5 Deposition Worksheet.

A. Why Should a Deposition Be Taken?

1. To obtain information from party and non-party witnesses, including experts. It is really the only way to fully question and obtain admissions and statements from non-party witnesses.

2. To preserve testimony of witnesses who may be unavailable at the time of trial either because of death, illness, geographic unavailability or whose attendance at the trial cannot be compelled. C.C.P. § 2025(U)(3).

3. To evaluate and test out various themes of the case that you are in the process of developing.

4. To seek information which, while it may not be admissible, may lead to the discovery of admissible material.

5. To promote settlement by exposing weaknesses in the opposing party's case either through witness statements or admissions of a party.

6. To assess the demeanor of the deponent and determine what kind of witness the deponent will make.

7. To preserve for the record a percipient witness' early recollection of the event in question before it is subject to memory lapses. Earlier deposition testimony will be believed by a jury more than later witness testimony that is at variance with the earlier testimony.

B. Planning a Deposition

1. *When Should a Deposition Be Scheduled?* The defendant may serve a notice of deposition at any time after the defendant has been served or has appeared in the action, whichever occurs first. The plaintiff may serve a deposition notice on any date that is 20 days after the service of the summons or appearance by any defendant. C.C.P. § 2025(b).

The oral deposition of a party requires 10 days' notice. C.C.P. § 2025(f). The deposition of a non-party requires a "sufficient time in advance of the deposition" to allow the deponent a reasonable time to travel to the place of the deposition. C.C.P. § 2020(f). These basic rules give the attorney great leaway in determining when to schedule depositions. Of course, the closer in time the deposition is taken to the event or occurrence, the fresher the memory of the deponent will be. In general, the more important the testimony of the deponent the later in the schedule that particular deponent should be placed in order to gather as much information as possible on which to question that particular deponent. This highlights the importance of preparing a discovery plan and planning the sequence of deposing various witnesses and parties, so that the depositions may be taken while the memory of important witnesses is fresh.

2. *Where Should it Be Held?* The deposition of a person, whether or not a party to the action, shall be taken at a place that is, at the option of the party giving notice of the deposition, either within 75 miles of the deponent's residence, or within the county where the action is pending and within 150 miles of the deponent's residence, unless the court orders otherwise. C.C.P. § 2025(e)(1). Convenience and tactical considerations will usually dictate the location of the deposition. Attorneys usually feel more comfortable in their own office and opponents may feel less comfortable in the office of the opposition, especially if they have to travel a long distance to get there. However, consideration should be given to neutral or uncommitted witnesses in order not to alienate these uncommitted witnesses. In such cases, consider holding the deposition on neutral ground such as in the court reporter's office or another convenient location. Consider deposing an expert witness at the expert witness' offices in order to facilitate the expert witness' referral to documents and text needed for his testimony.

3. *Who Should Be Present?* Typically, the attorneys, the deponent, and the court reporter will be present. A party has a right to be present for all depositions.

4. *How is Attendance Compelled?* The party desiring to take the oral deposition of any person shall give notice in writing which shall state:

a) the address where the deposition will be taken;

b) the date of deposition selected under C.C.P. § 2025(f) and the time it will be commenced;

c) the name of each deponent and the address and telephone number, if known, of any deponent who is not a party to the action;

d) the specification with reasonable particularity of any materials or category of materials to be produced by the deponent.

In practice, attorneys commonly stipulate in writing to set the time and place of the deposition. C.C.P. § 2021.

5. *Who Can and Should Be Deposed?* A party can take a deposition of any person or organization, including a corporation, partnership, association or governmental agency. C.C.P. § 2025(a). The decision as to who should be deposed should be made on a case by case basis after weighing the relative importance of the testimony of the deponent against the expense and the chance of negative consequences of deposing such a person. Consider deposing the following:

a) Adverse Party. Depose the adverse party in almost every case. The deposition of the adverse party gives the attorney the opportunity to evaluate the adverse party's claims, the manner in which the party can express and justify those claims and the general demeanor and believability of the party. It also gives the attorney the chance to evaluate the opposing counsel in the case.

b) Adverse Non-party Witness. While the deposition of an adverse non-party witness carries with it the danger of preserving harmful evidence, it is usually worth the risk to gain full knowledge of this negative testimony and preserve it in order to help counsel prepare for cross examination at the trial. It is also an opportunity to see how the adverse witness holds up to a cross examination type of questioning. Again, it gives the attorney a chance to evaluate the deponent as a potential witness.

c) The Friendly Non-party Witness. Consider deposing a friendly non-party witness if there is a chance that the friendly non-party witness for whatever reason, may not be able to be present at trial. It also may be helpful in settlement negotiations to have a permanent record of the friendly non-party witness' testimony in support of your case. C.C.P. § 2034.

d) Expert witnesses. Consider taking the deposition of an expert witness as soon as it is determined that a particular expert will testify at the time of trial. Usually there will be a brief period of time in which to take the deposition of the expert witness so such deposition must be taken as expeditiously as possible.

C. **Preparing to Take a Deposition.** Prior to the deposition:

1. Analyze all pleadings to determine the specific factual issues in controversy.

2. Review all informal discovery and fact investigations.

3. Review all previous formal discovery including interrogatories and previous depositions.

4. Review all relevant documents and exhibits and organize them in the order they will be used during the deposition.

5. Determine what other documents or records you need; obtain them, and review them and put them in the order they will be used during the deposition.

6. List the objectives of this deposition in order of importance.

7. Consult with an expert if the deposition will involve areas of special skill, expertise or is highly technical.

8. Make an outline or checklist of every area of inquiry. The outline should normally be organized in chronological order but consider an order in which you proceed directly with the most critical areas or an order in which you proceed in a non-confrontational way leading up to the controverted issues.

D. Beginning the Deposition

1. At the time of going on the record the examiner should state for the record the stipulation or notice which brought about this particular deposition. The opposing attorney or attorneys at this time can make any objections to the notice of the deposition for the record.

2. One should not merely agree to the usual stipulations. Any stipulations regarding the procedure of the deposition should be spelled out in their entirety.

The following are some of the usual stipulations which are often presented. One should have them spelled out and closely consider them.

1. Stipulation that an instruction to the deponent not to answer a question shall constitute a refusal to answer the question for purposes of a motion to compel. See C.C.P. § 2025(h), (o). This is appropriate for a party deponent, but not for a non-party deponent because opposing attorney cannot instruct a non-party who is not his client not to answer.

2. Stipulation that all objections under C.C.P. § 2025(m)(2) except to the form of the question are reserved until the time of trial. It should be noted that regardless of the stipulations, counsel should always object to questions involving privilege or work product. C.C.P. § 2025(m), Evidence Code § 912A.

3. Stipulation that an objection by one party is deemed an objection by all parties for purposes of reserving objections until the time of trial. This can be harmless or dangerous. It is best to rely on your own objection so as to avoid sanctions.

E. What Instructions Should Be Given to Deponent?

The examiner should make sure that the record reflects that the deponent fully understands the nature and importance of the proceeding and what is expected of the deponent during the course of the proceeding. The record should also reflect that the deponent is competent to testify and is under no infirmity which would affect his or her testimony. The admonition to the deponent should include:

1. Identity and representative capacity of the examiner taking the deposition;

2. That the testimony is being given under oath and that the deponent has the duty to tell the truth under penalty of perjury;

3. That the deponent is to answer all questions audibly;

4. That if the deponent does not understand the question, he is to ask the examiner to repeat or rephrase the question and that if the deponent answers the question it will be assumed that the deponent understood the question;

5. That the testimony will be transcribed by the reporter and everything said will be reported and that the deponent will have an opportunity to review the deposition and make changes to it if necessary but any changes may be commented on at the time of trial;

6. That the deponent is not under any medication or taken any drugs or has any medical or physical infirmity that would impair his or her ability to understand and answer questions asked;

7. That the deponent can request a recess for medical or any other reasons.

F. How Should Objections Be Handled?

The deponent's attorney is usually limited to objecting to the form of the question. C.C.P. § 2025(m)(3). The attorney should simply make the objection, e.g., "The question is vague and ambiguous." The objection will be noted by the reporter. In practice, the examiner when faced with an objection such as vague or ambiguous, will usually rephrase the question to make sure that there can be no later claim that the deponent did not understand the question or he will insist on an answer as asked. All objections made at the deposition are simply noted by the court reporter, except those that are coupled by a instruction by counsel not to answer the question. An instruction not to answer will usually be made on the grounds of privilege or work product which are waived if not raised. C.C.P. § 2025(m). If the deponent refuses to answer the question after being instructed by his attorney not to answer the question, the examiner has the option of adjourning the deposition to seek a court order under C.C.P. § 2025(o) or of completing the examination on other matters. C.C.P. § 2025(m)(4). The usual practice is for the deposition to proceed on all other matters and for the examiner to notice a hearing to compel answers to deposition questions. This notice may be given orally at the time of the deposition or the examiner may serve a notice of motion in writing after the deposition is over. The importance of preparation for the deposition and proceeding properly with the deposition cannot be overemphasized since under C.C.P. § 2025(t) *you can only depose a witness once.*

G. Questioning Tactics and Strategies

1. *Use a Structured Approach.* Your deposition outline should contain general headings with a list of specific information needed under each general heading. A successful structured approach that is used by many attorneys is to begin questioning by asking open-ended questions to which the deponent provides narrative answers. The narrative answers should be followed up with specific close-ended questions seeking further specific information and/or confirming or denying the existence of specific facts discussed in the narrative. One can then review the facts derived from the narrative and ask yes or no questions to confirm particular points.

2. *Listen Carefully to Everything the Deponent Says and Follow Up on Statements Made.* Always appear interested and curious and encourage the deponent to talk. Listen closely to the responses and ask follow up questions. The more the deponent talks the more information you receive. Very talkative witnesses often disclose either damaging information or say something inconsistent with their own previous statements or the deposition statements of others.

3. *Ask Easy to Understand Questions.* Besides being subject to objection, questions that are vague, ambiguous or unclear tend to have little impact when read at the time of the trial.

4. *Ask Who, What, When, Where, Why and How Questions.* Using a structured approach, ask open-ended questions followed by closed-ended questions designed to elicit information regarding who, what, where, when and how, of the matter in question.

5. *Clarify Dates and Times.* Make sure the deponent understands the time frame and gives accurate testimony regarding dates and time.

6. *Always Inquire About the Sources of Information.* It is important to always determine what basis or foundation the witness has to make the statements he or she is making. (E.g., the witness saw an event or heard something happen.)

7. *Require the Witness to Respond to All Questions.* If the witness says I don't remember, ask questions designed to help the witness remember certain things. This could include reciting another witness' version of what happened and asking if the witness agrees with it, or using previous statements or relevant documents to refresh recollection.

8. *Ask about Opinions, Emotions or Attitudes.* Ask the witness how he feels about the case or other people involved in the case.

9. *Ask About Other Witnesses, Documents or Evidence.* The purpose of the deposition is to learn everything that the deponent knows about the case, including knowledge of other people who may have knowledge regarding the case and the location and contents of other documents that may be relevant to the case.

10. *Where Appropriate, Have the Deponent Draw a Diagram.* In almost any case where the deponent is a percipient witness, the witness should be asked to draw a diagram of the scene or to verify that a given diagram is true and accurate.

11. *Ask Leading Questions for Purposes of Obtaining an Admission From the Deponent.*

12. *Assess Effectiveness of Witness.* Throughout the process you should be continuously observing and assessing the demeanor and believability of the deponent.

13. *Review and Verify Testimony.* Toward the end of the deposition review the main points testified to by the deponent to verify his version of the facts and to determine if there are any inconsistencies. This can be done by summarizing in your own words the testimony and asking the deponent if this statement is correct.

H. Representing the Deponent

1. *Preparing the Deponent for Deposition.* Attorneys who represent the deponent should do the following:

   a) Review the case file and all relevant information with the deponent.

   b) Explain what will happen in the deposition.

   c) Explain the function of the court reporter.

   d) Give the identities of all of those who are likely to attend the deposition.

   e) Rehearse anticipated deposition questions.

   f) The deponent should be instructed regarding how to act when objections are made. The attorney should be especially mindful and be prepared to make objections invoking privilege or work product. The deponent should be instructed ahead of time not to answer certain questions that are privileged or regard work product.

   g) The following specific instructions should be given to the deponent on how to answer questions at the deposition.

   (1) Listen to each question carefully. If you don't understand the question, tell the attorney you don't understand the question. Never guess at an answer.

   (2) If you don't know the answer to the question, say "I don't know."

   (3) If you don't remember the answer to the question, say "I don't remember."

   (4) If the question can be answered with a simple yes or no, say yes or no. Do not elaborate.

   (5) If you would like to confer with your attorney before answering, ask the examiner if you may confer with your attorney.

   (6) Answer only the question asked. Don't add facts you think the other attorney ought to know.

   (7) Don't argue with the attorney and don't let the attorney upset you.

   (8) If at any time you feel a recess would help, ask for a recess.

   (9) Avoid using superlatives such as "never" or "always" because they can provide a basis for effective cross-examination by opposing counsel.

   (10) Avoid obscenities and racial or sexual slurs.

   (11) Correct any errors that come to your attention during the course of the deposition.

   (12) Always tell the truth.

2. *Protecting the Deponent.* Protect the deponent from improper questioning. If necessary, the attorney can suspend the deposition to seek a protective order on the grounds that the examination is being conducted in bad faith or in a manner that unreasonably annoys, embarrasses or harasses the witness. C.C.P. § 2025(n).

3. *Instructing the Client Not to Answer.* Instructing the deponent not to answer at the deposition is a decision not to be made lightly. If counsel allows the deponent to answer a sensitive question, a privilege may be waived. On the other hand, if there are insufficient grounds for the objection, the attorney may be sanctioned on a motion to compel. In order to instruct your client not to answer the question, you must be very sure of your grounds and must make the record clear as to the basis for instructing your client not to answer.

4. *Whether to Question the Deponent at the End of the Examination.* It is usually not advantageous to question your own client at the deposition. It may be useful, however, if the deponent has made some admissions or statements in the deposition that need clarification or if you want to strengthen your case in the eyes of the opposing attorney for purposes of early settlement.

5. *Handling the Deposition Transcript.* The party noticing the deposition must pay the cost of the transcript, C.C.P. § 2025(p). The person taking the deposition shall send written

notice to the deponent and the party that the original transcript of the deposition is available for reading and signing. Unless the deponent and all parties agree to waive the reading and signing of the transcript of the testimony, the deponent has thirty days from receipt of this notice to change the form or the substance of the answer to any question. C.C.P. § 2025(q)(1). If a deposition is not signed by a deponent, the deposition is given the same force and effect as a signed deposition. C.C.P. § 2025(q)(1).

It is preferred practice for the deponent to review the deposition within the time allotted and make all necessary changes and to sign the deposition. The original of the signed deposition should be transmitted to the attorney for the party who noticed the deposition. C.C.P. § 2025(s)(1).

6. *Use of the Deposition at Trial.* At the trial or any other hearing in the action, any part or all of the deposition may be used against any party who was present or was represented at the taking of the deposition. C.C.P. § 2025(u)(1). The deposition may be used by any party for purposes of impeaching the testimony of the deponent as a witness. C.C.P. § 2025(u)(1). Also, the deposition of any person or organization including any party to the action may be used for any purpose if the court finds that the deponent is unavailable at the time of trial as defined by C.C.P. § 2025(3).

2.6 WRITTEN DEPOSITIONS C.C.P. § 2028

Deposition by written questions is a discovery device whereby a party can obtain answers to written questions from another party or from any person or organization who is not a party to the action. It may be taken in California, in another state or even in another nation. C.C.P. § 2028(a). This discovery device provides information without the expense of oral depositions and without the problems of written interrogatories. This device has limited use because of lack of flexibility and the difficulties inherent in preparing written questions and receiving full and adequate responses.

A. Procedure for Use. To use written depositions the examiner must notice the written depositions pursuant to C.C.P. § 2028(a). The examiner shall designate the deposition officer (usually a court reporter) and the deponent shall appear before the deposition officer and the deposition officer shall ask the questions and record the testimony of the deponent in response to the questions. The procedures for objecting to written deposition questions are, of course, different from the procedure used in objecting during oral depositions in which counsel are usually present. For objection procedures see C.C.P. § 2028(d), (e), (f).

B. Advantages of Written Depositions. A written deposition is the only way one may receive answers to written questions from non-party witnesses. While non-party witnesses can sometimes be conveniently deposed by oral examination, circumstances may sometimes make such oral depositions either not possible or economically unfeasible. It is a way of avoiding the expense of travelling to a distant place to take the deposition of a minor witness. The main benefit of the written deposition is to save attorney time and expense to the client. It is best suited for circumstances in which hard data or authentication of documents is needed. It can also be used to lay foundation for admission of documentary evidence.

C. Disadvantages of Written Depositions. Written depositions have all the disadvantages of interrogatories in that an uncooperative or hostile witness is able to give unresponsive or useless answers without the opportunity to follow up on the questions. One is not able to judge the demeanor and credibility of the witness. The response to the answers may be merely responses prepared for the deponent by his or her attorney.

2.7 PRODUCTION OF DOCUMENTS, THINGS AND PLACES C.C.P. § 2031

A party may demand that any other party produce and permit the party making the demand to inspect and to copy, photograph, test or sample any document or tangible things that are in the possession, custody or control of the party on whom the demand is made. C.C.P. § 2031.

A party may also demand that any other party permit the entrance on any land or other property that is in the possession, custody or control of the person on whom the demand is made and to inspect and to measure, survey, photograph, test or sample the land or other property or any designated object or operation on it. C.C.P. § 2031(a)(3). See Form 2-6 Production of Documents/Things Worksheet.

A. Manner of Request and Demand. The party demanding inspection of documents, things or places must do the following:

1. Designate the documents tangible things or land or other property to be inspected either by specifically describing each individual item or by reasonably particularizing each category of item.

2. Specify a reasonable time for inspection that is at least 30 days after service of the demand.

3. Specify a reasonable place for making the inspection.

4. Specify any related activity that is being demanded in addition to an inspection or copying as well as the manner in which the related activity will be performed. CCP 2031(c).

B. Responses C.C.P. § 2031(f). Within 20 days of service of the request, the party on whom an inspection demand has been directed shall respond separately to each item or category of item by a statement that the party will:

1. Comply with the particular demand for inspection and any related activities.

2. File a statement that the party lacks the ability to comply with the demand for inspection of a particular item or category of item. A representation of an inability to comply with the demand for inspection shall affirm that a diligent search and a reasonable inquiry has been made in an effort to comply with a demand. The statement shall specify whether the inability to comply is because a particular item or category has never existed, has been destroyed, has been lost, misplaced, or stolen or has never been or is no longer in the possession, custody or control of the responding party. C.C.P. § 2031(f)(2).

3. Object to the particular demand. C.C.P. § 2031(f)(3).

If the responding party objects to the demand for inspection of an item or category of item, the response shall identify any document, tangible thing or land falling within any category of item in demand to which an objection is being made and set forth the specific grounds for the objection. If the objection is based on privilege, the particular privilege shall be stated. If an objection is based on claim that the information is protected work product, the claim shall be expressly stated. C.C.P. § 2031(d).

If an objection is made to the inspection two things can happen. If efforts to informally resolve the disputed matters fail, the demanding party may move to compel under C.C.P. § 2031(1). Or the responding party may move for a protective order against unwarranted annoyance, embarrassment or oppression or undue burden or expense. C.C.P. § 2031(e).

2.8 REQUESTS FOR ADMISSIONS

Requests may be served only on parties to the case. C.C.P. § 2033(a). Requests for admissions can be a most valuable discovery tool and save great time and expense both in discovery and at trial. Admissions can force the opposing party to enter into serious settlement negotiations and finalize the case in your favor. See Form 2-7 Request for Admission Worksheet.

A. Subject Matter. Requests for admissions are used to:

1. Establish a fact or legal proposition.

2. Obtain some information that cannot be controverted.

3. Limit issues for trial.

4. Establish uncontested facts for purposes of motion for summary judgment.

5. To save deposition time and costs.

6. To save trial time and costs.

7. To eliminate surprise at trial.

8. To eliminate the need to call a trial witness.

B. Number of Requests. Requests for admissions are generally limited to 35 that do not relate to the genuineness of the documents. Any party may ask leave of court for more than 35 requests for admissions. C.C.P. § 2033(c)(1).

C. Form and Format. C.C.P. § 2033.5 sets forth the format to be used for request for admissions and the Judicial Council has published a blank form for use. See West's Cal. Forms, Form FI–100.

The basic objective is to get the opposing side to admit to the truth of facts and genuineness of documents. To this end the request should be drafted using simple, concise and precise words. The best requests for admissions seek a "yes" or "no" answer or a specific response that avoids misleading characterizations.

C.C.P. § 2033(c)(5) requires that each admission shall be full and complete in and of itself. No preface or instruction shall be included with the set of admissions. Make certain that each Request for Admission stands by itself and is clearly and precisely stated so that the answer can be used at trial. For each Request for Admission, define each possibly ambiguous term that is used to make certain of the meaning of the word or words in the request. Any term that is "specially defined" in a set of requests for admissions must be typed in capital letters whenever it appears. C.C.P. § 2033(c)(5).

Define every term used in the requests for admissions in each individual request for admission so as to avoid any conflict with the requirements of § 2033(c)(5). Put important phrases into capital letters.

D. Responses to Request. The party responding to a set of requests for admissions must respond within 30 days after the set was served unless time has been shortened or extended by court order.

A responding party may:

1. Admit matters either expressly or as clearly qualified.

2. Deny in whole or in part.

3. Qualify a response by stating that the responding party lacks sufficient information or knowledge to either admit or deny.

4. Object to the request.

5. Seek a protective order.

6. Seek an extension of time to respond.

7. Fail to respond and have the request become automatic admissions. C.C.P. § 2033(f)(7).

E. Failure to Respond. A failure to respond waives any objection to the requests and is deemed an admission of all of the requests for admissions. However, the court may relieve the responding party from this waiver and deemed admissions if it is satisfied that the party's failure to serve timely responses was a result of mistake, inadvertence or excusable neglect. CCP 2033(k).

F. Grounds for Objections. The usual objections apply to requests for admissions. These include:

1. The question is not relevant.

2. The question asks for privileged information.

3. The party does not have sufficient information after reasonable inquiry to affirm or deny.

4. The question asks for attorney work product.

5. The request exceeds the numerical limit.
6. The request is unintelligible.

All other objections, and privileges applicable to discovery are applicable to requests for admissions.

G. Use of Admission at Trial C.C.P. § 2033(n). Any admission admitted in response to a request for admission is conclusively established against the party making the admission in the pending action unless the court has permitted withdrawal or amendment of that admission. C.C.P. § 2033(n).

Any party that has requested the admission can quote the response to the admission or the lack of response to the admission that admits the fact at the time of trial and such facts are conclusively presumed to be correct. The genuineness of documents either agreed to by the request for admissions or not denied in requests for admissions are conclusively presumed to be genuine. C.C.P. § 2033(n), BAJI (7th ed.) No. *2.08*.

2.9 PHYSICAL OR MENTAL EXAMINATION C.C.P. § 2032

Any party may obtain discovery by means of a physical or mental examination by a licensed physician or other appropriate licensed health care practitioner. See Form 2–8 Physical Examination Worksheet.

A. Who May Be Examined. A party to the action, or a natural person under the legal control of a party in any action in which the mental or physical condition of that party or other person is in controversy in the action. C.C.P. § 2032(a).

B. When Appropriate. In any case in which a plaintiff is seeking recovery for personal injuries, any defendant may demand one physical examination of the plaintiff providing the examination does not include any diagnostic test or procedure that is painful, protracted or intrusive and is conducted at a location within 75 miles of the residence of the examinee. C.C.P. § 2032(c)(2).

C. Procedure to Be Followed. CCP 2032(c) provides a straightforward procedure by which a defendant may obtain a physical examination of a plaintiff in a personal injury case. The demands shall specify the time, place, manner and conditions and the identity of the examining physician. C.C.P. § 2032(c)(5).

D. Response to Demand for Physical Examination. The plaintiff in response to a demand for a physical examination may:

1. Comply with demand as stated;
2. Comply with demand with specified modifications; or
3. Refuse to submit to the examination and give specific reasons for the refusal.

All responses which demand specified modifications or refusals should be coupled with specific reasons for the modifications or the refusal or the attorney may be subject to sanctions under C.C.P. § 2032(c). As in all other discovery procedures, the party may seek a protective order.

2.10 LIMITING DISCOVERY

C.C.P. § 2017(c) gives discretion to the judge to limit discovery on a case by case basis. It provides that, "The court shall limit the scope of discovery if it determines that burden, expense or intrusiveness of that discovery clearly outweighs the likelihood that the information sought will lead to discovery of admissible evidence." However, one who seeks to limit discovery does so at their own risk. The court may impose a monetary sanction under 2023 against any party, person or attorney who unsuccessfully opposes a discovery motion. C.C.P. § 2023(b)(1).

The scope of discovery hinges not so much on a definition of relevance, but on a balancing of the relevance of the subject matter against the burden and expense of discovery.

A. Privileged Matters Not Discoverable. Privileged matters are not discoverable. C.C.P. § 2017(a). The following are the most commonly asserted privileges:
1. Confidential lawyer/client communications. Evid.C. § 254.
2. Confidential marital communications. Evid.C. § 280.
3. Confidential physician/patient communications. Evid.C. § 994.
4. Penitent/clergyman communications. Evid.C. §§ 1033 to 1034.
5. Confidential psychotherapist/patient communications. Evid.C. § 1014.
6. Trade secret privilege. Evid.C. § 1060.
7. Federal and State Income Tax Returns. Revenue and Taxation Code §§ 19282, 26451.

In addition to the above statutory privileges, California law recognizes the privilege of the right of privacy. Claims of right of privacy are decided on a case by case basis. Board of Trustees v. Superior Court, 117 Cal.App.3d 516, 174 Cal.Rptr. 160 (1981).

B. Attorney Trial Preparation Materials (Attorney Work Product) Not Discoverable. The work product of an attorney is not discoverable unless the court determines that denial of discovery will unfairly prejudice the party seeking the discovery in preparing that party's claim or defense or will result in an injustice. Any writing that reflects an attorney's impressions, conclusions, opinions, or legal research or its theories shall not be discoverable under any circumstances. C.C.P. § 2018(b) and (c).

Trial preparation materials are defined as writings prepared in anticipation of litigation or for trial. Factors that influence their discoverability include: 1) why were the materials gathered; 2) who prepared the materials; 3) when were they prepared? American Mutual Liability Ins. Co. v. Superior Court, 38 Cal.App.3d 579, 113 Cal.Rptr. 561 (1974).

C. Protective Orders. While objections to discovery attempts may be raised in response to interrogatories or at the deposition, it is better practice to anticipate such objections and to move for a protective order. This can be done at the time the request is made, or may be done in anticipation of discovery. The general authority for protective orders can be found in C.C.P. §§ 2017(c) and 2019(b). Section 2019(b) provides that if the discovery sought is unreasonably cumulative or duplicative, or is obtainable from some other source that is more convenient, less burdensome or less expensive or the selected method of discovery is unduly burdensome or expensive, the court may limit such discovery pursuant to a motion for protective order by a party or other affected person. In addition, each particular discovery device or method has a corresponding provision providing for protective orders. Depositions, C.C.P. § 2025(i); Interrogatories, C.C.P. § 2030(e); Inspection of Documents, C.C.P. § 2030(e); Physical Examination, C.C.P. § 2032(g)(1); Requests for Admissions, C.C.P. § 2033(e); Exchange of expert witness information, C.C.P. § 2034(e).

In moving for a protective order, the party requesting the protective order must do so through a motion procedure with supporting points and authorities and has the burden of showing good cause for issuance of a protective order.

2.11 ENFORCING DISCOVERY REQUESTS

A. Initial Failure to Respond. If a party fails to respond, gives an incomplete answer, objects or refuses to answer, counsel should first contact opposing counsel by phone with a follow up letter to try to resolve the discovery request. Ask for clarification of reasons for the failure to adequately respond or for further basis for the objection. Every effort should be made to resolve the dispute by meeting and conferring before bringing a motion to compel. Failure to confer with an opposing attorney in a reasonable and good faith attempt to informally resolve any dispute concerning discovery before bringing a motion to compel is considered a misuse of discovery process and, regardless of the outcome of the motion, the party or attorney who fails to confer will be subject to sanctions. C.C.P. § 2023(a).

Any attempt to meet and confer and any conference should be memorialized in a letter to the attorney summarizing the attempt to meet, the results of any conference and any agreements or disagreements which still exist after the conference.

B. Continued Failure to Respond

1. *To Compel Answers to Depositions.* CCP 2025(e)(4). To compel a deponent who refuses to answer a deposition question the examiner may:

   a) Give proper oral notice of the motion to compel at the time of refusal during the Deposition. C.C.P. § 2025(n); or

   b) Complete the deposition and set a hearing at a later date by proper written notice (see local rules for preferred practices for each jurisdiction). The court may order the deponent to answer the questions and sanction the refusing party and attorney for failure to answer. The sanction may include expenses, including attorney fees and more drastic sanctions if the conduct continues. C.C.P. § 2025(n), (o).

2. *To Compel Answers to Interrogatories.* C.C.P. § 2030(1). A propounder of interrogatories must file a motion to compel further answers within 45 days of the service of the response. The motion must be accompanied by Points and Authorities and a declaration showing that the meet and confer requirements have been met. The party bringing the motion has the burden to show that the response is insufficient or unresponsive. The court may order further responses and sanction the party who failed to respond. Further failures to respond may result in more serious sanctions including dismissal.

3. *To Compel Production of Physical Evidence.* C.C.P. § 2032(c)(7). To compel production of documents the requester must file a notice of motion to compel production of documents within 45 days of any response or date due for response. The motion must be accompanied by Points and Authorities and declarations showing good cause justifying the demand and a declaration showing a good faith attempt at informal resolution. The court shall impose a monetary sanction against any party who unsuccessfully makes or opposes such a motion. C.C.P. § 2032(n). The court may impose further sanctions including dismissal if the party fails to comply with the order to produce documents.

4. *To Compel Admissions.* C.C.P. § 2033(1). Requests for admission have an advantage as a discovery device because they are self-executing. That is, if the party does not respond after being given proper notice within 30 days of service, the requests are deemed admitted unless the court sets aside the admission because of mistake, inadvertence or excusable neglect. C.C.P. § 2033(a)(n).

C. Seeking Sanctions.
Almost every motion to compel discovery should be coupled with a request for sanctions. C.C.P. § 2023 sets forth acts which are considered a misuse of the discovery process for which sanctions may be imposed.

A motion for sanctions shall contain:

1. Notice of motion identifying every person, party and attorney against whom the sanction is sought.

2. A specification of the sanction sought.

3. Points and Authorities in support of motion.

4. Declaration setting forth the following:

   a) Attempts to meet and confer to settle dispute.

   b) Facts showing "willfulness" on part of opposing attorney.

   c) Facts supporting amount of any monetary sanction sought. C.C.P. § 2023(c).

Upon a showing that a party has misused the discovery process, the court may impose:

1. *Monetary Sanctions.* Guilty party to pay expenses and attorney's fees incurred by anyone as a result of that conduct. C.C.P. § 2023(b)(1).

2. *Issue Sanctions.* The court may order that designated facts shall be taken as established in the action in accordance with the claim of the party adversely affected by the misuse of discovery. C.C.P. § 2023(2).

3. *Evidence Sanctions.* The court may prohibit a party from introducing designated matters in evidence. C.C.P. § 2023(3).

4. *Terminating Sanctions.* A court may issue a terminating sanction by one of the following orders:

   a) An order striking the pleadings.

   b) An order staying further proceedings.

   c) An order dismissing the action.

   d) An order rendering a default judgment against the offending party. C.C.P. § 2023(b)(4).

2.12 AVOIDING MONETARY SANCTION AND TERMINATING SANCTION

A. Respond Promptly to All Requests for Discovery. Do everything you can as soon as you can. If you have a problem supplying requested information, call the opposing attorney and explain the problem. Convince the opposing attorney you are doing all you can do to comply and that you are acting in good faith. Enter into agreements and stipulations that may settle disputes.

B. Meet and Confer Whenever Possible. The courts do not want to spend time on discovery problems. The courts want the attorneys to work out the problems. If the attorneys don't—one of them is probably going to be sanctioned. If you meet and confer and do all you can but still have good faith reservations about giving information (e.g., privilege, work product) the court will see it as a good faith dispute regarding applicable law and not order sanctions.

C. Do Not Withhold Evidence. The attorney must disclose all evidence that he is aware of that is at all relevant to the case. There are serious sanctions for failure to do so. Generally, withholding information should be limited to privileged material and attorney work product.

D. Comply With Court Orders. While an attorney may have a good faith belief that certain information is not discoverable, once a court has ruled and ordered production, it must be done.

Normally, the sanction for losing a motion to compel will be monetary sanctions. That's out of the attorney's pocket. The sanction for failure to produce after a court order can be a "terminating sanction." That means the client loses his or her case and the attorney has failed to fulfill the most important duty of an attorney; that is to faithfully and fully represent the client to the best of his or her ability.

DISCOVERY WORKSHEET

Case _____   File _____

1. What facts are needed to prove the existence or non-existence of the substantive elements of the causes of action or affirmative defenses:

   _____

   _____

   _____

2. What are the possible sources of such information?

                 Name   **Address or Location**

   a. Parties _____

   b. Witnesses _____

   c. Documents _____

   d. Experts _____

   e. Records _____

   f. Things or places _____

3. What facts are needed to prove opposing party's case?

   _____

   _____

   _____

4. What are the sources of such facts?

                 Name   **Address or Location**

   a. Parties _____

   b. Witnesses _____

   c. Documents _____

   d. Experts _____

   e. Records _____

   f. Things or places _____

Form 2–1

DISCOVERY PLAN

Case _____   File _____

List below the discovery device to be used in the order in which you plan to use it:

Discovery Device **To Whom** **For What Purpose**

1. _____ _____ _____
   _____
   _____
   _____

2. _____ _____ _____
   _____
   _____
   _____

3. _____ _____ _____
   _____
   _____
   _____

4. _____ _____ _____
   _____
   _____
   _____

5. _____ _____ _____
   _____
   _____
   _____

6. _____ _____ _____
   _____
   _____
   _____

Form 2-2

Discovery Device   To Whom   For What Purpose

7. _____ _____ _____
                             _____
                             _____
                             _____

8. _____ _____ _____
                             _____
                             _____
                             _____
                             _____

9. _____ _____ _____
                             _____
                             _____
                             _____
                             _____

10. _____ _____ _____
                             _____
                             _____
                             _____
                             _____

11. _____ _____ _____
                             _____
                             _____
                             _____
                             _____

12. _____ _____ _____
                             _____
                             _____
                             _____

Form 2–2 (continued)

FACTUAL INVESTIGATION WORKSHEET

Case _____ File _____

1. WITNESS INTERVIEWS

   Name _____ Interviewer _____

   Date _____ Impression of Witness _____

   Fact Summary _____
   _____
   _____
   _____

   Statement Provided _____
   _____

   Name _____ Interviewer _____

   Date _____ Impression of Witness _____

   Fact Summary _____
   _____
   _____
   _____

   Statement Provided _____
   _____

   Name _____ Interviewer _____

   Date _____ Impression of Witness _____

   Fact Summary _____
   _____
   _____
   _____

   Statement Provided _____
   _____

   Name _____ Interviewer _____

   Date _____ Impression of Witness _____

   Fact Summary _____
   _____
   _____
   _____

   Statement Provided _____

Form 2–3

FACTUAL INVESTIGATION WORKSHEET

Case _____   File _____

2. SOURCES TO LOCATE WITNESSES AND INFORMATION

   Telephone Directory _____   Employees _____

   Department of Motor Vehicles _____   Friends _____

   City Directory _____   Relatives _____

   County Recorder _____   _____

   Other _____   _____

3. DOCUMENTS

   Statements _____   Bills, Receipts _____

   Writings _____   Photographs _____

   Contracts _____   Diagrams _____

   Leases _____   Coroner's Report _____

   Police Reports _____   Transcript of Traffic
       Court Hearings _____

   Highway Patrol
      DMV Records _____   Business Records _____

   Weather Newspaper
      TV Reports _____   Government
      Documents _____

   Court Records _____   Medical Records _____

   Advertising Brochures
      Warranties _____   Hospital Records _____

       Employee Records _____

   Videotapes _____

       Movies _____

4. PHYSICAL EVIDENCE _____

   _____

5. SCENE _____

   _____

6. OTHER INVESTIGATION _____

   _____

Form 2–3—(Continued)

INTERROGATORIES WORKSHEET

Case _____ File _____

Party	Date Served	Subject Matter	Answers Due	Answers Received	Motion to Compel Deadline

Form 2–4

DEPOSITION WORKSHEET

Case _____ File _____

DEPOSITION PLANNING

I. a. Prospective Deponent _____

    b. Notice or stipulation _____

    c. Location _____

    d. Date Time _____

    e. Purpose/Facts needed: _____

_____

_____

II. a. Prospective Deponent _____

    b. Notice or stipulation _____

    c. Location _____

    d. Date Time _____

    e. Purpose/Facts needed: _____

_____

_____

III. a. Prospective Deponent _____

    b. Notice or stipulation _____

    c. Location _____

    d. Date Time _____

    e. Purpose/Facts needed: _____

_____

_____

DEPOSITIONS COMPLETED

Deponent Transcript	Reviewed	Signed	Filed	Abstracted

Form 2–5

PRODUCTION OF DOCUMENTS/THINGS WORKSHEET

Case _____ File _____

Party	Date Served	Items Sought	Response Due	Response Received	Motion to Compel Deadline—Follow up

Form 2–6

REQUEST FOR ADMISSION WORKSHEET

Case _____ File _____

Party	Date Served	Requests	Response Due	Response Received	Deemed Admitted

Form 2-7

PHYSICAL EXAMINATIONS WORKSHEET FOR PLAINTIFF SEEKING PERSONAL INJURY DAMAGES C.C.P. SECTION 2032

Case _____ File _____

Date Motion	Date Response	Contents of Demand	Response to Demand	Motion to Compel Compliance	Protective Order Sought	Court Ruling

Form 2–8

Chapter 3
TRIAL FRAMEWORK

Table of Sections

Sec.
3.1 Analysis of Self.
    A. Verbal Analysis.
    B. Mental Analysis.
    C. Physical Analysis.
    D. Coping With Stress.
3.2 Analysis of Opponent.
3.3 Analysis of the Judge.
3.4 Analysis of Courtroom.
3.5 Analysis of Court Personnel.
3.6 Trial Brief.
    A. Need for a Trial Brief.
    B. Contents of Trial Brief.
3.7 Arriving in the Assigned Court and Chambers Conference.
    A. Court Personnel.
    B. Conduct in Chambers Conference.
3.8 Attorney's Trial Conduct.
    A. Avoiding Familiarity.
    B. Names.
    C. Interruptions.
    D. Approaching the Witness/Bench.
    E. To Stand or Sit.
    F. "Off the Record."
    G. Demeanor.
    H. Dress.
    I. Drama.

Forms
3–1 Opposing Lawyer Log.
3–2 Judge Log.
3–3 Courtroom Log.
3–4 Clerk Log.
3–5 Bailiff Log.
3–6 Trial Brief Worksheet.

3.1 ANALYSIS OF SELF

A. Verbal Analysis. Diction, pace, tone and volume will affect the fact finder's ability to understand what an attorney says. The attorney's eloquence and vocabulary will also have an influence. Poor grammar, stammers, and fillers, (i.e., "Ok, uhuh, uh," and "I see") reduce the lawyer's effectiveness. Word choice will likewise affect the jurors' ability to understand the case. Words should be selected that are simple and easy to understand.

B. Mental Analysis. An attorney's mental assets and mental strengths need to be taken advantage of while methods are developed to compensate for liabilities and weaknesses. For example, many attorneys overly rely on written notes for trial presentations because they believe they need memory aids. Practice, concentration, confidence, and a memory outline will usually suffice to overcome this or other perceived inabilities.

C. Physical Analysis. The appearance of an attorney and the image an attorney wishes to convey must be consistent for optimum persuasiveness. An attorney who wishes to be perceived as a professional, organized, and orderly advocate must appear that way.

The fact finder will be influenced to some degree by the dress and physical comportment of the attorney. Avoid flashy or sloppy clothes. Your physical appearance must be consistent with the image message you are trying to convey.

Posture, mannerisms, and habits affect the attorney's ability to communicate and persuade. Twitches, scratching, toe-tapping, swaying, knee-jerking, eyeglass jabbing, hand waving, scribbling, doodling, and paper shuffling games may detract from a presentation.

Body language may also affect what the fact finder perceives. The more consistent the content of the message is with the attorney's body language, the more credible the attorney will be. Various postures convey different messages to different individuals. Assume a posture that is comfortable, yet professional in appearance.

D. Coping With Stress. All trial attorneys will suffer stress from various sources. To maintain a proper, balanced attitude toward trial work each attorney must cope with the stress of being an advocate. Therefore:

1. Before accepting a trial, reflect on the reasons for taking the case and what your expectations are.

2. During the preparation of a case, involve the client in making decisions and avoid overcontrolling the case.

3. Do not worry about events or matters that cannot be controlled. Learn to let go and accept what cannot be changed.

4. Expect that relationship with family, friends, and colleagues will be disrupted and advise them accordingly.

5. Anticipate that some family members or friends may emotionally withdraw or be resentful.

6. Maintain a balanced relationship with the client throughout the trial.

7. Discuss feelings and attitudes with family and friends.

8. Monitor the trial workload to avoid becoming overworked.

9. Delegate appropriate responsibility and tasks to support staff.

10. Learn not to unnecessarily interfere and second guess decisions.

11. Avoid alcohol, pills, and drugs and other sources of escape.

12. Discuss a case thoroughly with the client after a verdict or decision.

13. Celebrate victories and accept losses.

14. Plan a break after a major trial.

3.2 ANALYSIS OF OPPONENT

The persuasive assets and liabilities of an opponent will affect the presentation and effectiveness of a case. Consider:

1. Level of experience.
2. Talent.
3. Presence and demeanor.
4. Reputation.
5. Relationship with the judge.
6. Habits and preferences.
7. How that attorney will be perceived by the jury.

Maintain records of various experiences with different lawyers, especially for attorneys who are encountered infrequently or intermittently. The log book which appears in Form 3–1 provides a method of maintaining these records. Information about an opposing lawyer may need to be obtained from other sources. Colleagues, law clerks, bailiffs, and other individuals, who know the lawyer may be helpful in providing needed information.

3.3 ANALYSIS OF THE JUDGE

Familiarity with the judge's strengths and weaknesses will help the attorney guide the case. Consider:

1. What are the strengths and weaknesses of the judge as judge?
2. How does the judge handle evidentiary rulings.
3. How does the judge run the courtroom?
4. What special demands may the judge place on lawyers?
5. Has the judge heard any similar cases?
6. What is the educational and professional background of the judge?
7. What is the judicial philosophy of the judge?

Maintain some of this information about judges in a written format. The log book which appears in Form 3–2 provides a method of recording this information. This retained information may be useful in future cases and for other lawyers in the office who have not appeared before a particular judge. Information about a new judge or a judge who has not presided over one of the attorney's cases may be obtained by talking with the law clerk, court reporter, clerk, bailiff, or by asking the judge.

3.4 ANALYSIS OF COURTROOM

Learn the physical setting and become comfortable and familiar with the acoustics, distances, spaces, and general layout of the courtroom. What can and cannot be done in the courtroom will affect how and where the attorney stands during examination and argument and how the attorney presents exhibits. The jury and judge need to have unobstructed views of the attorney, the witness, and exhibits. Some courtrooms have interferences, such as traffic, fan noise, uncomfortable jury chairs, and other problems that the attorney needs to be aware of before proceeding with a case. The log book appearing in Form 3–3 allows an attorney to build a record of the courtrooms as a reminder of what can and cannot be done in each room. Draw a diagram of the courtroom layout immediately after the first physical inspection.

3.5 ANALYSIS OF COURT PERSONNEL

Take into consideration the influence that the court reporter, clerk, and bailiff may have on a case. A court reporter will record the trial proceeding, usually on a steno machine and sometimes backed up with an audio recording system, and will mark exhibits. The clerk will usually provide the oath to the witnesses, perform general clerical duties during the trial, and may mark and handle exhibits. The bailiff will usually be responsible for maintaining order in the courtroom and will be responsible for the jury during selection and deliberation. The preferences, characteristics, and practices of these individuals may affect the manner in which a case proceeds. The log books contained in Forms 3–4 and 3–5 provide a means to record some helpful information.

3.6 TRIAL BRIEF

A. Need for a Trial Brief. While not specifically required by any Rule of Court or Code of Civil Procedure, a trial brief should be submitted in all cases except the very routine and simple. If the case is worth going to trial, it is worth doing a trial brief. If you do not submit a trial brief and your opponent does, you will be at a great disadvantage. The trial brief explains the facts, law, and evidence involved in the case, identifies the trial witnesses, details any stipulations, describes any pre-trial motions, and should include references to other trial matters such as the anticipated length of the trial. The purpose of the trial brief is to present in one cohesive document an overall perspective of the case from which the judge can gain an understanding of the case that he cannot readily gain from a mere review of the court file.

B. Contents of Trial Brief. A general trial brief may consist of concise memos regarding various issues. These memos may be separated from the main brief and submitted to the court as individual issue-oriented trial memos. A good trial brief should include:

1. A short statement of the case, including the origin of the lawsuit; a statement of the court proceedings held regarding the case so far, including any motions brought, the disposition of any motions and a procedural history of the case.

2. A brief statement of the facts (e.g., "This case arises from a collision which occurred . . .").

3. A statement briefly describing the parties (e.g., "Plaintiffs are John and Joan Nome, a married couple who purchased real estate from the defendants, Rubble Real Estate Agency").

4. A statement of the claims and defenses as asserted in the pleadings, including all allegations admitted by defendant, and/or admitted by plaintiff by way of affirmative defenses and all issues previously adjudicated by the courts in motions.

5. A statement of the facts that the attorney expects his or her evidence to show and a recitation of the opponent's factual contentions and rebuttal to those contentions.

6. A listing of the witnesses who will testify and a brief description of the substance of their testimony.

7. A brief statement of all legal arguments with citations and, where needed, excerpts from pertinent authorities. In a judge trial, it is important to give a full discussion of the substantive law issues which are central to the case. In jury trials, present authority for particularly important jury instructions that you anticipate will require argument.

8. A discussion of evidentiary issues which are expected to arise with a statement of position on each issue, the authority for the position, and anticipated offers of proof where necessary.

9. In cases involving complex issues of damages, include a detailed statement of damages with support for each damage claimed.

10. Finally, include a conclusion summarizing the statement of the case, the issues in contention, substantive law issues, the proposed resolution of evidentiary questions, and a summary of the damages claimed. See Form 3–6, Trial Brief Worksheet.

3.7 ARRIVING IN THE ASSIGNED COURT AND CHAMBERS CONFERENCE

A. Court Personnel. When arriving at your assigned courtroom, the first people you will meet are the court clerk and the bailiff. You will probably also meet the court reporter. These three people are important to the judge, important to the process of the trial, and very important to you. These people know how this particular courtroom is run, the particular idiosyncracies of this judge, and have their own particular preferences and rules regarding what procedures should be followed. Be courteous, respectful, and become friends with them as soon as possible. They are useful sources of information. When you first report to the trial department, give the court clerk the court file on the action and your business cards. Also give the clerk the time estimate for the trial. Determine from the court clerk, the bailiff, and the court reporter as much information as you possibly can, regarding the following areas: (1) any special preferences or procedures used by the trial judge in conducting the trial; (2) how the trial judge conducts the chambers conference; (3) the procedure in which this court wants the exhibit marked; and, (4) the mechanical and physical details related to the conduct of the trial, e.g., use of electrical outlet for slides or tape recorders, lecterns, stands for exhibits, storage of files, blackboards, bulletin boards, projectors.

Also obtain some information regarding jury procedures, the manner in which the court reporter or clerk would like the exhibits pre-marked and the times that the judge likes to start, take breaks, and proceed.

B. Conduct in Chambers Conference. The first order of business in the chambers conference is to make sure the judge has a copy of your trial brief. The judge may want some time to read this alone, or he may read it in the presence of both attorneys and ask questions as he reads the trial brief. While the chambers conference usually starts off in a very informal manner, there are important topics to discuss and important issues to resolve in the chambers conference. The informality of the setting and the tone should not distract the attorney from attending to the details that must be addressed at the chambers conference which could be extremely important in the outcome of the case.

The following is a list of subjects to consider in a chambers conference and are given in the form of a chambers conference check list based on Los Angeles Superior Court Civ. Trials Manual §§ 18, 21, and 25.

1. Whether the judge knows any of the parties or witnesses, or demonstrates any reasons for disqualification, either for cause or peremptorily.

2. Determine whether settlement possibilities should be explored and, if so, whether a further settlement conference is advisable.

3. Determine whether the issues in the case may be narrowed or modified by stipulations or motions. If there are any stipulations of fact or law, they should be made on the record.

4. Determine if there are any time problems in presentation of the case, e.g., picking witnesses out of order, adjourning for periods of time because of previous commitments of counsel, witnesses, or the court; and, generally setting the timetable for the proceedings.

5. Discuss and agree on housekeeping matters and schedule of the trial to include:

a) daily beginning and ending times;

b) recess policy;

c) use of exhibits to include use of exhibits on opening, procedure for marking and introduction into evidence, and procedure for publishing exhibits to the jury.

6. Determine whether there exists a potential for bifurcation of the trial for determination by the judge on certain issues and determination of other issues by a jury (e.g., statute of limitations determination made by judge, liability and damages determination made by jury).

7. Determine jury selection issues such as:

a) pre-instruction of jury;

b) voir dire questions judge will ask;

c) any specific requests as to method and order of examination of prospective jurors;

d) method of exercising challenges of prospective jurors;

e) the number of jurors and the number of alternate jurors.

8. Discuss evidentiary issues including:

a) whether any motions to exclude specified evidence or references to it will be requested;

b) whether any unusual or critical legal or evidentiary issues are anticipated during the course of the trial.

9. Discuss witness issues:

a) problems in order of presentation of witnesses;

b) convenience or availability of witnesses.

10. Discuss privilege or competence of witnesses.

11. Discuss jury instructions including:

a) when jury instructions are due;

b) when will jury instruction conference be held;

c) when will jury instructions be given to the jury (e.g., before or after closing argument);

d) will jury receive a written copy of jury instructions during their deliberations;

e) whether counsel may refer to the jury instructions that will be given by the judge during opening argument;

f) whether the judge will give some preliminary jury instructions prior to opening argument.

The following miscellaneous procedural issues may be discussed in the chambers conference: the use of an unusual demonstration; the use of unusual or inflammatory testimony; visiting the scene of the incident, accident, or crime; courtroom seating in multi-party cases; position used by counsel for opening-closing argument and examination of witnesses; the necessity to request to approach witnesses for direct or cross-examination.

In the course of the chambers conference, the judge may rule on certain motions regarding bifurcation, order of proof, and other pertinent procedural and substantive issues. All such rulings should be made in the presence of the court reporter with reasons given for such rulings.

Remember that the judge will form his or her first impression of the merits of your case and of you during the chambers conference. This first impression may strongly shape the judge's perception of the case and you throughout the trial. The attorney who makes a good impression on the judge as to the merits of the case and his or her ability to present such a case and knowledge of law and procedure has gained the first advantage in the proceedings to follow. Judges want to decide the case fairly and need to be guided in their decisions of law and fact. The attorney who appears competent and has set forth the case in an understandable, logical, rational, and legally sound manner will naturally be deferred to when the judge has difficult decisions to make. While the attorney can gain a tactical advantage by prevailing in motions and stipulations in the chambers conference, the most important advantage the attorney can take from a chambers conference is that the judge recognized him as prepared, competent and believable.

3.8 ATTORNEY'S TRIAL CONDUCT

The attorney's conduct will affect the way persons react to that attorney and, as importantly, to the client. Below are some general guidelines for attorney conduct.

A. Avoiding Familiarity. During trial, do not display familiarity with the judge, jurors, parties, witnesses, or other counsel. The expression of familiarity in the advocacy setting may be viewed as improper.

B. Names. Never address the judge by first name in the courtroom, but rather as "your Honor" or "the Court." Do not address the attorneys or jurors by their first name during trial. It is advisable, and required in some jurisdictions, to refrain from addressing witnesses by their first name to avoid any suggestion of improper familiarity. Some witnesses, such as children, may be appropriately referred to by their first name. Some attorneys will prefer to call witnesses by their first name in an attempt to personalize the witness or for other strategic reasons. Permission from the court to use first names should be obtained if the practice of the judge is unknown.

C. Interruptions. Do not interrupt an argument, questions, or response unless objectionable or unduly prejudicial. An examining attorney should wait until a witness has completed an answer before asking another questions and should not repeat the witness' answer to a prior question before asking another question.

D. Approaching the Witness/Bench. Do not wander around the courtroom, approach a witness, or approach the bench without first requesting permission from the judge unless the attorney knows that the judge does not require such a request. Some judges require the attorneys to sit at counsel table or stand at a lectern during direct and cross-examination. Other judges require the attorneys stand at certain positions for a bench or sidebar conference.

E. To Stand or Sit. Courts vary in their requirements regarding whether counsel should stand or sit during various stages of the trial. Counsel usually stand during opening statement and closing argument. Some jurisdictions require counsel to stand during examination and the making of objections. Other jurisdictions allow the attorneys to remain seated.

The decision where to stand or where to sit and the seeking of permission from the judge should be based upon an analysis of where in the courtroom the attorney will be most effective in presenting information or making an argument.

F. "Off the Record." Address any request by counsel to read or mark an exhibit or to be "off the record" to the court and not the reporter or clerk. Usually the reporter will stop recording only if the judge so indicates.

G. Demeanor. Always act with respect for the court and all participants in the trial. This professional demeanor should not prevent counsel from becoming assertive, insistent, or aggressive in appropriate situations. Do not indicate by facial expressions, body language, head shaking, gesturing, shouts, or other conduct any disagreement or approval of evidence, rulings, or events that happen during the trial. During the time the opposing lawyer makes a presentation or conducts questioning, refrain from reacting, either verbally or non-verbally, to statements and responses.

H. Dress. Many attorneys dress according to a standard of decorum they believe is expected of them by the judge and jury. The dress of an attorney should not become an issue which detracts attention from the client's case. Some attorneys prefer to wear a distinctive, but professional piece of clothing during a trial to help the jurors remember and identify the attorney.

I. Drama. Preparation for trial requires the attorney to play dual roles. The attorney is a technician in that he must satisfy all of the procedural and evidentiary rules of law in order to get his case before the finder of fact. He is also a performance artist in that he must act as a producer, director, writer, and lead actor in a performance which is designed to sway an audience composed of the jury and judge.

The truly successful trial attorney must perform both of these roles. One must be a technician to get the case before the finder of fact, and one must be a performing artist to convince the finder of fact.

Many trials are presented in a boring, uninteresting, and unpersuasive way because attorneys fail to understand the importance of treating the presentation of the case as a human drama. Remember the elements of drama, including human interest, excitement, suspense, resolution of conflict, and basic human values.

OPPOSING LAWYER LOG

Case: _____ File _____

Name of Attorney _____

1. Firm or affiliation

    a. Number of attorneys: _____

    b. Number of attorneys assigned per case: _____

    c. Reputation for staff and backup capability: _____
       _____
       _____

    d. Firm's general reputation:

        1. Negotiation: _____

        2. Discovery: _____

        3. Deposition: _____

        4. Trial: _____

2. Attorneys' strong points: _____
   _____
   _____

3. Attorneys' weak points: _____
   _____
   _____

4. Idiosyncrasies or predictable behavior: _____
   _____
   _____

5. Proficiency, competency

    a. Generally: _____

    b. Evidence: _____

Form 3–1

5. Proficiency, competency—Continued

    c. Procedure: _____

    d. Law and motion: _____

6. Negotiation

    a. Aggressive: _____

    b. Cooperative: _____

    c. Conciliatory: _____

7. What is this attorney's trial record?

    a. How many judge trials? _____

    b. Verdicts: _____

    c. How many jury trials? _____

    d. Verdicts: _____

    e. Is there reason to believe he/she is afraid to take a case to trial? _____

8. Discovery

    a. Prepared or not prepared? _____

    b. Extensive or cursory? _____

    c. Aggressive or cooperative: _____

    d. Allows extensions? _____

9. Prepare trial brief? _____

10. Trial skills

    a. Strong points: _____

    b. Weak points: _____

    c. Presentation skills: _____

    d. Likability to jury: _____

Form 3–1 (continued)

JUDGE LOG

Case _____ File _____

Name of Judge _____

1. Educational and professional background, including previous practice: _____
_____

2. Special courtroom rules: _____
_____

3. Evidence, rulings:

    a. Strong points: _____
    _____

    b. Weak points: _____
    _____

    c. Special considerations: _____
    _____

4. Procedure, rulings:

    a. Strong points: _____
    _____

    b. Weak points: _____
    _____

5. Special ethical requirements: _____
_____

6. Idiosyncrasies or philosophical bent: _____
_____

7. Previous verdicts in this type of case: _____
_____

8. Other: _____
_____

Form 3-2

COURTROOM LOG

Court and Department: _____

Diagram Courtroom in space below:

1. Acoustics: _____

2. Dimensions: _____

3. Layout (place on diagram the following):

   a. Bench

   b. Lectern

   c. Tables

      1. Number of counsel tables: _____

      2. Number of chairs for each: _____

      3. Court clerk: _____

Form 3–3

3. Layout (place on diagram the following)—Continued

    4. Court reporter: _____

    5. Bailiff: _____

  d. Jury box

  e. Witness box

4. Technical capabilities (note on diagram the following):

  a. Outlets: _____
  _____

  b. Overhead project: _____
  _____

  c. Screen: _____
  _____

  d. Shadowbox for X-rays: _____
  _____

  e. Chalkboard or white board: _____
  _____

  f. Easels: _____
  _____

  g. Microphones: _____
  _____

  h. Lighting: _____
  _____

  i. Interference:

    a. Traffic: _____
    _____

    b. Other noise: _____
    _____

  j. Air conditioning, heating: _____
  _____

Form 3–3 (continued)

CLERK LOG

_____
           (name)

1. Strong points _____
   _____
   _____
   _____

2. Weak points _____
   _____
   _____
   _____

3. Idiosyncrasies _____
   _____
   _____
   _____

4. Helpfulness _____
   _____
   _____
   _____

5. Expectations of lawyer behavior _____
   _____
   _____
   _____

6. Other thoughts _____
   _____
   _____
   _____

Form 3–4

BAILIFF LOG

_____
             (name)

1. Strong points _____
   _____
   _____

2. Weak points _____
   _____
   _____

3. Efficiency _____
   _____
   _____

4. Special rules _____
   _____
   _____

5. Helpfulness _____
   _____
   _____

6. Idiosyncrasies _____
   _____
   _____

7. Other thoughts _____
   _____
   _____
   _____

Form 3–5

TRIAL BRIEF WORKSHEET

1. Statement of Case:

   a. Date of filing: _____

   b. Origin of suit: _____

   c. Procedural history: _____
   _____
   _____
   _____

   d. Motions and rulings: _____
   _____
   _____
   _____

2. Summary of Facts: _____
   _____
   _____
   _____
   _____
   _____
   _____
   _____

3. Description of Parties: _____
   _____
   _____
   _____
   _____
   _____
   _____

Form 3-6

4. Claims and Defenses from pleadings which are still at issue: _____
   _____
   _____
   _____
   _____
   _____
   _____
   _____
   _____

5. Summary statement of what your parties evidence will show and rebuttal to opposing parties anticipated contentions: _____
   _____
   _____
   _____
   _____
   _____
   _____
   _____
   _____
   _____

6. List of witnesses who will testify and substance of their testimony

   Witness: _____

   Substance of Testimony: _____
   _____
   _____

   Witness: _____

   Substance of Testimony: _____
   _____

Form 3–6 (continued)

Witness: _____

Substance of Testimony: _____
_____
_____

7. Legal arguments (including jury instructions) with citations: _____
_____
_____
_____
_____
_____
_____
_____

8. Evidentiary issues with authority for exclusion or inclusion of evidence: _____
_____
_____
_____
_____

9. Statement of damages with support for each damage claimed: _____
_____
_____
_____
_____
_____
_____

10. Conclusion: _____
_____
_____

Form 3–6 (continued)

Chapter 4
MOTIONS

Table of Sections

Sec.
4.1 Scheduling a Case.
  A. Superior Court Trial Settings: Basic Steps.
  B. Setting Cases in Municipal and Justice Court.
  C. Assignment to Trial Department.
4.2 Judge Removal.
  A. Be Prepared for a Peremptory Challenge.
  B. Challenge With Caution.
4.3 Motion in Limine.
4.4 Motion to Amend Pleadings at Trial.
4.5 Motion for Continuance.
4.6 Motion to Strike.
4.7 Motion to Admonish the Jury to Disregard the Testimony.
4.8 Motion for Non-suit.
4.9 Motion for Directed Verdict.
4.10 Motion Argument Preparation.
  A. Time.
  B. Court Proceedings.
  C. Memoranda.
  D. Written Order.
  E. Time and Manner of Making Motions.
4.11 Motion Argument Presentation.
  A. The Facts.
4.12 Motion Argument Techniques.
  A. Conversational Approach.
  B. Preface.
  C. Structure.
  D. Substance of Argument.
  E. The Law.
  F. Factual Descriptions.
  G. Notes.
  H. Visual Aids.
  I. Interruptions.
  J. Candor and Compromise.
  K. Questions by the Judge.
  L. Involving the Judge.
Forms
4–1 Motion In Limine Worksheet.
4–2 Trial Motion Worksheet.

4.1 SCHEDULING A CASE

Many rules, rulings, standing orders, customs and statutory procedures govern the conduct of a trial and how a matter gets to trial. California rules are quite specific and must be followed to the letter. The rules for scheduling a Superior Court setting and a Municipal

Court setting differ and each local jurisdiction has its own local rules regarding the setting of trials. The California Rules of Court dealing with the setting of cases for trial are set forth in California Rules of Court 209–226 and constitute the basic provisions for setting the case for the trial calendar. One must also follow the local fast track rules to the letter. These may differ from the rules of court. Some jurisdictions consider the local rules to be controlling. Govt.Code §§ 68600–68615.

A. Superior Court Trial Settings: Basic Steps. (Caveat: Local fast track rules, where applicable, may supercede much of what is presented in this section.)

1. *At Issue Memorandum.* The first step in the trial setting process is for the party who desires to set the case for trial (usually the plaintiff) to file and serve an At Issue Memorandum. Some jurisdictions also require a Certificate of Readiness in this period.

Under California Rule of Court 209, the At Issue Memorandum shall contain at a minimum: (1) title and number of the case; (2) the nature of the case; (3) that all essential parties have been served with process and the case is at issue as to those parties; (4) whether the case is entitled to legal preference; (5) whether a jury trial is demanded; (6) the time estimated for trial; and (7) the names, addresses and telephone numbers of the attorneys for the parties or of parties appearing without counsel. Cal.Rules of Court 209.

2. *Arbitration Status Conference.* In most jurisdictions an Arbitration Status Conference must be held within 30 to 90 days after the filing of the At Issue Memorandum. Cal.Rules of Court 211(a).

At the Arbitration Status Conference, the court can: (1) order the case removed from the civil active list if it determines it is not yet ready to be set for trial; (2) order the case placed on the arbitration hearing list; (3) set the case for trial if the case can be set for trial within 90 to 120 days after the conference or at an earlier time if the parties agree or if the court orders; (4) schedule a trial setting conference if the case would not be ready for trial within 120 days, but can be given a certain trial date within 120 days to 180 days after the status conference; (5) schedule a pre-trial conference if required by local rules; or (6) set a status conference if the case cannot be set for trial, trial setting conference or pretrial conference as required by California Rules of Court 211C; and (7) conduct settlement discussions whenever appropriate.

3. *Settlement Conference.* A settlement conference must be set within three weeks before the date set for trial for any case estimated at longer than five hours. Trial counsel, parties, and persons having the authority to settle the case are required to personally attend the conference unless excused by the court for good cause. Local rules can impose additional obligations. Cal.Rules of Court 222.

Failure of any attorney to comply with the California Rules of Court, Local Rules of Court, and Orders, or to participate in good faith in any conference under the rules, is considered an unlawful interference with proceedings of the court and will be dealt with by the court with sanctions. Cal.Rules of Court 227.

4. *Continuances.* Continuances before or during a trial are disfavored and an attorney should not count on getting a continuance unless extreme circumstances exist. Cal.Rules of Court 375A.

B. Setting Cases in Municipal and Justice Court. The first step in setting a Municipal or Justice Court case for trial is filing and serving a Memorandum to Set the Case for Trial. This memorandum is similar to the At Issue Memorandum required in Superior Court. Preprinted At Issue Memorandum Forms are usually available from the local municipal court clerk. In Municipal and Justice Courts, cases are chosen from the civil active list in the order in which they were filed and are set for trial during the succeeding month. Cal.Rules of Court 509A. There are no specific procedures set forth in the California Rules of Court for Pretrial, Trial Setting, or Settlement Conferences. See California Rules of Court 506–515, Local Municipal Court Rules for specific details.

C. Assignment to Trial Department. In both Superior and Municipal Courts, the assignment to the trial department takes place at the calendar call for trial which is held on the morning of the scheduled date of the trial. California Rules of Court 223B and 511C. Cases on the calendar ready for trial are transferred to departments that are available on that particular day. California Rules of Court 223B and 511C. If no trial departments are available, cases usually will be "trailed" on the calendar until the trial department becomes available. Trailed cases usually take precedence over other cases of the same class on the master calendar. California Rules of Court 223C and 511D. It is essential that trial counsel determine the current practice in the presiding or master calendar department of the court in question. Check the applicable local rules.

4.2 JUDGE REMOVAL

The California Code of Civil Procedure provides for two ways to disqualify a judge from hearing a matter. C.C.P. § 170 sets forth that which must be shown in order to disqualify a judge for cause. C.C.P. § 170.6 provides for a peremptory challenge of the judge.

A challenge for cause under C.C.P. § 170 requires an evidentiary showing of prejudice, while a peremptory challenge under C.C.P. § 170.6 requires only a conclusionary affidavit or declaration to the effect that the declarant cannot or believes that he or she cannot receive a fair and impartial trial before the challenged judge.

A. Be Prepared for a Peremptory Challenge. Under C.C.P. § 170(d) a motion to disqualify a judge must be made at "the earliest practicable opportunity." When a case is assigned to a trial department on the morning of the calendar call, a challenge to the trial judge under C.C.P. § 170.6 must be made immediately on the assignment. This presents a serious logistic and tactical problem. Because the attorney does not know which judge will be assigned until the very moment of assignment at the beginning of the trial, it is necessary for the attorney to know which judges to challenge. Usually, the attorney must come equipped with the applicable preemptory challenge form and affidavit ready for filing at the very time the trial judge is assigned.

B. Challenge With Caution. The decision to file a preemptory challenge against a judge is not to be taken lightly, because such a challenge may be taken personally by the judge. The attorney may have to appear in front of this same judge on a later occasion with no opportunity to challenge. If a preemptory challenge is granted, which is essentially automatic, there is no assurance the next judge assigned to the case will be more desirable and there is a limit of one challenge in a case. C.C.P. § 170.6. A challenge for cause under C.C.P. § 170 requires an affidavit setting forth the interest the judge has in the case. There is no assurance that the motion will be granted. If denied, the judge will remain the trier of fact.

Prior to assignment to a trial judge counsel should do as much investigation as possible regarding judges that may be predisposed against his or her case. Counsel should consult whatever sources are available including other attorneys and published sources of information on the background of the judges. See, e.g., *Profiles of Judges*, L.A. Daily Journal.

Conflicts may become apparent in the pre-trial chambers conference. The judge himself may state facts which could lead to a challenge for cause under C.C.P. § 170, or make statements that would lead the attorney to believe that the judge should be challenged under C.C.P. § 170.6 (peremptory challenge). This is another reason why the attorney should always have a preemptory challenge form ready to be filled out and sworn under penalty of perjury or be prepared to bring a challenge for cause. If the attorney has a good faith belief that the judge cannot impartially try this particular matter, the attorney may have a duty to his client to file for disqualification of the judge under either a C.C.P. § 170 for cause, or C.C.P. § 170.6 peremptory challenge.

4.3 MOTION IN LIMINE

A motion in limine requests the court in advance of a proceeding to make an order determining questions of procedure or evidence or restricting conduct of the participants. The motion is used primarily to preclude parties, their counsel, or witnesses from communicating or disclosing to jurors or prospective jurors irrelevant or otherwise inadmissible matters that are so prejudicial or confusing that their effect cannot be nullified by a subsequent admonition by the court. The motion can also be used by a party who hopes to gain admission of some controversial evidence, but is not sure that it can be admitted. This will give that party an opportunity to get a ruling on the admissibility of the evidence so that the attorney can prepare the case based on the admissibility or inadmissibility of the proferred evidence. Although no specific statutory authority exists for a motion in limine, the motion has been approved and encouraged by the appellate courts Hyatt v. Sierra Boat Co., 39 Cal.App.3d 325, 337–339, 145 Cal.Rptr. 47, 54–55 (1978).

Such a motion should be considered in any jury trial in which the attorney anticipates serious questions being raised regarding admissibility of key evidence. See Form 4–1 Motion in Limine Worksheet.

4.4 MOTION TO AMEND PLEADINGS AT TRIAL

As a general rule, the issues for a trial and the relief awarded is limited to that set forth in the pleadings. However, a trial judge has the power to allow amendment of pleadings at trial in furtherance of justice, on whatever terms may be proper. C.C.P. §§ 473, 476. Such amendment may be granted at the outset of the trial, during the course of the trial, or even after all evidence has been presented and the case has been submitted for decision. When it appears necessary to the court, the court may postpone the trial after an amendment of the pleadings. C.C.P. § 473.

In requesting a substantial amendment to a pleading before the commencement of the trial, written notice of the motion and the proposed amendment is ordinarily required. C.C.P. §§ 471.5, 473. California Rules of Court 327. However, when a party moves at trial to amend a pleading to conform to proof, notice is not required.

An attorney, who, in preparing for the trial, realizes that the proof that he offers or will be offering is at variance with the pleadings, must decide whether to bring a motion to amend at the outset of the trial, or to attempt to introduce evidence on issues outside of the scope of the pleading during the trial, or make a motion to conform to proof. If there is serious variance between the pleadings and the proof offered at the time of trial, it is suggested that the attorney bring a formal motion to amend at the outset of the trial. To do so later runs the risk of having the motion to amend to conform to proof denied at a time when little can be done. The safer course is to make a formal motion to amend a pleading at the earliest opportunity.

4.5 MOTION FOR CONTINUANCE

"Continuances before or during trial in civil cases are disfavored. The date set for trial shall be firm." California Rule of Court 375. The court is empowered to grant continuance for good cause. Good cause requires a showing of an unanticipated or unavoidable emergency situation that cannot be resolved by means other than a continuance. (California Rules of Court, Rule 375A; referring to Section 9 of the Standards of Judicial Administration). Counsel should not count on being granted a continuance and a motion for continuance should be made only if counsel is unavailable due to illness, death, engagement in another trial or other unavoidable circumstances. (California Rules of Court, Division 1, Standards of Judicial Administration, Section 9; For other grounds see California Rules of Court, Division 1, Standards of Judicial Administration, Section 9; C.C.P. §§ 595, 595.2, 473, 576, 594.)

4.6 MOTION TO STRIKE

A motion to strike is a procedure for excluding improper evidence from the record that could not or was not excluded by objection. The party who fails to make a proper and timely motion to strike evidence waives the right to assert that the evidence is inadmissible. Evid.C. § 353A.

1. *Non-responsive Answer.* "Answers that are not responsive shall be striken on motion of any party." Evid.C. § 766. A motion to strike a non-responsive answer should be used against an inadmissible and damaging statement that a witness volunteers either through inadvertence or improper coaching.

2. *Improper Questions Answered Too Quickly for Objection.* When the question is asked and an answer is given so quickly that an objection cannot be made, a motion to strike is proper. In reality, the motion to strike really doesn't do anything, since the matter remains in the record and the jury has already heard it. It is made to preserve the matter on appeal.

3. *When to Make Motion to Strike.* A motion to strike must be "timely made" Evid.C. § 353(a). It should be made during or immediately following the answer. It should be coupled with a request to admonish the jury to disregard the testimony.

In the case of conditionally admitted evidence, the motion should be made as soon as it appears that the condition has not been met (e.g., foundation for admission of evidence not made).

4.7 MOTION TO ADMONISH THE JURY TO DISREGARD THE TESTIMONY

A motion to strike should almost always be coupled with the request that the judge admonish the jury to disregard the stricken evidence. If the impropriety of introducing the evidence is sufficiently clear, it may be appropriate to request the judge to admonish the attorney and/or the witness from referring to such material again. If the improper matter is so prejudicial that its disclosure makes a fair trial impossible, counsel should move for mistrial.

4.8 MOTION FOR NON-SUIT

A motion for non-suit is essentially a demurrer to the evidence in that it tests the legal sufficiency of the plaintiff's evidence. The motion is appropriate when it is clear that the evidence to be presented or already presented is not sufficient to entitle the plaintiff to relief under any applicable theory. It may be made either: (1) after the plaintiff's opening statement, or (2) after plaintiff's presentation of the evidence. C.C.P. § 581C(a). The motion for non-suit may be made as to specific causes of action or as to the plaintiff's suit in its entirety. If the motion for non-suit is granted, the judgment of non-suit usually operates as an adjudication upon the merits unless the court orders otherwise. C.C.P. § 581C. Form 4–2 Trial Motion worksheet may be used before trial to anticipate a motion for non-suit and during trial to prepare for and bring the motion.

4.9 MOTION FOR DIRECTED VERDICT

A motion for directed verdict is similar to a motion for non-suit in that it is appropriate when the evidence is not legally sufficient to support a verdict for an adverse party. It may be used as to an individual cause of action or the entire action. It differs in that the motion for directed verdict is based on an examination of all the evidence presented by all parties, and may be made by plaintiff, as well as defendant. C.C.P. § 630. Plaintiff's motion for directed verdict should be granted when all of the essential elements of a prima facie cause of action are established by uncontradicted evidence and the evidence is legally insufficient to sustain any defense asserted by the defendant. Defendant's Motion for Directed Verdict may be granted when there is no evidence to substantiate an essential element of plaintiff's cause of action, or where defendant's affirmative defenses are established by uncontradicted evidence. Form 4–2 Trial Motion worksheet may be used before trial to anticipate a motion for directed verdict and during trial to prepare for and bring the motion.

4.10 MOTION ARGUMENT PREPARATION

The preparation of an argument in support of or in opposition to a motion requires the same degree of preparation as any other facet of trial advocacy. The judge will expect an attorney to be prepared. An opposing attorney will evaluate a lawyer's performance during motion argument and assess that lawyer's trial skills and capabilities. If it is a motion in limine, it may be the first time the opposing attorney will have a chance to evaluate your oral advocacy skills.

A. Time. All pre-trial motions have specified time limits for noticing the motions, serving the papers on the opposing side, and filing papers with the court. Before preparing or filing any motion first consult the applicable California Code of Civil Procedure, California Rules of Court, and the most recent version of the local rules relevant to the particular motion you are filing. The subject of pre-trial motions is beyond the scope of this book. For an excellent discussion of pre-trial motions, see California Civil Procedure Before Trial, Vol. 2 Chap. 23, Cal. CEB, 1978, June 1988 Supplement.

B. Court Proceedings. While a motion in limine should generally be made with notice to the opposing side and points and authorities served and filed in support of the motion in limine, other trial motions which arise during the course of the trial are usually presented orally. It is preferred practice to anticipate the bringing of such motions and to have appropriate points and authorities in support of your oral motions ready to be submitted to the judge for his review to help decide the issues raised in the motion.

C. Memoranda. Most judges will require some written legal authority supporting or opposing the granting of a motion. The memorandum should be brief and contain a summary of the facts and the legal authority supporting the position asserted by the attorney. Most trial judges will not be inclined to read a lengthy detailed memo. A one or two-page memo is often sufficient. Many of the legal issues that you anticipate raising in motions during trial, can be discussed in the trial brief submitted to the judge at the beginning of the trial.

A memorandum may also be submitted to the court after a motion argument if some issues were brought up during argument which were not briefed and which need briefing to assist a judge in making a decision. An attorney may suggest that a memorandum and reply memorandum be submitted to the court, or a judge may request such submissions from the attorneys.

D. Written Order. Always submit a proposed written order for any motion presented.

E. Time and Manner of Making Motions. In a non-jury trial, any motion can be made in open court at the appropriate time. In jury trials, counsel should request the opportunity to present a motion in open court and ask permission to approach the bench for a sidebar conference and either argue the motion at sidebar, or excuse the jury so argument can be heard in court or in chambers.

4.11 MOTION ARGUMENT PRESENTATION

An effective and efficient presentation in support or in opposition to a motion must address the following question: What information does the judge need to decide the motion in favor of my client?

A. The Facts. Many motions revolve around questions of law. Facts may not make a significant difference in the outcome of the motion. Many other motions will depend upon the development of the facts. The presentation of facts in a motion hearing often occur by the submission of declarations.

When declarations are submitted in support or in opposition to a motion, there may be no need for the client or any witness to attend the hearing. When an attorney believes that additional evidence or live testimony is necessary or may be preferable, the party or the witnesses with such information should attend the hearing. When a judge believes that the granting or denial of a motion will turn on a fact which neither party has submitted to the court, it may be necessary to continue the motion hearing or present the information by way of declaration after the motion hearing terminates.

4.12 MOTION ARGUMENT TECHNIQUES

The techniques of motion argument do not significantly differ from other oral argument situations. The appropriate techniques to be employed depend upon the judge's familiarity with the motion, the type of motion presented, the position asserted by the opposing lawyer, and the time available.

A. Conversational Approach. Many lawyers will present an oral argument in a formal way as if they were debating. This approach may not be as effective as a conversational approach in which the attorney converses with the judge instead of arguing with an opponent.

An attorney, to be an effective "conversationalist" in this setting needs to adopt a persuasive style, display familiarity with the facts and the law, exude confidence, and persist when necessary. Rapport, eye contact, voice tone, diction, pace, gestures, and other factors will influence the effectiveness of a presentation.

B. Preface. An attorney should preface the substance of an argument with a brief outline of what will be covered. This will enable the judge to follow the argument. The judge may suggest that certain matters need not be covered because the judge is familiar with them or may have already resolved them. A judge may also postpone asking questions about a matter until that point is reached in the argument.

The preface should include a short description of the motion, its grounds, and the relief sought. The moving attorney may also wish to provide the court with some background regarding the nature and history of the case to put the motion in perspective. An opposing lawyer may present information if the moving party fails to do so.

C. Structure. The optimum structure for an argument will depend significantly on the type of motion presented. Any lengthy argument must be carefully ordered so that it can be easily followed by a judge. The motion, memorandum, proposed order, affidavits, or other moving papers may provide a structure for the argument.

D. Substance of Argument. An explanation of the facts and the law mixed with reason, logic, emotion, and equity will comprise the content of a presentation. Some techniques that may increase the persuasive value of an argument include the following considerations:

1. Should the strongest position be asserted first, with the second strongest position last, with other weaker positions explained in between?

2. Should key words, phrases, or positions be emphasized and repeated throughout the argument?

3. Is the motion a routine request, an unusual request, or a common request?

4. Should the failure or refusal of the opposing attorney to cooperate with the moving lawyer in resolving or compromising the issues of the motion be mentioned?

E. The Law. Legal explanations should be accurate and understandable. Many arguments lose their effectiveness because the attorney exaggerates the applicable law and explains it in a confusing way. Legal matter may be argued if it can be explained more effectively in oral argument, rather than in a brief. Long quotes and specific citations should be avoided during oral argument. These should be in the trial brief or points and authorities. An attorney should be able to explain the legal positions without having to bore a judge by reading from some authority.

F. Factual Descriptions. A description of the facts should include a complete and accurate recitation of the relevant evidence. Some attorneys will provide the court with factual information that does not appear in an affidavit, in the file, or on the record. The opposing attorney should point out to the judge the inadequacy of this information and the inappropriateness of the attorney's attempt to testify or provide evidence in an improper manner. Some attorneys may exaggerate the facts to match a point of law. This tactic will usually backfire, because the inherent weakness of such a position will be readily apparent to the opposing lawyer and to the judge.

G. Notes. The argument should never be read to a judge. A set of notes outlining the essential points of an argument may be used during a presentation as a guide. The absence of notes may indicate lack of preparation and may make a complete and logical presentation difficult. Whatever notes an attorney uses should not distract from the presentation of the argument.

H. Visual Aids. Visual aids such as diagrams, charts, graphs, exhibits, and other devices may help present an argument and may assist the judge in understanding the argument. The opposing lawyer should be advised and permission of the judge should be sought prior to the hearing to avoid problems at the hearing and to prevent any waste of time in preparing visual aids that may not be used.

I. Interruptions. Interrupting the opposing attorney and the judge should be avoided. It is unprofessional and discourteous to interrupt opposing counsel unless the statements are prejudicial, bear no relation to the motion, or mischaracterize something that requires immediate correction. Many judges will admonish an attorney who unnecessarily interrupts. It may be more effective for a lawyer to note any misstatements of fact or law and comment on any inappropriate statement after the opposing lawyer has completed an argument. A lawyer should direct all statements to the judge and avoid arguing with opposing attorney. A lawyer may request the court to admonish opposing counsel for making disparaging statements.

J. Candor and Compromise. An attorney must be candid during argument. If the facts and supporting law provide the judge with the discretion to grant or deny a motion, a moving party should not contend that the judge has only one option. If the facts and supporting law provide a party with a reasonable position, an opposing lawyer should not unrealistically argue that precedent requires only one result. Many judges will view the hearing as an opportunity to force the attorneys to negotiate a resolution to the problem. Attorneys who argue set positions during a motion hearing must be prepared to propose or accept alternative positions to resolve a matter.

K. Questions by the Judge. Questions asked by the judge should always be answered at the time asked and should rarely be postponed until later. The judge will expect an immediate answer and may not listen to the continuing argument until the question has been answered.

An attorney should directly answer a question and avoid hedging or qualifying a response. An attorney should also attempt to provide an answer in a light most favorable to a position. An attorney must also be prepared, if necessary, to concede a point in a response and attempt to place that concession in perspective and continue on with another point.

L. Involving the Judge The attorney should prepare and present an argument that involves the judge in the motion. Some judges are more active than others during oral argument. Effective presentations develop an interchange between that attorney and the judge. The more the judge participates, the better the judge's understanding of the case. The attorney may want to invite questions from the judge to involve the judge as much as possible.

MOTION IN LIMINE WORKSHEET

Case: _____ File: _____

A. Evidence sought to be excluded: _____
_____

   1. Summary of argument to exclude evidence: _____
_____

   2. Statutory authority: _____
_____

   3. Case authority: _____
_____

B. Evidence sought to be admitted: _____
_____

   1. Summary of argument to admit evidence: _____
_____
_____

   2. Statutory authority: _____
_____

   3. Case authority: _____
_____

   4. Offer of proof to show relevance needed: _____
_____

      a. If so, what should be shown by offer: _____
_____

      b. Declarations needed? _____

         If so, of whom? _____

      c. Witness testimony needed: _____

         If so, who? _____

Form 4-1

TRIAL MOTION WORKSHEET

Case _____   File _____

Date _____   Judge _____

A. <u>Motion for non-suit:</u>

    1. Why is plaintiff's evidence insufficient as a matter of law to state a cause of action? CCP Section 581(c).

        a. First cause of action: _____
_____
_____

        b. Second cause of action: _____
_____
_____

        c. Third cause of action: _____
_____
_____

        d. Entire case: _____
_____
_____

    2. When should motion be brought? _____

        a. What omissions in opening statement would warrant bringing motion after opening statement: _____
_____
_____
_____
_____

Form 4–2

3. What omissions in the presentation of plaintiffs evidence would warrant bringing motion after closing of plaintiff's case? _____

_____

_____

_____

_____

_____

4. What do you anticipate plaintiff will omit which would give rise to motion for non-suit?

_____

_____

_____

_____

_____

B. Motion for Directed Verdict CCP Section 630

   1. Plaintiff's case:

     a. Are all elements of prima facie cause of action established by uncontradicted evidence and insufficient evidence exists to sustain any affirmative defense?

       If so, list causes of action and why:

       (1) First cause of action: _____

_____

_____

       (2) Second cause of action: _____

_____

_____

       (3) Third cause of action: _____

_____

_____

Form 4–2 (continued)

(4) Entire case: _____

_____

_____

(5) Lack of evidence for affirmative defenses: _____

_____

_____

_____

2. Defendant's Case: Is there no credible evidence to substantiate an essential element of plaintiff's causes of action or are defendant's affirmative defenses established by uncontradicted evidence? If so,

    a. For which causes of action was no credible evidence presented, and why? _____

_____

_____

    b. Which affirmative defenses are uncontradicted? _____

_____

_____

_____

Form 4-2 (continued)

Chapter 5
PREPARING FOR AND PRESENTATION OF EVIDENCE

Table of Sections

Sec.
5.1 Witness Logistics.
    A. Excluding Witnesses at Trial.
    B. Use of Interpreters.
    C. Compelling Attendance for Testimony at Trial.
5.2 Court Intervention.
    A. Court Appointed Experts.
    B. Court Witnesses.
5.3 Expert Witnesses.
    A. When to Use an Expert.
    B. Who Is an Expert?
    C. Qualifying the Expert.
    D. Knowing the Subject Area.
    E. Preparing the Expert on the Law of the Case.
    F. Preparing the Expert on the Facts of the Case.
    G. Opinion Testimony.
    H. Sources of Information.
    I. Hypothetical Questions.
    J. Questions and Answers.
    K. Opinions.
    L. Explaining Technical Terms.
5.4 Preparation of Witnesses.
    A. Meeting the Witness.
    B. Gathering Information.
    C. Witness Satisfaction and Effectiveness.
    D. Preparation for Direct and Cross-Examination.
    E. Providing the Witness With Guidelines for Testifying.
    F. Witness' Dress.
    G. Rehearsal.
    H. Ensure Attendance.
    I. Client Guidelines.
5.5 Problems With Foundation.
    A. Foundation Questions.
    B. Foundation Checklist.

EXHIBITS

Sec.
5.6 Types of Exhibits.
  A. Real Evidence.
  B. Demonstrative Evidence.
  C. Visual Aids.
5.7 Purposes.
5.8 Relevancy Considerations.
  A. Threshold Test—Is the Exhibit Logically Relevant?
  B. Is the Exhibit Legally Relevant?
5.9 Selecting Exhibits.
5.10 Foundation for Exhibits.
5.11 Legal Foundation.
  A. Tangible Objects and Properties (Including Products, Clothing, Appliances, and Weapons).
  B. Chain of Custody.
  C. Documents.
  D. Business Correspondence (Including Letters, Memos, and Notes).
  E. Business Records (Including any Memorandum, Report, Writing, or Data Compilation).
  F. Copies.
  G. Electronic Recordings (Including Audio and Video Recordings).
  H. Test Results (Including X-ray Films and Laboratory Analysis).
  I. Photographs (Including Prints, Slides, and Movies).
  J. Diagrams (Including Charts, Models, Drawings, Overhead Transparencies and Similar Illustrative Aids).
  K. Past Recollection Record.
  L. Stipulations.
  M. Statements of Admissions in Judicial Proceedings.
  N. Discovery Information.
  O. Self-Authenticating Documents.
5.12 Persuasive Foundation.
5.13 Stipulating to Foundation.
5.14 Exhibit Systems.
5.15 Planning Introductions.
  A. Preparing the Witness.
  B. Preparing for Possible Objections.
  C. Supplementing Exhibits.
5.16 Presentation and Delivery.
  A. Professional Presentation.
  B. Practical Problems.
  C. The Steps to Introduction of Exhibits.
  D. Variation in Word Usage.
  E. Leading Questions.
  F. Finessing the Foundation.
  G. Location.
  H. Voir Dire Examination.
5.17 Offer and Use of Requests for Admissions.
5.18 Offer and Use of Stipulations.
5.19 Evidence Summaries.
5.20 Judicial Notice.
5.21 Matters to Be Heard Outside the Presence of the Jury.

Forms
5-1 Professional/Expert Witness Log.
5-2 Expert Testimony Planning Worksheet.
5-3 Witness Preparation Worksheet.
5-4 Exhibit Selection Worksheet.
5-5 Exhibit Foundation Worksheet.
5-6 Trial Exhibits Chart.

Forms
5-7 Exhibit Introduction Checklist.
5-8 Trial Proof Worksheet.

5.1 WITNESS LOGISTICS

A. Excluding Witnesses at Trial. The exclusion of witnesses at trial is a tactical decision that is made by the attorney based upon the circumstances of the case. An attorney may request that the court exclude future witnesses from the courtroom to prevent them from hearing other witnesses' testimony. Evid.C. § 777. The rationale for this motion is that the later witness may be subconsciously influenced to conform his or her testimony to the earlier testimony heard. A more significant consideration is that the witness will not have heard the cross-examination of the attorney regarding the particular subject matter area and cannot prepare responses. Evid.C. § 777(b) provides that a party to the action cannot be excluded under this section. Also, Evid.C. § 801(b) indicates that an expert witness cannot be excluded from the trial if his opinion is to be based on hearing the testimony of the witnesses appearing at the trial. It provides that the expert opinion may be based on matter perceived "by or personally known to the witness or made known to him at . . . the hearing, whether or not admissible."

B. Use of Interpreters. A witness may need an interpreter in order to testify. A judicial proceeding must be conducted in English. C.C.P. § 185. Evid.C. § 752(a) provides that an interpreter shall be sworn when a witness is incapable of hearing or understanding English or is incapable of communicating in English, so as to be directly understood.

Requests for interpreters or translators should be made in advance of trial and, in most jurisdictions, the attorney should look to the list of recommended court interpreters provided by most counties in the State of California. Gov't.C. § 68562. The trial court in those counties which have a list of interpreters utilize only the services of those recommended interpreters, unless good cause is found by the judge for the appointment of an interpreter not on the approved list. It is recommended practice to use an interpreter from the list of court-approved interpreters, since interpreters are "treated as expert witnesses and subject to the same rules of competency in examinations as are experts generally." Comment to Evid.C. § 352.

C. Compelling Attendance for Testimony at Trial. The attorney of record may sign and issue a subpoena to require the attendance before the court in which the action or proceeding is pending or at the trial of an issue. C.C.P. § 1985. The witness who fails to abide by a subpoena may be subject to a contempt citation and arrest. C.C.P. § 1991.

There are certain procedural requirements which must be adhered to in order for the subpoena to be enforceable by contempt. (See C.C.P. § 1985 through 1996.) The attorney who subpoenas a witness should make diligent efforts to obtain the witness' appearance or to determine the reasonableness of the witness' failure to appear.

5.2 COURT INTERVENTION

A. Court Appointed Experts. The court on its own motion or on the motion of any party, may appoint an expert witness to testify in a case. Evid.C. § 730. The court may fix the compensation for such services rendered by any person appointed by the court and the fact of the appointment of an expert witness by the court may be revealed to the trier of fact. Evid.C. § 722.

B. Court Witnesses. The court, on its own motion or on the motion of any party, may call witnesses and interrogate them the same as if they had been produced by a party to the action, and the parties may object to the questions asked by the judge and to the evidence aduced by the examination by the judge, the same as if the witnesses were called and examined by an adverse party. In addition, all witnesses called by the court may be cross-examined by all parties to the action. Evid.C. § 775.

5.3 EXPERT WITNESSES

Although all witnesses share some characteristics, the expert witness requires some special considerations. See Form 5-1 Professional/Expert Witness Log.

A. When to Use an Expert. The scientific, technical, or other specialized knowledge of an expert may assist the fact finder in understanding the evidence or determining a fact in issue. Certain fields of expertise are well recognized such as medicine, engineering, economics, ballistics, fingerprints, and accounting. Evid.C. §§ 801–802, 702.

B. Who Is an Expert? A person who has some expert knowledge gained by skill, experience, training, or education may be qualified as an expert. Evid.C. §§ 702, 801(b), 802.

C. Qualifying the Expert. The rules of evidence require that an expert witness be qualified in the area in which the expert will be testifying. Evid.C. §§ 702, 720, 802. The judge must determine whether a person is an expert based upon that individual's qualifications. The jury should hear the expert's qualifications to judge the expert's credibility. The expert may testify only in those areas in which qualified. Evid.C. §§ 720, 802.

An opposing lawyer may offer to stipulate to an expert's qualifications. An attorney should not usually accept this stipulation because the jury will need to hear all of the background qualifications of the expert. However, a witness with marginal qualifications or lower qualifications than the other side's expert, might be more credible with stipulated qualifications. In either case, the qualifications should be presented in an interesting, tasteful, and non-bragging fashion.

D. Knowing the Subject Area. Know the subject on which the expert will testify as well as the expert. The attorney will need to be educated, trained to read relevant materials, and become thoroughly familiar with that area of expertise.

E. Preparing the Expert on the Law of the Case. Explain the law of the case to the expert. This will allow the expert to frame an opinion that meshes with the law.

F. Preparing the Expert on the Facts of the Case. The attorney will often explain the facts of the case to an expert, establishing a mind-set from which to proceed. The examination and opinion may then be prepared with an understanding as to how the attorney views the case. However, remain open to the expert's ideas. Talking to the expert may provide new ideas and concepts and correct mistaken ideas.

G. Opinion Testimony. An expert must testify to the sources of information supporting an opinion, to the opinion, and to the bases of the opinion. Evid.C. § 802. Opinion based on matter that is not a proper basis for such opinion is inadmissable. Evid.C. § 803.

H. Sources of Information. An expert may rely upon several sources of information including:

1. Personal firsthand information.

2. Data obtained from other experts, documents, treatises, files, persons, and other sources of hearsay as long as such data is the type reasonably relied upon by an expert. See Evid.C. § 804.

3. Trial or deposition testimony.

4. Hypothetical questions.

I. Hypothetical Questions. Prepare hypothetical questions in advance with the assistance of the expert. Hypothetical questions should be written so that no mistakes are made. They should be accurate, complete, simply phrased, and as short as possible. They are helpful but not required in order for an expert to give an opinion. Because they are often boring and open to attack on cross-examination they should be carefully structured and cautiously used. Hypotheticals may be used when the expert does not have personal knowledge of all of the facts necessary to form an opinion and the attorney is certain that all of the facts contained in the hypothetical will have been or be established by the evidence presented. It is best for the expert to testify to an opinion based on personal knowledge whenever possible.

J. Questions and Answers. Experts will often be permitted to give lengthy explanatory answers. The attorney will also be permitted to ask questions calling for narrative responses.

K. Opinions. An expert may testify to a number of opinions, including one that embraces the ultimate issue to be decided by the trier of fact. Evid.C. § 805. A case may involve a major opinion and several subordinate or minor opinions. Some judges may expect the attorney to elicit an opinion by asking the traditional questions: Do you have an opinion based upon a reasonable degree of expert certainty? What is that opinion?

L. Explaining Technical Terms. Understand and know how to pronounce all of the expert's technical terms. Learn how to explain the technical terms in plain English. If testing is involved, the expert must explain why the testing was done and the validity of the result. See Form 5–2 Expert Testimony Planning Worksheet.

5.4 PREPARATION OF WITNESSES

The preparation of the witness will begin at the initial interview, long before trial. Every contact with a witness should be viewed as an opportunity to prepare that witness for trial.

A. Meeting the Witness. Consider several factors for a witness preparation meeting:

1. How will the meeting be structured?
2. Will the attorney structure the meeting or just let it happen?
3. What other ways are there to structure the meeting?
4. Is there a particular impression the attorney wants to convey to the witness?
5. How will the attorney prepare for the meeting?
6. Will the attorney know everything there is to know about the case, or will more information be gathered?

B. Gathering Information. During the meeting with the witness your object is to find out what the witness knows or does not know, and who this person is. To determine this information, consider using one or more of the following methods:

1. Let the witness give a semi-narrative description.
2. Set up specific responses with questions.
3. Establish a mind-set with the witness by telling your view of the case or theme first.
4. Show the witness statements made by other witnesses.
5. Explore any "skeletons" that may be hanging in the witness' closet so that they may be assessed for purposes of meeting attacks on credibility by the other side.
6. Uncover any bias or prejudice the witness may have toward the client, other party, or case.
7. Take a declaration or other signed statement from the witness.

C. Witness Satisfaction and Effectiveness. A satisfied and informed witness may be more effective and persuasive at the trial. Initial and subsequent contacts that an attorney has with a witness will affect the witness' impression of the attorney and of the case. Factors which will influence the witness' perceptions include:

1. Who conducts the preparation? Does the witness feel important because the attorney conducts the preparation?
2. When does preparation occur? Will the witness be more comfortable if the preparation takes place at a time convenient to the witness?
3. Where does the preparation occur? The location, the office, furniture, and physical layout will also affect the impression of the witness.
4. Why does the preparation take place? Do the witnesses understand their role in the trial and the issues in the case to the extent necessary to be effective witnesses?

D. Preparation for Direct and Cross–Examination. A witness must know what is expected and what will happen at trial. The lawyer must know how the witness will perform. Areas to be covered with a witness before the trial include:

1. The application of the oath and the need to tell the truth.
2. The facts the witness knows.
3. A review of the exhibits the witness will identify and laying foundation for admission.
4. Appropriate demeanor at the trial.
5. The need for the witness to answer questions in a conversational style using his or her own vocabulary.
6. The role of the lawyers, the judge, the court reporter, the clerk, and the bailiff.
7. When to appear in court.
8. Whether the witness should sit in the courtroom before being called and remain after testifying.
9. Areas of likely cross-examination.
10. Objection and witness' possible response.

An attorney may need to or wish to provide witnesses with additional information. If the witness is a client, obviously that person will need to be involved in all aspects of the case. An attorney may decide to explain to some witnesses the theme and theories of the case, the purpose of the witness' testimony, and other information about the case. This knowledge may help the witness be more effective and credible at trial, but may also provide additional areas that can be explored on cross-examination. Preparation must be conducted to avoid the appearance of having overly influenced the testimony of the witness.

Whatever approach taken, the witness should be prepared to testify in a natural and not memorized manner. Witnesses may be prepared individually, in sets, during one interview or during several interviews. These decisions will depend upon the type of case, the witness' ability, and the time available.

Some witnesses may have problems which require special consideration before trial. A child witness, a person with a communication, physical, or mental handicap, the extremely nervous witness, the obnoxious witness, and other types of witnesses may need special care during preparation. A doctor, linguist, therapist, or interpreter may be necessary.

E. Providing the Witness With Guidelines for Testifying. The best way to have a witness live up to the attorney's expectations is to inform the witness of what those expectations are. Some of the instructions the witness should be given include:

1. The need to maintain some eye contact with the jury or judge.
2. The need to maintain eye contact with the examining attorney:
    a) Whom to look at during direct examination and cross examination; and
    b) The dangers of looking at the lawyer too much, as if looking for clues about what to say.
3. The attorney's role of protecting the witness from opposing counsel.
4. The dangers of becoming angry or losing control.
5. The importance of telling the truth and not exaggerating.
6. The benefits of appearing honest and sincere.
7. The necessity of not answering a question that is not understood.
8. The avoidance of speculation or inappropriate opinions when answering questions.
9. The need to decline to answer a question if the witness does not know the answer.
10. The problems created by being non-responsive or volunteering information.
11. An explanation of technical terms used during the trial.
12. The obligation of the attorney to control the case.

F. Witness' Dress. The credibility of a witness will be affected to some degree by the witness' attire. Generalizations about the type, color, and quality of clothing that should be worn are difficult. Principles that help guide individual decisions include:

1. The theme and theories of the case. The dress of a witness should be consistent with the role of that witness in establishing or reinforcing the theme and theories of the case.

2. The personality of the witness. Overdressing or underdressing may adversely affect the believability of a witness.

3. The expectations of the fact finder. The jurors or judge will have certain expectations based on community standards about how people should dress. Neatness is an example of such an expectation. Regardless of the type, color, or quality of clothing, if the witness dresses neatly, the fact finder will be more comfortable listening to that witness.

G. Rehearsal. A well-prepared witness should be comfortable with the role to be played at trial. Preliminary hearings and depositions serve as rehearsal vehicles. Some of the considerations in rehearsal include:

1. The witness should know which questions will be asked, and should not be asked "surprise" questions at trial.

2. The witness may need to understand the theories of the case and the purpose of the testimony.

3. The witness should not be coached to "parrot" answers.

4. The witness should realize that the examination at trial may differ because of changing trial strategies.

5. The rehearsal should take place far enough in advance of the trial so that the witness will be able to incorporate the attorney's suggestions.

6. The witness should avoid the rehearsed look.

7. The witness should be comfortable with exhibits.

H. Ensure Attendance. After preparation and before the trial, the attorney should instruct the witness to keep the attorney informed concerning the witness' whereabouts and any new information or ideas concerning the case. Develop a system to assure that all witnesses have been contacted and subpoenaed if necessary. Subpoenaing all witnesses, even favorable witnesses, will ensure attendance and make the witnesses appear more neutral. A subpoena must be accompanied by a witness and mileage fee. C.C.P. §§ 2064, 2065. See Form 5-3 Witness Preparation Worksheet.

I. Client Guidelines. A client who sits at the counsel table during trial should be told that:

1. The party will be periodically watched by the jurors and the judge and should always be conscious of being observed.

2. The party should periodically maintain eye contact with jurors and the judge. This helps personalize the client.

3. The client should not interrupt the attorney during trial unless necessary or when the attorney seeks advice. The client may be advised to communicate in writing during the trial.

4. The client should pay attention throughout the trial, concentrate on the evidence and arguments, and watch the judge and jury to catch anything the attorney might miss.

5.5 PROBLEMS WITH FOUNDATION

A. Foundation Questions. Foundation questions are preliminary questions that establish a basis for the introduction of further evidence. Foundation questions are necessary to show that certain evidence is admissible and to assist the fact finder weighing the value of the evidence. There are several categories of evidence requiring specific foundation.

1. *Qualifications of Witness.* Foundation questions must establish the personal knowledge of a witness for that witness to be competent to testify. Evid.C. §§ 400, 700, 403.

2. *Sources of Information.* Foundation questions will be necessary to explain how, when, and where a witness saw an event firsthand. Evid.C. §§ 702, 403.

3. *Conversations.* Foundation questions to establish the admissibility of a conversation include where and when the conversation took place and who was there. Telephone conversations require further foundation establishing how the witness identified the voice (prior conversations) or know who the speaker was (by dialing a phone number). Evid.C. §§ 702, 403.

4. *Opinions and Conclusions.* Foundation questions are necessary to describe the basis for a witness' opinion. Evid.C. §§ 800. A non-expert witness, for example, can state that a person appeared drunk if they can testify to the person's glassy eyes, alcohol, breath, slurred speech, staggered walk, and other observations supporting that conclusion. People v. Ruiz, 265 Cal.App.2d 766, 71 Cal.Rptr. 519 (1968).

5. *Documents.* Foundation questions are necessary to establish the authenticity of a document. Before introducing a document, it must be shown that the exhibit is what it purports to be. Evid.C. §§ 1401(a), 403.

B. Foundation Checklist. The specific foundation required will vary depending upon the type of evidence. A checklist of required points will make certain that a foundation has been established. The following factors will satisfy nearly all foundation requirements for direct examination.

1. *Is the Witness Competent?*

a) Is the person capable of expressing himself or herself so as to be understood? Evid.C. § 701(a)(1).

b) Is the person capable of understanding his duty to tell the truth? Evid.C. § 701(a)(2).

c) Has it been established that the witness has personal knowledge of the matter? Evid. C. § 702(a).

2. *Is the Evidence Relevant?*

a) Is the evidence logically relevant? Does the evidence, including evidence relevant to the credibility of a witness, have any tendency in reason to prove or disprove any disputed fact that is of consequence to the determination of the action? Evid.C. § 210.

b) Is the evidence legally relevant? Evid.C. § 352. Is the probative value of the evidence outweighed by the probability that its admissions will:

1) necessitate undue consumption of time?

2) create substantial danger of undue prejudice?

3) confuse the issues? or,

4) mislead the jury?

Unless a foundation is laid addressing these issues the judge can exclude the evidence as legally irrelevant evidence. Evid.C. § 352.

3. *Is the Witness Qualified to Testify to an Opinion?*

a) If a lay witness, is the opinion testimony rationally based on the perception of the witness and helpful to a clear understanding of his testimony? Evid.C. § 800.

b) If an expert witness, does the opinion testimony relate to a subject that is sufficiently beyond common experience that the opinion of an expert would assist the trier of fact, and is such opinion based on knowledge and information that is of a type reasonably relied upon by an expert in forming an opinion upon the subject? See Section 5.3 Expert Witnesses. Evid.C. § 801.

4. If the proferred evidence is a writing, has the best evidence rule been complied with by providing an original? Evid.C. § 1506. If not, do any of the following exceptions apply?

a) The original is lost or stolen. Evid.C. § 1501.

b) The original is not available by use of the court's process. Evid.C. § 1502.

Preparing for and Presentation of Evidence 5–9

c) The writing does not address a controlling issue and it is inexpedient to require its production. Evid.C. § 1504.

d) The original is a public record. Evid.C. §§ 1506 & 1507.

e) There is no genuine question as to authenticity of an original when a duplicate of the original is offered. Evid.C. § 1511. See Chapter 6, Section 6.4J.

5. *Is the Exhibit Authentic?* What evidence will be presented sufficient to sustain a finding that the writing or exhibit is what the proponent claims it is? Evid.C. § 1400.

6. *Is the Evidence Non-hearsay or a Hearsay Exception?* See Chapter 6, Section 6.4L for discussion of hearsay.

EXHIBITS

5.6 TYPES OF EXHIBITS

There are three main types of exhibits that are covered in this section—real evidence, demonstrative evidence, and visual aids.

A. Real Evidence. Real evidence refers to those exhibits that are directly probative concerning one or more issues in the case. They are a "real" part of the event or transaction. Real evidence might include a gun, documents such as a contract, clothing, or other tangible items. Real evidence is usually admitted into the jury room.

B. Demonstrative Evidence. Demonstrative evidence consists of those exhibits that are admitted for illustrative purposes only. Demonstrative evidence has no probative value in and of itself. Rather, its two primary purposes are to help a witness testify and clarify the evidence for the jurors. Demonstrative evidence commonly includes diagrams, charts, graphs, and models. Demonstrative evidence may be admitted into the jury room in the discretion of the trial judge.

C. Visual Aids. Visual aids refer to a group of exhibits that are used by the attorney during opening statement, closing argument and infrequently during testimony. Visual aids help the attorney present and summarize the case before the jury. Visual aids are not admitted into evidence and do not go with the jury into the deliberation room. Commonly used visual aids include a chart summarizing a plaintiff's injuries, an outline of a summation written on a blackboard, or an outline of testimony.

5.7 PURPOSES

People learn most of what they know through their sense of sight. Society, in general, has been transformed by modern media into a visual society. The predominance of listening as the primary means of learning has passed. Attorneys must and have responded to these changes.

The use of exhibits helps attorneys present more persuasive cases. Exhibits give the jury and judge a focal point on which to center their attention. Exhibits also help the attorney gain and maintain the attention of both the jury and judge and focus that attention on the theme of the case. The use of exhibits also gives the impression that the attorney is prepared, serious, and has developed some expertise regarding the subject area.

5.8 RELEVANCY CONSIDERATIONS

A. Threshold Test—Is the Exhibit Logically Relevant? Exhibits meet the threshold test if it has any tendency in reason to prove or disprove any disputed fact. Evid.C. § 210. The burden of establishing relevance is on the proponent of the evidence.

B. Is the Exhibit Legally Relevant? Relevant exhibits may be excluded if the probative value is outweighed by the danger of its being unfairly prejudicial, cause undue consumption of the court's time or confuse or mislead the jury. Evid.C. § 352.

In determining the relevancy of an exhibit it is usually self-apparent whether an exhibit is logically relevant. "Evidence" is defined quite broadly in the California Evidence Code to include writings, material objects or other things presented to the senses that are offered to prove the existence or nonexistence of a fact. Evid.C. § 140.

The critical question usually is, is the proffered evidence unduly prejudicial? If the exhibit is a picture of a particularly gruesome injury where the nature and extent of the injury has already been admitted, it is proper for the court to exclude such evidence because the probative value is outweighed by its tendency to prejudice the jury.

5.9 SELECTING EXHIBITS

Before trial, careful consideration should be given to how and when exhibits will be used. A prepared professional presentation of an exhibit can be a persuasive part of a case. On the other hand, a sloppy, unprepared presentation of an exhibit can mislead or confuse the fact finder.

Every exhibit should be designed and chosen for maximum impact. When deciding whether to use a particular exhibit an attorney should consider:

1. The necessity of using the exhibit;
2. The degree to which the exhibit supports the case;
3. Whether the exhibit is relevant;
4. Whether the witness will be able to testify more effectively;
5. Whether there is adequate foundation;
6. Whether the exhibit will detract the jury's attention from the witness' testimony or from the case as a whole;
7. Whether the exhibit will confuse the jury; and
8. Whether the exhibit is unnecessarily cumulative or repetitive.

See Form 5–4 Exhibit Selection Worksheet.

5.10 FOUNDATION FOR EXHIBITS

The introduction of each exhibit must be supported with foundation questions. These questions vary from exhibit to exhibit but, in general, the attorney should seek responses which establish the existence, identity, authenticity, and accuracy of the exhibit. Become familiar with the requisite foundation questions. A well developed technique of introducing exhibits will be invaluable during trial. A competent presentation will be necessary to meet the minimum grounds for admissibility. An effective presentation will enhance the weight afforded the exhibits by the jurors. A prepared list of foundation questions will prevent a step from being omitted and will overcome any possible objections. See Form 5–5 Exhibit Foundation Worksheet.

There are two levels of foundation that must be met during a trial. The first is the legal foundation and the second is the persuasive foundation. Evid.C. §§ 403, 405. The judge will usually determine whether the legal foundation has been established and an exhibit is admissible. The jury will review the persuasive foundation and determine the importance of the exhibit.

5.11 LEGAL FOUNDATION

Different types of exhibits have differing elements of foundation. The elements of foundation for several different types of exhibits are presented below. Evid.C. §§ 402 and 403.

A. Tangible Objects and Properties (Including Products, Clothing, Appliances, and Weapons). Elements to be proved through evidence:

1. The exhibit is relevant to the case.
2. The witness recognizes and can identify the exhibit.
3. The witness can recall what the exhibit looked like at the previous relevant time.

Preparing for and Presentation of Evidence 5–11

  4. The exhibit is now in the same or substantially the same condition as when the witness saw it at the previous relevant time.

B. Chain of Custody. A chain of custody may be required where an object is not unique or capable of identification through the senses to establish that it is the very same object. There are two primary ways of establishing an unbroken chain of custody:

  1. The exhibit at all times has been in the safe, continuing and sole possession of one or more individuals; or

  2. The exhibit bears a unique mark, was distinctively marked or was sealed and placed in a safe or other tamper-proof container.

C. Documents. Elements of foundation include:

  1. The document is relevant to the case.

  2. The document contains a signature, was handwritten, or bears some other identifying characteristics.

  3. The signature, handwriting, or characteristic belongs to or identifies a person.

  4. The witness saw the person sign or write the document; or

    a) the witness knows, is familiar with, or can recognize the signature or handwriting; or

    b) the witness recognizes and can identify the characteristics of the document; or

    c) the witness is a party and admits signing, writing, or the contents of the document; or

    d) a handwriting expert states that the signature or writing is by a certain person or that the characteristics of the document identify it.

  5. The document is authentic.

  6. The document is an original or an admissible duplicate or other copy.

  7. The document is now in the same condition as when it was made and has not been altered.

  See Chapter 6.

D. Business Correspondence (Including Letters, Memos, and Notes). Business correspondence has the same foundation requirements as documents. Some correspondence may require additional foundation evidence to prove it was sent or received. In these instances, the elements that need to be proved in addition to those listed in Section 5.11 C. of this chapter include:

  1. The correspondence was addressed to a certain person.

  2. The witness saw or signed the original and any carbon or photocopy of the original.

  3. The witness placed the correspondence in an accurately addressed delivery envelope; or the witness supervised a person who in the normal course of their business mails such correspondence.

  4. The envelope was placed in a mailbox or given to another carrier; or the witness supervised a person who in the normal course of business mails such envelopes.

  5. The photocopy or carbon of the original is an accurate copy.

  6. The original correspondence was never returned to the sender or was received by the addressee. See Chapter 6.

E. Business Records (Including any Memorandum, Report, Writing, or Data Compilation). Records maintained in the ordinary course of business may be introduced through a witness who does not have personal knowledge of the recorded information but does have personal knowledge concerning the business recording process. Evid.C. § 1271 allows the introduction of this information by establishing the foundation elements detailed in that rule. The term "business" includes any business, hospital, institution, organization, association, profession, occupation, and calling of every kind including non-profit agencies. Evid.C. § 1270.

The content of business records may include any facts, acts, events, conditions, opinions, or diagnosis that are relevant to the case. The elements to be established under Evid.C. §§ 1270, 1271 include:

1. The writing was made in the regular course of a business;

2. The writing was made at or near the time of the act, condition or event;

3. The custodian or other qualified witness testifies to its identity and the mode of preparation; and,

4. The source of information and time of preparation were such as to indicate its trustworthiness. Evid.C. § 1271.

F. Copies. Modern office equipment and practice create accurate copies of original documents and records. The original may be the most persuasive and should be offered to prove its content. Evid.C. § 1500. A copy may be routinely admitted unless it is of questionable authenticity or it would be unfair to admit a copy. Evid.C. § 1511. A copy may also be admissible if the original has been lost or destroyed, is in the possession of the opponent, or is otherwise not obtainable. Evid.C. §§ 1501–1509. If there is a question raised, the elements to establish the foundation for a copy include:

1. The copy is relevant to the case.

2. An original did once exist.

3. A copy was made from the original.

4. The copy is an authentic and accurate duplicate of the original.

G. Electronic Recordings (Including Audio and Video Recordings). The elements to be proved to establish a sufficient foundation for the introduction of recordings include:

1. The electronic recording is relevant to the case.

2. The operator of the equipment was qualified to run the equipment.

3. The recording equipment was checked before its use and operated normally.

4. The witness heard or saw the event being electronically recorded.

5. After the event had been recorded, the witness reviewed the tape and determined that it had accurately and completely recorded the event.

6. The witness can recognize and identify the sounds or images on the recording.

7. The recording is in the exact same condition at the time of trial as it was at the time of the taping.

H. Test Results (Including X-ray Films and Laboratory Analysis). The results from tests, x-rays and other procedures will require special foundation information to be introduced at trial. The elements to be established include:

1. The exhibit is relevant to the case.

2. The witness is qualified to operate the equipment.

3. There exists a procedure which regulates the testing, x-ray, or analysis process.

4. The witness personally conducted or supervised an operator who conducted the testing, developed the x-rays, or completed the analysis.

5. The equipment was in normal operating condition.

6. The witness can recognize and identify the results, x-rays, or analysis.

7. The results, x-rays, or analysis are in the same condition as when they were completed.

I. Photographs (Including Prints, Slides, and Movies). The elements to be proved by evidence include:

1. The photograph is relevant to the case.

2. The witness is familiar with the scene displayed in the photograph at the relevant time of the event.

3. The photograph fairly and accurately depicts the scene at the time of the event.

J. Diagrams (Including Charts, Models, Drawings, Overhead Transparencies and Similar Illustrative Aids). Various types of demonstrative evidence will be useful during the presentation of a case. The elements of foundation for the introduction of diagrams include:

1. The witness is familiar with the scene or event.

2. The witness recognizes the scene depicted in the diagram or is familiar with the exhibit.

3. The diagram will assist the witness in explaining testimony or will aid the jury in understanding the testimony.

4. The diagram is reasonably accurate (or is drawn to scale) and is not misleading.

K. Past Recollection Record. A witness who, at the time of trial, does not have a recollection of an event may have previously made a record of that event. Evid.C. § 1237 permits a recorded recollection to be introduced at trial. The elements to establish the foundation of past recollection recorded exhibits include:

1. The witness has no present recollection of the event;

2. The recorded statement was made at a time when the fact recorded in the writing actually occurred or was fresh in the witness' memory;

3. The record was made by the witness, or under the direction of the witness for the purpose of recording the event;

4. The witness testifies that the statement is a true statement of such facts; and

5. The witness authenticates the writing as an accurate record of the statement. Evid.C. § 1237.

After laying this foundation, the statement may be read to the jury, but the writing itself is not entered into evidence unless offered by an adverse party. Evid.C. § 1237(4)(b).

L. Stipulations. Any written stipulations the attorneys may have made that have been entered into the minutes pursuant to C.C.P. § 283(1) may be introduced during the trial. Stipulations entered into by counsel that are not illegal or contrary to public policy are binding on the court. The attorney who wishes to introduce the evidence must request permission from the court to read or have someone read the contents of the stipulation.

M. Statements of Admissions in Judicial Proceedings. Statements of admissions made by parties in the course of judicial proceedings are admissible against the party making them whether made in pleadings, in other writings, orally, or in a former trial of the same action. Evid.C. §§ 1290; 1230, 31 Cal.Jur. 305, Section 236. An admission made in a pleading, whether by affirmative allegation, or by failure to deny an allegation, may be offered into evidence during the direct or cross-examination of the witness, if the witness is the party who made the admission. It may be directly read to the jury during the offering party's case in chief, or can be used and read on cross-examination.

N. Discovery Information. Information gained from formal discovery including Depositions, Answers to Interrogatories, Request for Admissions and products of Requests for Documents and Things may be introduced as evidence during the trial. See Section 5.17 herein for discussion of an admission of discovery information at the time of the trial.

O. Self-Authenticating Documents. Extrinsic evidence of the authenticity of certain documents and exhibits is unnecessary under certain circumstances. These self-authenticating documents and exhibits include:

1. *Authentication by Content.* A writing may be authenticated by evidence that the writing refers to or states matters that are unlikely to be known to anyone other than the person who is claimed by the proponent of the evidence to be the author of the writing. Evid. C. § 1421.

2. *A Public Document Under Official Seal.* A seal is presumed to be genuine and the document is authenticated if it purports to be the seal of any agency of the US, a nation

recognized by the executive power of the US, a public entity in a nation recognized by the executive power of the US, or a court of admiralty or maritime jurisdiction. Evid.C. § 1452.

3. *A Document Under Official Seal of a Notary Public Within Any State of the US.* Evid. C. §§ 1452(f), 1543(c).

4. *Acknowledged Writings.* A certificate of the acknowledgment of a writing is prima facie evidence of the facts recited in the certificate and the genuineness of the signature of each person who has signed the certificate. Evid.C. § 1451.

5.12 PERSUASIVE FOUNDATION

Persuasive foundation is testimony that enhances the credibility and weight of an exhibit. In a jury trial, the persuasive foundation will be as important as the legal foundation. The legal foundation for an exhibit may be quite simple to meet. However, the attorney may want to expand, simplify, or clarify the foundation to increase the weight that the jury gives the exhibit.

5.13 STIPULATING TO FOUNDATION

The legal foundation elements may be stipulated to by the attorneys thereby avoiding the need to ask detailed foundation questions. Stipulations will significantly reduce trial time and should be voluntarily entered into between counsel if there is no real dispute concerning the authenticity or accuracy of the exhibits. For example, hospital records will often be entered into evidence by stipulation because these records will usually be reliable. Judges often suggest that attorneys agree to the admissibility of reliable exhibits.

5.14 EXHIBIT SYSTEMS

An adequate exhibit system should record exhibits offered by any party. The system should include the necessary foundation elements; a list of the witnesses needed to lay the foundation, and a chart showing exactly where each exhibit is in the process of introduction. See Form 5–6 Trial Exhibits Chart. The exhibit system should keep track of opposing counsel's exhibits in order to prevent exhibits from being presented that have not been introduced into evidence. A good exhibit system will be important where more than one witness must be used to lay the foundation for an exhibit. The exhibit tracking system should easily identify exactly where a particular exhibit is in the process of introduction. Has the exhibit been marked? Has it been offered? Has the exhibit been accepted? See Form 5–6 Trial Exhibits Chart.

5.15 PLANNING INTRODUCTIONS

A. Preparing the Witness. The witness that will be used to introduce the evidence should be familiar with the questions and answers that will be necessary to introduce the exhibit and should be comfortable with handling or testifying about the exhibit. Exhibits that are introduced smoothly are perceived as more credible by the jury.

B. Preparing for Possible Objections. An objection, whether sustained or overruled, slows the presentation of the exhibit and the case. Delays caused by opposing counsel's objections may make the exhibit less effective. Advance preparation to overcome potential objections to the use and introduction of exhibits will make the presentation more effective.

Possible objections to exhibits include:
1. Prejudicial or gruesome. Evid.C. § 352.
2. Cumulative or repetitious. Evid.C. § 352.
3. Exhibit is not the same or similar to what it is claimed to be. Evid.C. § 1406.
4. Lack of authentication and identification. Evid.C. § 1401.
5. Violation of best evidence rule. Evid.C. § 1500.
6. Misleading or inaccurate. Evid.C. § 352.
7. Waste of court's time or undue delay. Evid.C. § 352.

Preparing for and Presentation of Evidence 5–15

8. Exhibit does not assist the witness nor aid the jury. C.Evid.C. § 350.

9. Inadmissible hearsay. C.Evid.C. §§ 1200–1205.

Sometimes it will not be possible to overcome an objection. In cases in which the exhibit may not be admissible into evidence because of some procedural or technical grounds, consider ways of using the exhibit as a visual aid for illustrative purposes.

The jury will then have a chance to see the exhibit, but will not be able to take the exhibit into the jury room. The real value of using exhibits is to provide a visual context in which the jurors may understand the oral testimony or arguments. Using an exhibit as a visual aid is almost as effective and as persuasive as admitting it into evidence. Do not try this tactic if the proposed exhibit is overly prejudicial or gruesome because it risks the chance of a mistrial. Obtain the judge's approval before showing any exhibits to the jury.

C. Supplementing Exhibits. Consider additional preparations necessary before the exhibit can be adequately presented during the trial. These considerations might include whether:

1. The exhibit will stand by itself.
2. The exhibit should be enlarged.
3. An overhead projector would be more effective.
4. Copies should be made of the exhibit.
5. The exhibit should be passed to the jury, and if so, when.
6. Questions should be asked while the exhibit is being passed among the jury.
7. The exhibit is too offensive to be passed.
8. The judge will require that questions be asked while exhibits are being passed.
9. The exhibit should be mounted.
10. The exhibit can be left in the presence of the jury or must be put away.

5.16 PRESENTATION AND DELIVERY

A. Professional Presentation. Develop confidence in the material to be presented. The judge and jury will have certain expectations regarding the presentation of exhibits that should be satisfied. If a presentation does not live up to these expectations, the exhibit may be more damaging than helpful.

The attorney and the witness should be coordinated so that exhibits are marked appropriately, charts are flipped at the right time, the model works, and the overhead projector is plugged in. Know the courtroom, understand the limitations of the available space, and adapt accordingly.

B. Practical Problems. Be aware of the potential problems that can arise with exhibits during the trial. Most problems can be anticipated and prevented. Those that cannot will not be as disconcerting if the attorney has planned for that contingency. Below is a partial list of problems that arise with the use of exhibits:

1. Visuals may be poorly drawn and confuse the judge or jury.
2. Exhibits may be too bulky.
3. The preservation of the exhibit for appeal may be difficult.
4. Exhibits may be offensive (i.e., using a real skeleton instead of a model).
5. The experiment or demonstration in court may malfunction or fail.
6. The attorney may lose the continuity of a presentation if the judge disallows the exhibit or stops the demonstration before completion.
7. The jury may perceive the case as a case of rich versus poor if only one side uses exhibits.
8. Exhibits that are bizarre, too numerous, waste time, clutter, or confuse the presentation may hurt the case.

C. The Steps to Introduction of Exhibits. There are several crucial steps in the introduction of exhibits, including physical or documentary evidence that must be mastered. The attorney will need to:

1. Qualify the witness by laying a foundation to establish competency to testify and personal knowledge sufficient to identify the exhibit.

2. Either have the exhibit pre-marked for identification or request that the object be marked for identification at the time of the presentation of the exhibit. For example, "Your Honor, I request that this be marked as Plaintiff's Exhibit # 1 for identification." From this point on you can then refer to this object as the object "which has previously been marked Plaintiff's Exhibit # 1 for identification."

3. Show the object or exhibit to the opposing counsel. At the same time, you should say, "Let the record reflect that I am showing Plaintiff's Exhibit # 1 to the opposing counsel," (or establish that counsel has had an opportunity to review the exhibit).

4. Ask for permission to approach the witness.

5. Hand the object to the witness and ask the witness to examine the object.

6. Ask the witness to identify the item. For example, "I hand you Plaintiff's Exhibit # 1 for identification. Do you recognize it?"

7. Lay the necessary additional foundation needed for the introduction of that particular exhibit. If you want to use the exhibit or document as substantive evidence, your foundations should always cover at least the following elements:

   a) Authentication, including the facts showing the personal knowledge of the witness regarding the object, and that it is what she says it is;

   b) The object meets the requirements of the Best Evidence Rule, or meets one of the exceptions;

   c) The document or exhibit does not contain hearsay or that it meets one of the hearsay exceptions; and

   d) The object is relevant to the subject matter in controversy.

8. After laying the foundation, make a formal offer into evidence by referring to its exhibit number or letter, "Your Honor, I now offer Plaintiff's Exhibit # 1 for identification into evidence as Plaintiff's Exhibit # 1."

9. Respond to any objections opposing counsel may have to the exhibit.

10. If the exhibit is entered into evidence, show the exhibit to the jury. If the object is a document, request permission to have the witness read the pertinent parts to the jury. For example, "Your Honor, I request permission to have the witness read the first paragraph to the jurors."

If the object is physical evidence, request permission to hand the object to the jurors for their inspection. Consider and decide whether or not to have a particular exhibit sent to the jury room during the jury's deliberations. C.C.P. § 612. See Form 5-7 Exhibit Introduction Checklist.

D. Variation in Word Usage. The words used to introduce and describe an exhibit must be varied. "Boiler plate" terms that are repeated endlessly will bore the jury. Below are several ways of referring to exhibits:

1. This exhibit has been marked as Plaintiff's exhibit 1. . . .

2. I am handing you. . . .

3. You have in your hands. . . .

4. I have just handed you. . . .

5. Here is. . . .

6. I am showing you. . . .

A varied style will hold the jury's attention longer than the use of the same monotonous "buzz" word. However, some judges require certain "buzz" words. In these circumstances, use the phrases and words the judge requires. Whatever description is used, the reference should include the exhibit number or letter to protect the record.

E. Leading Questions. Leading questions may be allowed when laying the foundation for some exhibits. Leading questions may be necessary to elicit the precise elements of foundation required for the introduction of an exhibit. For example, it is proper to lead a witness who identifies a photograph by asking if the photo is a "fair and accurate" representation. Without such leading questions, laying the foundation for exhibits could take forever. See Evid.C. §§ 765, 767.

F. Finessing the Foundation. If there are a series of exhibits for which the foundations are similar, abbreviating the process of laying foundation after the first few exhibits have been introduced should be possible. The witness may be asked whether the response to the previous exhibit would be the same for additional exhibits. Once the judge and opposing attorney know that the attorney is prepared to present extensive foundation, the presentation of that foundation may not be necessary. This will speed up the process and reduce the potential for boredom.

G. Location. The attorney's position in the courtroom should maximize the clarity and impact of the exhibit. Each courtroom provides many possibilities for movement, stance, and positioning. Repetitious or blocking movements and positions diminish the effectiveness of the presentation. Where to place exhibits and where to stand will depend on a variety of factors including:

1. The ability of the attorney to stand without support from a table or lectern.
2. The ability of the witness to speak and be heard.
3. The size and impact of the exhibit.
4. The shape and acoustics of the courtroom.
5. Any constraints imposed by the trial judge.

H. Voir Dire Examination. Opposing counsel has the opportunity to examine the witness after an exhibit has been offered to determine if there is a basis for an objection. The questions that may be asked must seek to establish the lack of foundation required for an exhibit. The scope of this examination is very limited and only a minimal number of questions may be asked. Voir dire examination should not be used unless the exhibit will most likely be excluded. Cross-examination will provide the opportunity to ask questions to reduce the evidentiary effect of an exhibit.

5.17 OFFER AND USE OF REQUESTS FOR ADMISSIONS

Facts that have been affirmatively admitted in requests for admissions or have not been denied during the statutory period for denying such admissions and have not been set aside as a result of mistake, inadvertence, or excusable neglect (C.C.P. § 2033) may be presented to the fact finder in an affirmative way. Such requests for admissions can be read into the record at an appropriate time during the trial. Counsel, at that time, can request the judge to explain to the jury what the admissions are and the legal effect of their being admitted. BAJI 2.08 (7th ed.) contains the relevant jury instruction. However, at trial, a party charged with an admission can argue that the admission should be narrowly construed or given only limited effect. See Milton v. Montgomery Ward & Co., 33 Cal.App.3d 133, 138, 108 Cal.Rptr. 726, 728 (1973).

5.18 OFFER AND USE OF STIPULATIONS

Facts that have been stipulated to before or during the trial must be presented to the fact finder in an affirmative way. The attorney introducing the evidence must offer the evidence and request that the fact finder be informed in one of a variety of ways. Fact stipulations may be read to the jury by the attorney offering the evidence or by a neutral person, such as a clerk.

5.19 EVIDENCE SUMMARIES

Lengthy, complex, or factually complicated cases may necessitate the introduction of time-saving evidence summaries. The court may order, or the parties may stipulate to several types of summaries. These may include a summary of the testimony of a witness based upon a deposition, a summary list of exhibits and their contents, a summary outlines of information, or any other summary which makes the evidence more understandable for the jury.

5.20 JUDICIAL NOTICE

1. *What can be Judicially Noticed?* Judicative facts generally known within the territorial jurisdiction of the court or capable of accurate and ready determination by highly reliable sources may be judicially noticed by a court. Evid.C. §§ 451, 452. Generally, the court *must* take judicial notice of certain specified decisional, constitutional, and public statutory law of the State of California and of the United States, and of facts and propositions of generalized knowledge that are so universally known that they cannot reasonably be subject to dispute. Evid.C. § 451. The court *may* take judicial notice of facts and propositions that are not reasonably subject to dispute and are capable of immediate and accurate determination by resort to sources of reasonably, indisputable accuracy and other specified decisional, constitutional, and statutorial language of any state of the United States and the resolutions and private acts of the Congress of the United States and of the legislature of this state. See Evid. C. § 452 for other facts of which the court may take judicial note, and § 457 for notice requirements.

2. *Use of Noticed Facts.* The use and reading of admissions, stipulations, transcripts of depositions, and evidence summaries should be planned so that the admission of such evidence has a maximum impact on the jury and follows in a logical order the presentation of the other evidence in the case. The same is true of the use of judicial notice. It is preferred practice to ask the court to take judicial notice of a fact by way of a motion in limine prior to the beginning of a trial so that the attorney knows what facts can be conclusively established by judicial notice, and which facts need to be established either through admission, stipulations, deposition testimony or direct testimony of witnesses.

5.21 MATTERS TO BE HEARD OUTSIDE THE PRESENCE OF THE JURY

1. Concise and relatively uncontroversial objections may be made within the hearing of the jury, but arguments on the objections should be made at sidebar conference outside of the hearing of the jury.

2. Offers of proof and supporting arguments should be made at a sidebar conference.

3. Proposed stipulations and bargaining, leading to agreement on stipulations should be either in chambers or in sidebar conference.

4. Motions and oral argument should either be in chambers or in the courtroom, without the jury.

5. Sensitive areas of evidence should be outside the presence of the jury. Questions, answers, exhibits, statements, or arguments that may be prejudicial or inflammatory or inadmissible should be brought to the attention of the opposing counsel and trial judge outside of the hearing of jurors, before they occur.

PROFESSIONAL/EXPERT WITNESS LOG

_____
(name)

_____
(title or profession)

1. Strong points _____
   _____

2. Weak points _____
   _____

3. Idiosyncrasies _____
   _____

4. Qualifications (Attach resume or curriculum vittae)

   a) Education _____
      _____

   b) Honors _____
      _____

   c) Experience

      i) Generally _____
         _____

      ii) Area of expertise _____
          _____

   d) Specialty _____
      _____

   e) Academic appointments _____
      _____

   f) Publications _____
      _____

Form 5–1

4. Qualifications (Attach resumé or curriculum vittae)—Continued

    g) Continuing professional education _____

    _____

    h) Other background _____

    _____

5. Testimony

    a) Previous testimony _____

    _____

        i) What side _____

        ii) How helpful or damaging _____

        _____

    b) Style, presentation, appearance _____

    _____

    c) Quality of content _____

    _____

    d) Prepared _____

    e) Credibility _____

    f) Honesty _____

    g) Cost expense _____

    h) Availability _____

    _____

    i) Cross-examination _____

    _____

    j) Other _____

    _____

Form 5–1 (continued)

EXPERT TESTIMONY PLANNING WORKSHEET

Case _____   File _____

Name of expert witness: _____

Fee Agreement: _____

1. Qualifications: (see Form 5–1) _____
   _____
   _____
   _____
   _____
   _____

2. How, when, where did expert become involved: _____
   _____
   _____
   _____
   _____
   _____

3. Opinions: _____
   _____
   _____
   _____
   _____
   _____

4. Basis of Opinion: _____
   _____
   _____
   _____
   _____

Form 5–2

5. Sources of Opinion: _____
   _____
   _____
   _____

6. Foundation necessary to testify as expert: _____
   _____
   _____
   _____
   _____

7. Foundation necessary to testify to ultimate fact at issue: _____
   _____
   _____
   _____
   _____
   _____

8. Exhibits to be introduced: _____
   _____
   _____
   _____
   _____

9. Foundation needed for exhibits: _____
   _____
   _____
   _____
   _____

10. Probable cross-examination areas: _____
    _____
    _____
    _____
    _____

11. Redirect examination: _____
    _____
    _____
    _____

Form 5–2 (continued)

WITNESS PREPARATION WORKSHEET

Case _____ File _____

1. Name of case _____ Date of incident _____

2. Name of witness _____

3. Address _____

4. Phone: _____ home _____ work/office

5. Employer _____

6. Written statement taken: _____

    a. When: _____

    b. By whom: _____

    c. Declaration or sworn affidavit: _____

    d. Has witness reviewed and approved statement: _____

    e. Statement and attach copy: _____
        _____
        _____

7. Deposition taken _____ When: _____

    Represented by counsel: _____ Who: _____

    Deposition transcript reviewed by witness: _____

    Any changes made? _____ If so, what changes: _____
    _____

    Deposition signed: _____ Date of signing: _____

8. Is witness: _____ friendly _____ hostile _____ neutral

9. Has witness been prepared for trial testimony by:

    Plaintiff attorney: _____ Name: _____

    Defendant attorney: _____ Name: _____

    Own attorney: _____ Name: _____

Form 5–3

10. Appearance Date: _____

   Date witness prefers to appear: _____

   Date witness cannot appear: _____

   Subpoena necessary or advisable: ___ yes   ___ no

   Has subpoena been served: ___ yes   ___ no

11. Type of Witness:

   ___ Eye witness   ___ Expert

   ___ Exhibit/Chain of possession   ___ Lay

   ___ Event—before, during, after   ___ Other

12. Purpose of witness: _____

   _____
   _____
   _____
   _____

13. Expected testimony of witness: _____

   _____
   _____
   _____
   _____

14. Key questions to ask this witness: _____

   _____
   _____
   _____
   _____

Form 5–3 (continued)

15. **Exhibits to Be Introduced by Witness**   **Foundation Needed for Exhibit**

1. _____   _____
   _____   _____
   _____   _____
   _____   _____

2. _____   _____
   _____   _____
   _____   _____
   _____   _____

3. _____   _____
   _____   _____
   _____   _____
   _____   _____

4. _____   _____
   _____   _____
   _____   _____
   _____   _____

5. _____   _____
   _____   _____
   _____   _____
   _____   _____

6. _____   _____
   _____   _____
   _____   _____
   _____   _____

7. _____   _____
   _____   _____
   _____   _____

Form 5–3 (continued)

EXHIBIT SELECTION WORKSHEET

Case_____   File_____

WHAT EXHIBITS WILL BE NECESSARY OR USEFUL?

1. Tangible Objects:

    ___ Clothing _____
    _____

    ___ Weapons _____
    _____

    ___ Products _____
    _____

    ___ Appliances _____
    _____

    ___ Others _____
    _____

2. Documents:

    ___ Letters _____
    _____

    ___ Memos _____
    _____

    ___ Correspondence _____
    _____

    ___ Contracts _____
    _____

    ___ Leases _____
    _____

    ___ Bills _____
    _____

    ___ Checks _____
    _____

Form 5–4

2. Documents—Continued

   ___ Other _____
   _____

3. Business Records _____
   _____

4. Computer Data _____
   _____

5. Audio/Visual Recordings _____
   _____

6. Test Results:

   ___X-rays   ___Laboratory Analysis

7. Photographs:

   ___Prints   ___Slides   ___Movies

8. Diagrams:

   ___Charts   ___Maps   ___Graphs   ___Drawings

9. Past Recollection Recorded _____
   _____

10. Exhibit Summaries _____
    _____

11. Demonstrations _____
    _____

12. Chain of Custody Problems _____
    _____
    _____
    _____

Form 5–4 (continued)

EXHIBIT FOUNDATION WORKSHEET

Case_____   File_____

EXHIBIT_____

Elements of Foundation	Which witness will provide	What witness will say
(1)		
(2)		
(3)		
(4)		
(5)		
(6)		
(7)		

EXHIBIT_____

(1)		
(2)		
(3)		
(4)		
(5)		
(6)		
(7)		

Exhibit marked ( )

Foundation completed ( )

Exhibit offered ( )   Accepted ( )   Rejected ( )

If rejected, offer of proof made ( )

Any pretrial rulings pertaining to this exhibit ( )

Form 5–5

TRIAL EXHIBITS CHART

Case _____ File _____

Court Exhibit Identification Number	Description of Exhibit	Offered By	Identified By	Introduced By	Received/ Denied	Offer of Proof Made

Form 5–6

EXHIBIT INTRODUCTION CHECKLIST

Case_____   File_____

_____ 1. Establish sufficient *foundation* for the witness to be able to *identify* the exhibit.

_____ 2. Have the exhibit *marked* or pre-marked before the trial.

_____ 3. Determine whether the judge requires permission to be obtained to *approach* the witness.

_____ 4. Establish for the record that counsel already has the exhibit or you are supplying it at this time.

_____ 5. Request that the witness *examine* the exhibit.

_____ 6. Have the witness *identify* the exhibit.

_____ 7. Lay the necessary foundation for the *introduction* of the exhibit.

        a. Authenticate _____

        b. Best evidence (if necessary) _____

        c. Relevant _____

        d. Non-hearsay (if necessary)

_____ 8. Offer the exhibit into evidence by referring to its exhibit number or letter.

_____ 9. Respond to any *objections* made by opposing counsel regarding the exhibit.

_____ 10. Publish the exhibit to the *fact finder*.

Form 5–7

TRIAL PROOF WORKSHEET

Check off the following table as you proceed with the presentation of your case. Make sure all of the necessary elements are proved before resting your case.

Elements to Prove Prima Facie Case	Key Facts to be Established	Method of Proof

Form 5–8

Chapter 6
OBJECTIONS

Table of Sections

Sec.
6.1 Purposes.
6.2 Preparation and Organization.
    A. When to Object.
    B. Examining Attorney.
    C. Anticipating Evidentiary Problems.
6.3 Objections Under California Evidence Code.
6.4 Objections Made to Exclude Evidence.
    A. Relevance Evid.C. §§ 210, 350–351.
    B. Legal Relevance Evid.C. § 352.
    C. Evidence Which Is Inadmissible Under the California Rules of Evidence.
    D. Privileges Evid.C. §§ 930–1060.
    E. Competence C.C.P. Section 701.
    F. Lack of Foundation Evid.C. §§ 400–406.
    G. Questioning by the Court Evid.C. § 775.
    H. Opinion Testimony Evid.C. §§ 800–805.
    I. Speculation Evid.C. §§ 702, 801.
    J. Best Evidence Rule Evid.C. §§ 1500–1511.
    K. Lack of Authentication Evid.C. §§ 1400–1454.
    L. Hearsay Evid.C. § 1200.
6.5 Objections to the Form of the Questions.
    A. Leading Evid.C. §§ 764, 767.
    B. Narrative Evid.C. § 765.
    C. Asked and Answered Evid.C. § 774.
    D. Cumulative Evid.C. § 352.
    E. Vague, Ambiguous, Misleading, Confusing or Unintelligible Evid.C. § 765.
    F. Multiple or Compound Questions Evid.C. § 765.
    G. Assuming Facts Not in Evidence Evid.C. § 765.
    H. Misstatement or Mischaracterization of Testimony or Evidence Evid.C. §§ 765, 774.
    I. Argumentative Evid.C. § 765.
    J. Improper Impeachment Evid.C. §§ 780, 785.
    K. Beyond the Scope Evid.C. §§ 761, 773.
6.6 Objections to Demonstrative Evidence.
    A. Misleading, Inaccurate or Distorting Evid.C. § 352.
    B. Lack of Foundation Evid.C. §§ 403–405.
    C. Waste of Court's Time/Undue Delay Evid.C. § 352.
    D. Evidence Does Not Aid or Assist Jury Evid.C. § 352.
6.7 Objections During Jury Selection.
    A. Mentioning Insurance Evid.C. 1155.
    B. Arguing or Indoctrinating Jurors About the Law.
    C. Arguing Facts.
6.8 Objections During Opening Statement.
    A. Explaining the Law or Instructions.
    B. Argumentative.
    C. Mentioning Inadmissible Evidence.

Sec.
6.8 Objections During Opening Statement—Continued
    D. Mentioning Unprovable Evidence.
    E. Personal Opinions.
    F. Misstating the Law.
    G. Referring to Insurance Coverage.
6.9 Objections During Closing Arguments.
    A. Misstating Evidence.
    B. Misstating Law and Quoting Instructions.
    C. Personal Opinions.
    D. Appealing to Jury's Bias or Prejudice.
    E. Appealing to Jury's Pecuniary Interests.
    F. Reference to Judgments Awarded in Similar Cases.
    G. Personal Attacks on Parties and Counsel.
    H. Prejudicial Arguments.
6.10 Presentation and Delivery.
    A. How to Object.
    B. Motion to Strike.
    C. Admonition to Disregard the Evidence.
    D. Offers of Proof.
    E. When an Offer of Proof Is Not Required.
Appendix. Common Legal Objections.
Forms
6–1 Objection Planning Worksheet.

6.1 PURPOSES

An objection is the procedure used to oppose the introduction of improper evidence, testimony, and argument or to oppose inappropriate behavior and procedures during the trial. An objection is both a strategic and tactical tool for the attorney. The main purpose of making evidentiary objections is to prevent damaging evidence or testimony, which is not admissible under the rules of evidence, from being introduced. Objections are also used to control the form of questions and to protect witnesses from harassment by the opposing attorney.

Another important purpose of objections is to make a record. A complete trial record is necessary to preserve objections for potential appeal. Sometimes objections can be used strategically to help a witness, to respond to a suggestion by the judge, to intimidate an inexperienced opponent, or for other tactical reasons. Whatever strategy the attorney uses, the overall effect should be consistent with the theories of the case.

6.2 PREPARATION AND ORGANIZATION

A. When to Object. As with every other aspect of the case, a thorough understanding of the facts and issues is necessary in order to make and anticipate objections. Many objections may be dealt with by a motion in limine brought, heard, and decided before the trial. In addition to the particular circumstances surrounding the case, the attorney should be familiar with the various types of objections.

The attorney will also want to consider when it is proper to object. Although much of the skill of objecting involves quick thinking and instant decision making at the trial itself, a more consistent strategy can be developed by considering when it is that the attorney will object to evidence.

An objection should seldom, if ever, be made when the testimony will be favorable or neutral to the case. The attorney should also consider how the objections affect the jury. Jurors often think that lawyers who object are hiding something from them. Also, an objection calls the jury's attention to the evidence that the attorney is attempting to exclude, tending to emphasize its significance.

Objections are best reserved for testimony or evidence that the attorney is reasonably certain will harm the case. An objection may unnecessarily highlight a problem, and objections should only be made when there is a good chance of the objection being sustained. The attorney will, regardless of the ruling on the objection, want to preserve the record in case of an appeal.

B. Examining Attorney. The examining attorney in preparing and presenting evidence must recognize possible objections that can be asserted and present evidence to avoid the objectionable matter. Skilled advocates will often conduct examinations with few or no objections.

C. Anticipating Evidentiary Problems. An attorney must anticipate evidentiary problems and plan how to handle them. Certain evidence may have some evidentiary infirmities. The attorney will need to consider how the evidence may be made admissible or alternative ways to introduce other evidence. The opponent may introduce inadmissible evidence and the attorney needs to prepare objections to such evidence. See Form 6–1 Objection Planning Worksheet.

6.3 OBJECTIONS UNDER CALIFORNIA EVIDENCE CODE

The California Evidence Code establishes many grounds for objections. (See Appendix List of Common Legal Objections.) Additional objections may be based on the rules of trial practice, civil or criminal procedure, case law, common sense, and fairness.

6.4 OBJECTIONS MADE TO EXCLUDE EVIDENCE

The following is a summary of the basic rules of California evidence which constitute the objections that can be made to exclude evidence. Cites are given to the applicable code section, and each applicable section should be thoroughly researched regarding the intracacies of the objection to be used.

A. Relevance Evid.C. §§ 210, 350–351. Relevant evidence means evidence having tendency in reason to prove or disprove any disputed fact that is of consequence to the determination of the action, including evidence relevant to the credibility of a witness or hearsay declarant. Evid.C. § 210. Only relevant evidence is admissible. Evid.C. § 350. All relevant evidence is admissible unless the probative value of the evidence is outweighed by the prejudicial effect or as otherwise provided by statute. Evid.C. §§ 351, 352.

Evidence is relevant if it has probative value. It must tend to prove or disprove a fact that is of consequence to the action. Further, the fact or issue that the evidence tends to prove or disprove must be in dispute in the action. Evidence of facts which have been stipulated to are not relevant in a trial for purposes of presenting further evidence of those facts. See Jefferson Evid.Bench Book § 21.2. Evidence relevant to the credibility of a witness or hearsay declarant is always considered relevant under the specific terms of Evid.C. § 210. Usually the logical relevancy or the logical irrelevancy of offered evidence can be ascertained from the evidence itself.

The majority of relevancy objections arise with the introduction of circumstantial evidence. They arise because the determination of the relevancy of circumstantial evidence requires a drawing of inferences that may be weak or remote. If the relevancy of the proffered evidence is not readily apparent, counsel should be prepared to make an offer of proof showing the relevancy of the testimony or evidence and linking it up with its probative value regarding disputed issues in the case.

B. Legal Relevance Evid.C. § 352. The court in its discretion may exclude evidence if the probative value of the evidence is substantially outweighed by the probability that the admission of the evidence will:

1. necessitate undue consumption of time; or
2. create substantial danger of undue prejudice; or
3. confuse the issues or mislead the jury. Evid.C. § 352. Opposing counsel may attempt to introduce evidence which, while logically relevant to the issues in dispute, raises a

substantial risk of unduly prejudicing, confusing or misleading the jury. When such evidence is presented, counsel should request the trial judge to use discretion to exclude the evidence as legally irrelevant. Evid.C. § 352.

An objection based on legal relevance under Evid.C. § 352 is often made to prevent the admission of photographs, videotapes and other visual exhibits that graphically display injuries or a scene. This evidence, while relevant, may so prejudice the jurors and confuse the real issues to the point where the jury may not be able to make a sound rational decision. A prompt objection should be presented, because once the jury has seen it, the evidence will be etched in their memories. This objection also applies to testimony and persons wishing to display their injuries in the courtroom. One should try to anticipate such evidence and bring a motion in limine.

C. Evidence Which Is Inadmissible Under the California Rules of Evidence. The following types of evidence have been determined by law to be legally irrelevant, regardless of their probative value.

1. *Improper Character Evidence.* Evid.C. § 1324. While evidence of a person's general reputation with reference to his character or a trait of his character in the community is admissible, such evidence is inadmissible when offered to prove his conduct on a specified occasion. Evid.C. §§ 1320, 1101–1104.

2. *Improper Habit Evidence.* C.C.P. §§ 1103–1105. Evidence of a trait of a person's character with respect to care or skill is inadmissible to prove the quality of his conduct on a specific occasion. Evid.C. § 1104.

3. *Subsequent Remedial Measures.* Evid.C. § 1151. Evidence of remedial or precautionary measures taken after the occurrence of an event are *inadmissible* to prove negligence or comparable fault in connection with such event. Evid.C. § 1151.

4. *Offers of Compromise.* Evid.C. Section 1152. Evidence that a person has offered to compromise, offered to furnish money, or any other thing, act or service to another, and evidence of any conduct or statements made in negotiations regarding the subject matter of the case is inadmissible to prove liability for the loss or damage or any part of it. Evid.C. §§ 1152 and 1153.5.

5. *Communications During Mediation Proceedings.* Evid.C. § 1152.5. Evidence of anything said, admissions made or documents prepared in the course of a mediation is inadmissible in evidence.

6. *Offer To Plead Guilty Or Withdraw Plea Of Guilty By Criminal Defendant.* Evid.C. § 1153. Evidence of a withdrawn plea of guilty or of an offer to plead guilty to the crime charged or to any other crime made by the defendant in a criminal action is inadmissible.

7. *Evidence Of Liability Insurance.* Evid.C. § 1155. Evidence that a person was, at the time a harm was suffered by another, insured against such loss is inadmissible.

D. Privileges Evid.C. §§ 930–1060. Privileges can be divided into three separate categories. They are:

1. Privilege not to testify against one's self;

2. Privileged communications; and,

3. Statutory privileges, involving proprietary rights, political rights and other policy considerations.

A valid objection based on privilege will bar the underlying privileged information from being disclosed. Privileges must be closely guarded from the very outset of any case. Failure to object to a question involving privilege waives the privilege.

1. *Privilege Not to Testify.* A person has a privilege to refuse to disclose any matter that may tend to be incriminating. Art. V, U.S. Constitution.

2. *Privileged Communications.* Evid.C. §§ 950–1047. In order to raise the objection of privileged communications the attorney must first address several questions. Was the discussion or matter subject to a recognized privilege? Was the communication made under

confidential circumstances? Is the privilege absolute or qualified? Has there been a waiver of the privilege? Has the privilege been asserted by the proper party?

Review Evid.C. §§ 950–1047 and court decisions regarding these questions.

- a) *Attorney/Client Privilege.* A communication made in confidence in the course of an attorney/client relationship is considered privileged information. The client has a privilege to refuse to disclose and to prevent another from disclosing such information. Evid.C. §§ 950–955. A lawyer who receives or makes a communication subject to privilege must claim the privilege whenever present when the communication is sought to be disclosed. Evid.C. § 955. There is no privilege if the services of the lawyer were sought in furtherance of a plan to commit a crime or a fraud. Evid.C. § 956.

- b) *Physician/Patient Communications.* This privilege prevents compulsory disclosure of confidential information transmitted between the patient and the physician. Evid.C. §§ 990–1007. This particular privilege has numerous exceptions. Review the applicable code sections before invoking this privilege to determine whether the case falls under one of the many exceptions. Evid.C. §§ 996–1007 enumerates the exceptions.

- c) *Psychotherapist/Patient Privilege.* Evid.C. §§ 1010–1028. This privilege prevents compulsory disclosure of confidential information transmitted between a patient and psychotherapist. This provision also covers licensed psychologists and physicians practicing psychiatry. While it has exceptions, the exceptions are not as extensive as the physician/patient privilege. See Evid.C. §§ 1017–1027 for exceptions to the privilege.

- d) *Privilege Not to Testify Against Spouse.* Evid.C. §§ 970–971. A married person has two privileges: (1) not to testify against his/her spouse in any proceeding; and, (2) not to be called as a witness in any proceeding to which his/her spouse is a party. Evid.C. § 971. The privilege is not applicable in a proceeding brought by or on behalf of one's spouse against another spouse or a proceeding to commit his/her spouse under the control of another because of the spouse's alleged mental or physical condition. Evid. C. § 972. For a waiver of privileges, see Evid.C. § 973.

- e) *Privilege for Confidential Marital Communications.* A spouse has a privilege during the marital relationship and afterwards to refuse to disclose a communication made in confidence between husband and wife. Evid.C. § 280. This privilege does not apply to communications in furtherance of a crime or fraud (Evid.C. § 91); commitment or similar proceedings (Evid.C. § 982); a proceeding brought by one's spouse against another spouse (Evid.C. § 984); and, certain criminal and juvenile court proceedings Evid.C. §§ 985–986.

- f) *Clergyman/Penitent Privileges.* Both a penitent and a clergyman, as defined in Evid. C. §§ 1033 and 1034, have a privilege to refuse to disclose a penitential communication made between the penitent and the clergyman in the course of a penitential communication. Evid.C. § 1033. "Penitential communication" means communications made in confidence to a clergyman who is authorized to hear such communications and who, under the tenets of his church, has a duty to keep such communications secret.

3. *Statutory Privileges.*

- a) *Privilege of a Voter Not to Disclose Vote.* Evid.C. § 1050.

- b) *Privilege for Information Acquired in Confidence by a Public Employee in the Course of His Duty and Not Open to the Public.* Evid.C. § 1040(a).

- c) *Privilege for Identity of a Person Who Informs a Law Enforcement Agency of an Apparent Violation of California or Federal Law.* Evid.C. § 1042.

- d) *Privilege Governing Newspaper Reporter's Immunity From Contempt for Failure to Disclose a Source of Information Procured for Publication.* Evid.C. § 1070.

E. Competence C.C.P. Section 701. The witness must be competent to give testimony. A person must be capable of expression concerning the matter so as to be understood either directly or through an interpreter and must be capable of understanding the duty of a witness to tell the truth. C.C.P. Section 701. More importantly, the witness must demonstrate that he has *personal knowledge* of the matters testified to and is able to remember and communicate what he observed. The ability of a witness to use verbal expression so as to be understood, and whether the witness understands the duty to tell the truth and is able to understand the significance of the oath, is usually self-apparent. Objections usually arise regarding lack of foundation to establish that the witness has personal knowledge of the facts with which the testimony deals.

F. Lack of Foundation Evid.C. §§ 400–406. The admissibility of proposed evidence often depends on proof of a preliminary fact. A preliminary fact is defined as a fact, the existence or nonexistence of which, determines the admissibility or inadmissibility of the evidence. Evid.C. §§ 400–405. If an attorney has not presented proof of a preliminary fact, an objection on the basis of the lack of foundation is appropriate. When a foundational problem is presented, counsel must first determine whether the required foundation is governed by Evid. C. § 403, or Evid.C. § 405.

Evid.C. § 403 applies if one of the following four foundation problems is presented:

1. relevancy;
2. personal knowledge;
3. authentication of a writing; or,
4. identity.

If one of these four problems is present, the judge makes the initial determination as to whether there is evidence sufficient to sustain a finding of the existence of the preliminary fact and may admit the evidence with an instruction to the jury that it must first determine if the preliminary fact exists and to disregard the evidence if the jury finds that the preliminary fact does not exist. Evid.C. § 403. In all other foundational questions, the judge shall determine the existence of the preliminary fact and shall admit or exclude the evidence without an admonition to the jury (e.g., expert witness testimony). Evid.C. § 405. Evid.C. § 403(b) allows the judge to admit evidence on the condition that the required foundation be supplied later in the trial.

Counsel should consider making appropriate lack of foundation objections wherever grounds appear to exist. In many cases, the opposing attorney may not have thought through all of the preliminary facts that must be established before evidence is admitted and a lack of foundation objection may make it difficult if not impossible to get the evidence admitted. Such objections may seriously impair opposing counsel's ability to present the case.

On the other hand, if the objection does not keep the evidence out but forces the opposing attorney to establish all the preliminary facts necessary to establish the foundation, the evidence may appear more credible. Sometimes the better tactical approach, when the missing element can be established, is to not object and argue the missing preliminary fact in summation especially when the judge has instructed the jury that it can ignore the evidence if it finds that a preliminary fact has not been established.

G. Questioning by the Court Evid.C. § 775. The court may call a witness and interrogate just as if the witness had been produced by a party to the action. The parties may object to any question asked of the witness by the court just as if the witness had been called and examined by an adverse party. Evid. Bench Book, 2nd Edition, Volume 1, Jefferson, Ca. Judge's Association, CEB 1982, Chapter 27, Rule 27.22, Page 836. The purpose of objecting to questioning by the court is to prevent the judge from taking over or unduly influencing the jury by questioning a witness. It is suggested that such objections be made out of the presence of the jury. Objecting to the judge's questions in front of the jury, may lead the jury to believe that counsel is trying to disrupt the fair administration of justice by the judge.

H. Opinion Testimony Evid.C. §§ 800–805

1. *Opinion Testimony by a Lay Witness.* Lay opinion testimony is limited to those opinions regarding matters rationally based on the perception of the witness and helpful to a clear understanding of the testimony. Evid.C. § 800.

Three elements should be present:

a) the matter is personally perceived by the witness;

b) the matter is subject to commonly understood interpretation; and,

c) the opinion is helpful to the jury's understanding of the testimony.

The following are examples of permissible lay opinions: The sanity of a person known well to the witness, The Estate of Holloway, 195 Cal. 711, 733 (1925); The value of property owned by a witness, Schroeder v. Auto Driveaway Co., 11 Cal.3d 908, 921, 114 Cal.Rptr. 622, 631, 523 P.2d 662, 672 (1974), and a witness' own intent, motive or knowledge, Cope v. Davison, 30 Cal. 2d 193, 200, 180 P.2d 873, 877 (1947).

2. *Opinion by Expert Witness.* Experts can give opinion testimony including an opinion on an ultimate issue in the case if the expert has been qualified regarding the area of expertise and the basis of his opinion. Evid.C. §§ 801, 805. The opinion must be related to a subject that is sufficiently beyond common experience such that the opinion of an expert would assist the trier of fact. The witness must show special knowledge, skill, experience, training and education and must state the basis for his opinion. Evid.C. §§ 800–802.

In making objections to expert witness testimony, counsel should center on the basic qualifications of the expert and more significantly on the basis for the expert opinion. Testimony in the form of an opinion that is based on matter that is not a proper basis for such an opinion is inadmissible. Evid.C. § 803. For example, an expert's opinion which assures an incorrect legal theory is not substantial evidence. Smith v. Workmen's Comp. App. Bd., 71 Cal.2d 588, 78 Cal.Rptr. 718, 455 P.2d 822 (1969).

I. Speculation Evid.C. §§ 702, 801. Any question that asks the witness to guess or engage in conjecture is objectionable. Words like "if", "should", "could", and similar phrases in a question may render a question susceptible to this objection.

J. Best Evidence Rule Evid.C. §§ 1500–1511. The traditional best evidence rule required that the original of a document or other writing be introduced at the trial. The rule has been the subject of many exceptions including allowing copies of lost or destroyed writings when the original is unavailable. Evid.C. § 1502. A copy is also admissible if the original of the writing is under the control of the opponent (Evid.C. § 1503); if it is a copy of a public writing (Evid.C. § 1506); a copy of recorded writing (Evid.C. § 1507); or, if it is a voluminous writing (Evid.C. § 1509).

The 1986 Amendment to the Evidence Code recognizes the use of modern copying machines by simply providing that a duplicate is admissible to the same extent as the original unless a genuine question is raised as to the authenticity of the original or in circumstances in which it would be unfair to admit the duplicate in lieu of the original. Unless there is any real question as to the authenticity of the original from which the copy was made, or there are questions of unfairness, a duplicate of a writing is admissible. Evid.C. § 1511.

However, it does appear that the proponent of a duplicate of a writing must lay a foundation as to the authenticity of the original from which the duplicate copy was made, if a genuine question of authenticity of the original is raised by the opponent. An objection to a copy would be based on no foundation as to the authenticity of the original. Evid.C. § 1511.

K. Lack of Authentication Evid.C. §§ 1400–1454. Evidence Code § 1401(a) requires authentication of a writing before it may be received into evidence. A writing includes handwriting, typewriting, printing, photostating, photographing, and every other means of recording upon any tangible thing. Authentication of a writing, whether an original or a copy, means the introduction of evidence that the court determines is sufficient for a trier of fact reasonably to find that such writing is what the proponent claims it to be; or proof by any other means provided by law that such writing is what the proponent claims it to be. This can be by stipulation; by the pleadings or by the use of a presumption of genuineness. (Id. Evid. Bench Book, Jefferson, Volume 2, Chapter 30, § 30.1, Rule 4, Page 1050, Rule 4). Lack of authentication is usually raised as a foundation-type objection. e.g., "objection, foundation, lack of authentication."

L. Hearsay Evid.C. § 1200

1. *Definition.* Hearsay evidence is evidence of a statement that was made other than by a witness while testifying at the hearing which is offered to prove the truth of the matter stated. Unless an exception is provided by law, hearsay evidence is inadmissible. Evid.C. § 1200. "Statement" means an oral or written verbal expression or nonverbal conduct of a person that is intended by the person as a substitute for oral or written verbal expression. Evid.C. § 225. The nonverbal conduct must be assertive in character. That is, there must be an intent to communicate some fact. Nonassertive conduct is not a "statement" and is therefore not hearsay. See Law Revision Commission Comments to Evid.C. § 1200.

Hearsay is excluded because at the time the statement was made the person was not under oath, there is no way for the fact finder to observe the credibility of the person when the statement was made, and it is not possible to cross-examine the person who made the statement. The statement is hearsay only if the statement is introduced to prove the truth of the statement or the assertive conduct.

The attorney should always ask, "What is the proponent of this evidence trying to prove with this statement or assertive conduct?" If a statement is being introduced solely for the purpose of establishing that a statement was made, the statement is not hearsay. People v. Warner, 270 Cal.App.2d 900, 76 Cal.Rptr. 160 (1969).

There are many exceptions to the rule excluding hearsay. The exceptions are based on the existence of two conditions:

a) the likelihood that the hearsay is reliable; and,

b) the need to receive the hearsay; that is, it contains such probative value that it will assist the trier of fact in making a proper determination.

2. *Exceptions To The Hearsay Rule.* Evid.C. §§ 1220–1341.

a) *Admissions.* Evid.C. § 1220. Admissions which include certain confessions and declarations are divided into eight separate exceptions to the hearsay rule.

   (1) A Personal Admission Of A Party. Evid.C. § 1220.

   (2) Adoptive Admissions; that is, evidence of a statement offered against a party, if the statement is one which the party, with knowledge of the content has by words or other conduct manifested his adoption or his belief in its truth. Evid.C. § 1221. E.g., witness says "you ran that stop sign", defendant says nothing, but appears to nod his head up and down.

   (3) Authorized Admission; a statement made by a person authorized by a party to make a statement concerning the subject matter. Evid.C. § 1222.

   (4) Admission Of A Co–Conspirator; a statement made by the declarant while participating in a conspiracy to commit a crime or civil wrong while participating with a party in that conspiracy. Evid.C. § 1223.

   (5) Statement Of Declarant Whose Liability Or Breach Of Duty Is In Issue. Evid.C. § 1224.

   (6) Statement Of A Declarant Whose Right Or Title Is At Issue. Evid.C. § 1225.

   (7) Statement By A Minor Child In An Action Brought By The Minor Child's Parents For The Child's Injury. Evid.C. § 1226.

   (8) Declarations Against Interests. Evidence of a statement by an unavailable declarant having sufficient knowledge of the subject is not inadmissible by the hearsay rule, if the statement made was so contrary to the declarant's pecuniary or proprietary interests or would so subject him to risk of civil or criminal

liability that a reasonable person in his position would not have made the statement if he did not believe it to be true. Evid.C. § 1230.

b) *Prior Inconsistent Statements of Witnesses.* A prior statement of a witness is admissible and may be used as substantive evidence of the truth of its content as well as for impeachment of the witness' credibility if the statement is inconsistent with his present statement and if the witness is given the opportunity to explain or deny the previous inconsistent statement pursuant to Evid.C. § 770.

c) *Spontaneous, Contemporaneous and Dying Declarations.* These statements appear to be reliable and are admissible when they are made in response to an event in a spontaneous fashion and without time or need to be fabricated.

  (1) *Spontaneous Statement.* Evid.C. § 1240. (Also known as excited utterances.) Spontaneous statements made by the declarant while the declarant was under the stress of excitement from witnessing an act or event may be used to describe or explain the act or event perceived by the declarant.

  (2) *Contemporaneous Statements.* Evid.C. § 1241. Statements offered to explain, or make understandable the conduct of declarant made by the declarant while the declarant is engaged in such conduct falls under the Contemporaneous Statement exception to the hearsay rule.

  (3) *Dying Declaration.* Evid.C. § 1241. Evidence of a statement made by a dying person respecting the cause and circumstances of his death is admissible if the statement was made upon the decedent's personal knowledge and under a sense of immediate impending death. Evid.C. § 1242.

  (4) *Statement of Mental or Physical State.* Evid.C. §§ 1250–1251. Statements made by a person regarding that individual's existing state of mind, emotion, sensation or physical condition (such as intent, plan, motive, design, mental feeling, pain and bodily harm) are admissible unless the statement was made under circumstances such as to indicate its lack of trustworthiness. Evid.C. §§ 1250–1252.

d) *Business Records.* Evid.C. § 1271. Evidence of writings made in the regular course of business made at or near the time of the act or event are admissible where a qualified witness testifies to its identity and mode of preparation and the circumstances are such to indicate its trustworthiness. Evid.C. § 1271.

e) *Record by a Public Employee.* Evid.C. § 1280. Evidence of a writing made by and within the scope of employment of a public employee made at or near the time of the act is admissible if the sources of information and method and time of preparation were such as to indicate its trustworthiness. Evid.C. § 1280.

f) *Record of Vital Statistic.* Evid.C. § 1281. Evidence of a writing made as a record of a birth, fetal death, death or marriage is admissible if the maker of the writing was required by law to file the writing in a designated public office and the writing was made and filed as required by law.

g) *Absence of Business and Public Entries.* Evid.C. §§ 1272, 1284. The absence of business and public records may prove the nonexistence of a fact.

h) *Judgment of Conviction of a Crime Punishable as a Felony.* Evidence of a final judgment, adjudging a person guilty of a felony is admissible in a civil action to prove any fact essential to that judgment. Evid.C. § 1300.

i) *Family History.* Statements concerning the declarant's own family history are admissible. Statements concerning the family history of another to whom the declarant was related by blood or marriage; entries in family records; reputation in the family concerning family history and the reputation in the community concerning a family's history are admissible. Evid.C. §§ 1310–1314.

j) *Church Records.* Evidence of a statement concerning a person's birth, marriage, divorce, death, parent and child relationship, race, ancestry, relationship by blood or marriage that is contained in a writing made as a record of a church, religious denomination or religious society is admissible. Evid.C. §§ 1310–1316. These include marriage, baptismal and similar certificates made by a clergyman, civil officer or other person authorized to perform such acts. Evid.C. § 1316.

k) *Statements Relating to Wills or to Claims Against an Estate.* Evid.C. § 1260. Statements by an unavailable declarant that he has or has not made his will, or has or has not revoked his will or that identify his will, is admissible if made under circumstances such as to indicate trustworthiness. Evid.C. § 1260.

l) *Reputation.* Statements concerning community history, or property interests may be admissible. These include:

   (1) Reputation concerning community history. Evid.C. § 1320.

   (2) Reputation concerning public interest and property. Evid.C. § 1321.

   (3) Reputation concerning boundaries or customs effecting land. Evid.C. § 1322.

   (4) Statements concerning boundaries by unavailable declarant who had sufficient knowledge of the subject. Evid.C. § 1323.

   (5) Reputation concerning character. Evidence of a person's general reputation with reference to his character or trait of his character at a relevant time in the community in which he resided is admissible as an exception to the hearsay rule. Evid.C. § 1324. Character evidence is admissible only when the question of character is relevant to the matter being litigated and is not precluded by policy restrictions. (Id. Evid.Bench Book, Jefferson, Volume 1, Chapter 18, § 18.5, Page 433.) Character evidence may not be used to prove that a person did a particular thing at a particular time.

m) *Evidence Contained in Writings Affecting Property.* Statements contained in conveyances or in wills are generally admissible if the matter stated in the writing was relevant to the purpose of the writing and would be relevant to an issue regarding an interest in the property. Evid.C. § 1330.

n) *Recitals and Ancient Writings.* Evid.C. § 1331. Statements contained in writings over 30 years old that have been generally acted on as true by persons having interests in the matter are admissible. Evid.C. § 1331.

o) *Statements Contained in Commercial, Scientific and Similar Publications.* Evidence of a statement, (other than an opinion) contained in published compilations generally used and relied upon as accurate in the course of a business as defined in Evid.C. § 1270 are admissible. Evid.C. § 1340.

p) *Statements Contained in Historical Works, Books and Science or Art, or Published Maps or Charts.* Statements made by neutral persons and offered to prove facts of general notoriety, are admissible under Evid.C. § 1341.

6.5 OBJECTIONS TO THE FORM OF THE QUESTIONS

The following objections should be made to control the examiner and to prevent the asking of questions which may result in improper, prejudicial or unintelligible answers. While these objections are not designed by statute to specifically exclude evidence, the thoughtful and timely use of these objections can exclude unduly prejudicial evidence and will allow for timely objections to exclude improper evidence. They can also be used in a proper manner so as to make it difficult for your opponent to present his case.

A. Leading Evid.C. §§ 764, 767. Generally, leading questions are not permitted during direct examinations. Leading questions are questions that are suggestive of the answer. (e.g., "and then Mr. Jones hit you, didn't he?") Leading questions are permitted in direct examinations under certain circumstances. These include: preliminary matters; noncontroversial, undisputed or inconsequential facts; topic transition; examination of an adverse or hostile witness; when the witness has poor communication skills; refreshing a witness' recollection and when asking a witness to contradict previous testimony. Evid.C. §§ 765, 767.

B. Narrative Evid.C. § 765. An objection may be made to a question that calls for or results in a narrative. A narrative question is a question that allows the witness to tell a long uncontrolled story. For example, "In your own words, Ms. Smith, tell the jury everything that happened to you on July 1." A narrative question is objectionable because it allows the witness to interject inadmissible testimony without giving the opposing attorney a reasonable opportunity to object. Sometimes a witness will give a narrative response to an otherwise permissible question and a narrative answer may be objected to as being a narrative answer or as being non-responsive. (See Chapter 9, Sec. E2.)

C. Asked and Answered Evid.C. § 774. If the question has been "asked and answered," the attorney may object to the question as repetitious. The purpose of this objection is to prevent the opposing attorney from gaining undue advantage by repeating favorable testimony in front of the jury. The form of the questions need not be absolutely identical in order to raise this objection. If the new question calls for an answer previously given the question is objectionable as repetitious.

D. Cumulative Evid.C. § 352. Cumulative evidence usually occurs when testimony regarding character and reputation is involved. Cumulative exhibits are most often photographs. Cumulative evidence is objectionable because it is repetitive, unnecessary, and a waste of time.

E. Vague, Ambiguous, Misleading, Confusing or Unintelligible Evid.C. § 765. A question must be reasonable, clear, and specific so that the witness knows what is being asked. (See Chapter 6, Sec. E3.)

F. Multiple or Compound Questions Evid.C. § 765. A multiple or compound question presents two or more questions within a single question. This type of question is objectionable because the answer will usually be ambiguous or confusing both in court and on review of the record. E.g., "Was the defendant wearing brown shoes and was he driving?"

G. Assuming Facts Not in Evidence Evid.C. § 765. This objection is often used to object to cross-examination questions that include facts which are in dispute or not in evidence. An examiner who faces this objection, may revise the question to eliminate the assumption of fact or may advise the court that the assumed fact will be proven later. If the latter course is taken, the assumed fact must be proven. If that fact is not proven later, the opposing attorney may request that the judge direct the jury to disregard such evidence.

H. Misstatement or Mischaracterization of Testimony or Evidence Evid.C. §§ 765, 774. Misstatement or mischaracterization of evidence and testimony is objectionable because it inaccurately describes evidence or draws inferences that are reserved for the jury's determination. This objection may be used to object to testimony as well as questions.

I. Argumentative Evid.C. § 765. Any question that is essentially an argument to the jury is objectionable. The role of the attorney is to question and not to testify. An argumentative question is recognized either by the fact that it elicits no new information or that it is a form of harassment. Argumentative questions often assume a sarcastic tenor, "Do you mean to tell me," or "Doesn't it seem preposterous that."

J. Improper Impeachment Evid.C. §§ 780, 785. Improper impeachment is an impermissible attempt to discredit a witness. Improper impeachment may occur in a variety of ways. A cross-examiner may improperly attempt to impeach the witness on a collateral matter, or with a prior statement that is not materially inconsistent.

K. Beyond the Scope Evid.C. §§ 761, 773. Cross-examination, redirect examination, rebuttal testimony, and rebuttal closing arguments are each limited in scope. Cross-examination is limited to the subject matter of the direct examination and other matters relating to the witness' credibility. If the cross-examiner wishes to go beyond the scope of the direct, the cross-examiner must usually recall the witness. The cross-examiner may, however, raise new matters in a non-leading way if the court permits.

The scope of direct examinations will usually be broad enough to permit inquiries on cross or re-direct that do not go beyond the scope of the examination. The issue of credibility may be sufficient in itself to justify most cross-examination questions. Usually judges view the scope of an examination liberally and permit wide ranging examinations as long as the questions are relevant to the case.

Redirect questions should be limited in scope to those new matters raised in cross-examination. Rebuttal testimony will be permitted to rebut evidence introduced during the opponent's case in chief. Rebuttal closing argument will be limited to new matters raised by the opponent's summation. Evid.C. §§ 761, 773.

6.6 OBJECTIONS TO DEMONSTRATIVE EVIDENCE

A. Misleading, Inaccurate or Distorting Evid.C. § 352. Demonstrative evidence should not mislead, confuse, or distort facts. Drawings that are not drawn to scale, photographs taken of a scene at a time far removed from the time of the incident, and other differences, can be misleading. The attorney should request to see demonstrative evidence prior to trial so that objections can be made before the jury is exposed to the evidence.

B. Lack of Foundation Evid.C. §§ 403–405. See Section 6.4F.

C. Waste of Court's Time/Undue Delay Evid.C. § 352. Sometimes the presentation of demonstrative evidence may be time consuming or require extensive preparation. In these instances, the value of the demonstrative evidence must be weighed against the cost of court time and delay. Demonstrative evidence that does not significantly add to the case will be rejected more frequently than demonstrative evidence that is crucial to the case.

D. Evidence Does Not Aid or Assist Jury Evid.C. § 352. Demonstrative evidence that does not aid or assist the jury is objectionable.

6.7 OBJECTIONS DURING JURY SELECTION

A. Mentioning Insurance Evid.C. § 1155. As a general rule it is improper to mention the existence or nonexistence of insurance coverage during jury selection. However, some judges permit inquiries on voir dire to determine bias, prejudice, or interest in insurance matters.

B. Arguing or Indoctrinating Jurors About the Law. Voir dire may not be used to argue the law. However, most judges will permit some general questions concerning the law. People v. Williams, 29 Cal.3d 392, 174 Cal.Rptr. 317, 628 P.2d 869 (1981).

C. Arguing Facts. Jury selection may not be used to argue the facts. An attempt to present the facts of the case during jury selection is objectionable. People v. Williams, 29 Cal. 3d 392, 174 Cal.Rptr. 317, 628 P.2d 869 (1981).

6.8 OBJECTIONS DURING OPENING STATEMENT

A. Explaining the Law or Instructions. Opening statement is intended to allow each party an opportunity to present its version of the case and what it expects to prove. Explaining the law or instructions is considered premature and is objectionable in most courts. Most judges, however, will permit some limited explanations if related to the facts and if counsel has the judge's approval ahead of time.

B. Argumentative. The opening statement should consist of a synopsis of the facts to be presented. The opening statement is usually confined, therefore, to a discussion of what will be proved. Argument is appropriate only in closing argument. Love v. Wolf, 226 Cal.App.2d 378, 38 Cal.Rptr. 183 (1964).

C. Mentioning Inadmissible Evidence. One of the main purposes of excluding certain evidence is to prevent the prejudicial effects of that evidence. Consequently, it is improper to discuss inadmissible or questionably admissible evidence during opening statements. This would include any evidence excluded by pretrial rulings or likely to be excluded by the rules of evidence. Love v. Wolf, 226 Cal.App.2d 378, 38 Cal.Rptr. 183 (1964).

D. Mentioning Unprovable Evidence. Mentioning unprovable evidence is tantamount to using fiction to prove a case. The attorney may only discuss evidence that can be proved. The test in these instances is one of good faith. Love v. Wolf, 226 Cal.App.2d 378, 38 Cal.Rptr. 183 (1964).

E. Personal Opinions. Phrases such as "I think" or "I believe" are objectionable. The jury should be left to decide the case on the evidence.

F. Misstating the Law. Cal.Rules of Prof.Cond. 7–105(1).

G. Referring to Insurance Coverage. Evid.C. § 1155.

6.9 OBJECTIONS DURING CLOSING ARGUMENTS

A. Misstating Evidence. Misstating or mischaracterizing the evidence is objectionable. If a description or characterization does not reflect the testimony and evidence given during the trial it is objectionable. Cal.Rules of Prof.Cond. 7–105(1).

B. Misstating Law and Quoting Instructions. Misstating the law, like misstating the evidence, is objectionable. Most judges allow attorneys to highlight, comment on, and explain instructions during closing argument. However, it is improper to read all the instructions verbatim. Cal.Rules of Prof.Cond. 7–105(1).

C. Personal Opinions. Personal opinions are not appropriate in closing argument. An attorney may not use phrases such as "I think" or "I believe."

D. Appealing to Jury's Bias or Prejudice. This includes ethnic prejudice, and appealing to sympathy and shock, Horn v. Atchison T & S F Ry., 61 Cal.2d 602, 39 Cal.Rptr. 721, 394 P.2d 561 (1964).

E. Appealing to Jury's Pecuniary Interests. References in a suit that taxpayers (including members of the jury) will have to pay the damages are objectionable. Brokopp v. Ford Motor Co., 71 Cal.App.3d 841, 861, 139 Cal.Rptr. 888, 900 (1977).

F. Reference to Judgments Awarded in Similar Cases. Salgo v. Leland Sanford, Jr. Bd. of Trustees, 154 Cal.App.2d 560, 317 P.2d 170 (1957).

G. Personal Attacks on Parties and Counsel. A trial should be a reasoned and rational decision-making process. Personal attacks in the courtroom do nothing to further this objective. Bus. & Pro.C. § 6068(f).

H. Prejudicial Arguments. Comments that have little or nothing to do with the facts are objectionable. An attorney may not ask the jury if they would "take $500,000 if they were offered it for their arm." Nor may an attorney say that if the defendant is not found guilty "he will continue to commit crimes."

6.10 PRESENTATION AND DELIVERY

A. How to Object

   1. It is best to rise when making an objection. Most judges will expect an attorney to stand and the extra second gained may help in framing an objection. Some judges may allow an attorney to remain seated or an attorney may request to remain seated.

   2. In order for an objection to be effective it must be timely. The objection must be made before the jury hears the testimony or sees the evidence. Also, a timely objection is necessary to preserve the objection for appeal. Evid.C. § 353(a).

   3. If a question is improper, the objection should be made before an answer is given. If an answer is improper, an objection and motion to strike should be made as soon as the problem becomes apparent. Evid.C. § 353(a).

   4. The proper way to object is simply to say "Objection" and then state the specific, precise legal grounds in one or a few words. Evid.C. § 353(a). E.g., "Objection, the question calls for hearsay." If the grounds for the objection are clear, it may be sustained without further explanation. If an explanation is requested, a further statement may be made.

   5. An objection may be sustained by the judge even if the attorney does not advance a specific reason if the ground for the objection is apparent from the content of the evidence. Evid.C. § 353(a), 354(a).

6. Usually the reason supporting an objection will be obvious from the judge's ruling. Evid.C. § 354(a). If the attorney is uncertain about the grounds for sustaining an objection the attorney may ask the judge to explain the ruling.

7. If an attorney wishes to argue an objection, the attorney should ask the court to be heard on the matter and approach the bench in a jury trial. Arguments or comments about the evidence should occur outside of the hearing of the jury.

8. It may be necessary to insist on a ruling to the objection. The attorney has a right to it. If the objection is sustained, the attorney may request a curative instruction. If the objection is overruled, the attorney should make sure that the legal basis for the objection is on the record to preserve the issue for appeal. Evid.C. § 353 and Comments to § 353.

B. Motion to Strike. If an answer has been given before an objection has been made and the objection is sustained, a motion to strike must be made. Failure to make a motion to strike waives the right to complain of the erroneous admission of evidence. Evid.C. § 353(a) LRC Comment.

C. Admonition to Disregard the Evidence A motion to strike should always be coupled with a request that the judge admonish the jury to disregard the stricken testimony. If the testimony is prejudicial and the impropriety of seeking its admission is clear, counsel may request the judge to reprimand opposing counsel. If the improper matter is so prejudicial that its disclosure makes a fair trial impossible, counsel should move for a mistrial. See California Trial Objection § 51.13 (Cal. CEB 1984).

D. Offers of Proof. When an objection is sustained, an offer of proof usually should be made to preserve rights on appeal. Evid.C. § 354(a). Offers of proof to overcome a sustained objection based on relevancy should be geared towards changing the judge's mind. There are two types of offers of proof. The first involves the attorney summarizing the proposed testimony on the record outside the hearing of the jury. Another method of making an offer of proof is to examine the witness in a question and answer dialogue out of the jury's presence. This method is time consuming, but has the advantage of completeness and accuracy. This method should only be used for a crucial part of the case, and when you think the judge may reverse his own relevancy ruling.

E. When an Offer of Proof Is Not Required

1. When the question itself makes clear the relevant purpose and substance of the evidence. Evid.C. § 354(a).

2. When previous trial court rulings, such as ruling out an entire area of questioning, makes the offer of proof futile. Evid.C. § 354(b).

3. When the evidence is sought through cross-examination. Evid.C. § 354(b).

COMMON LEGAL OBJECTIONS

I. OBJECTIONS TO EXCLUDE EVIDENCE
   (All cites are Cal.Evid.Code, unless otherwise noted)

Cal.Evid.Code Section

A. Irrelevant
   (Federal Rules of Evidence hereafter FRE 401) — 210, 350, 351
B. *Legally Irrelevant* (generally) — 210, 350, 352
   FRE 401–411
   - Probative Value Outweighed — 210, 352
   - Prejudicial — 350, 352
   - Improper Character — 786, 787, 1101–1102
   - Improper Habit — 1103–1105
   - Subsequent Remedial Measures — 1151
   - Offers of Compromise — 1152, 1154
   - Plea Bargains — 1153
   - Payment of Medical Expenses — 1152
   - Liability Insurance — 1155
   - Communications During Mediation Proceedings — 1152.5
C. *Privileges*
   FRE 501
   - Self Incrimination — 404, 940
   - Attorney/Client — 950–962
   - Physician/Patient — 990–1007
   - Spousal Testimony — 970–973
   - Marital Communications — 980–987
   - Clergy/Penitent — 1030–1034
   - Trade/Business Secrets — 1060
   - Informer Identity — 1040–1047
   - Official Information — 1040–1047
   - News Sources — 1070
   - Psychotherapist/Patient — 1010–1027
   - Voter — 1050
D. *Competence*
   FRE 601–602
   - Incompetence — 701(a), (b), 703, 704
   - Lack of Personal Knowledge — 702(a)
   - Lack of Memory — 702(a)
E. *Foundation*
   FRE 601–602
   - Lack of Foundation — 400–405, 701, 702
   - Improper Lay Opinion — 800
     FRE 701
   - Impermissible Opinion — 720, 800, 803, 804
   - Impermissible Conclusion — 720, 800, 805
   - Speculation — 702, 800
   - Expert Opinion
     FRE 702–705 — 720, 801, 802, 804, 805, 813
   - Unqualified Witness — 720, 802
   - Impermissible Opinion — 803, 804

Appendix

			Cal.Evid.Code Section
F.	*Authentication*		
	FRE 901–902		1400–1454
	Lack of Authenticity		1401
	Best Evidence Rule		
	FRE 1001–1007		1500–1511
	Unauthentic Copy		1500
	Non-genuine Original		1151
G.	*Parol Evidence*		C.C.P. 1856
H.	*Hearsay*		1200(a)
	Evidence of a Statement Made;		
	Not Under Oath by a Witness;		
	Not Subject to Cross,		
	To Prove the Truth of the Matter		1200, 1201
I.	*Exceptions to Hearsay Rule*		
	FRE 803, 804		
	1)	Admissions of party and other specified admissions	1220–1228
	2)	Declarations against interest	1230
	3)	Prior inconsistent statement	1235
	4)	Prior consistent statement	1236
	5)	Past recollection recorded	1237
	6)	Prior identification	1238
	7)	Spontaneous statement	1240
	8)	A contemporaneous statement	1241
	9)	A dying declaration	1242
	10)	Statements of mental or physical state	1250–1252
	11)	Statements relating to wills and to claims against estates	1260–1261
	12)	Business records	1270–1272
	13)	Official records and other official writings	1280–1284
	14)	Former testimony	1290–1292
	15)	Judgments	1300–1302
	16)	Family history	1310–1316
	17)	Reputation and statements concerning community history, property interest, and character	1320–1324
	18)	Recitals and writings effecting property interests	1330
	19)	Recitals and ancient writings	1331
	20)	Commercial, scientific and similar publications	1340–1341
	21)	Declarant unavailable as a witness in a serious felony criminal prosecution	1350

Appendix (continued)

		Cal.Evid.Code Section
II.	IMPROPER FORM OF QUESTION	
A.	*Leading*	764, 767
	FRE 611	
	Suggests the Answer	
	Lawyer Testifying	
B.	*Narrative*	765, 766
C.	*Asked and Answered*	774
	FRE 403, 611	
D.	*Vague*	765a
	FRE 401–403	
	Ambiguous	
	Confusing	
	Misleading	
	Unintelligible	
E.	*Multiple Questions*	765a
	Compound Question	
	FRE 611	
F.	*Assuming Facts Not In Evidence*	765a
	FRE 611, 701–704	
G.	*Misstatement of Evidence*	765, Rules of Prof.Cond. 7–105(1)
	FRE 611	765, 774
H.	*Argumentative*	
	FRE 611	765
I.	*Beyond Scope*	760–764, 772
	Cross Examination	761, 773
	Beyond Scope of Direct	760, 773, 774
J.	*Calls For Speculation Or Conjecture*	702

Appendix (continued)

OBJECTION PLANNING WORKSHEET

Case _____ File _____

A. Evidentiary questions to be resolved by motion in limine:

Opponent's Evidence Sought to Be Excluded	Reason/Argument	Authority

Your Evidence Sought to Be Admitted	Reason/Argument	Authority

B. Ruling on motion in limine:

Form 6–1

C. Objections to be asserted against opponent's evidence during trial:

Evidence	Reason/Argument	Authority

D. Anticipated objections by opponent:

Evidence	Reason/Authority for	Reason/Authority Against

Form 6–1 (continued)

Chapter 7

THE JURY SELECTION PROCESS

Table of Sections

Sec.
- 7.1 Description.
- 7.2 Purposes.
    - A. Obtaining Information About the Jurors.
    - B. Determining Attitudes.
    - C. Disqualifying a Juror.
    - D. Establishing Rapport.
    - E. Other Uses of Jury Voir Dire.
- 7.3 Procedure for Obtaining a Jury Trial.
- 7.4 Preparation and Investigation.
    - A. Advance Investigation.
    - B. Develop a Theory for Selection.
    - C. Selection Considerations.
- 7.5 Jury Selection Procedures.
    - A. Overview.
    - B. Voir Dire Procedures.
    - C. Jury Selection Topics to Be Discussed in Pre-trial Conference.
    - D. Voir Dire by Judge.
    - E. Voir Dire by Attorney.
    - F. Preliminary Instructions.
- 7.6 Selection Process.
    - A. Generally.
    - B. Notes.
    - C. Addressing the Jurors.
    - D. Areas of Questioning.
    - E. Selection of Question Areas.
    - F. Types and Forms of Questions.
    - G. Conduct of Voir Dire.
    - H. Rehabilitation.
- 7.7 Objecting to Improper Voir Dire Questions.
    - A. Improper Voir Dire.
- 7.8 The Final Selection Process.
    - A. Challenge for Cause C.C.P. § 225(a).
    - B. Peremptory Challenges.
    - C. Use of Client.
    - D. Alternative Jurors.
    - E. Making the Challenge.
    - F. Keeping Track of Challenges.

Forms
7-1 Jury Selection Worksheet.
7-2 Jury Seating Chart.
7-3 Jury Selection Chart.
7-4 Jury Challenge Worksheet.

7.1 DESCRIPTION

Jury selection is the process of removing the least acceptable persons from a pre-selected panel of jurors. With counsel of equal ability, the resulting panel will be as balanced as possible. This process usually involves questioning of prospective jurors by the attorneys or by the court. Questions asked during jury selection attempt to obtain information about the prospective juror's perceptions, opinions, experiences, and personalities. Each attorney then attempts to strike unfavorable jurors using challenges for cause and peremptory challenges.

7.2 PURPOSES

A. Obtaining Information About the Jurors. The attorney needs to acquire factual information about the jurors to support a challenge for cause and to form a basis for exercising peremptory challenges.

B. Determining Attitudes. Knowledge of attitudes and feelings, in addition to factual knowledge, is necessary in order to knowingly and intelligently select a jury.

C. Disqualifying a Juror. A juror may agree that because of apparent or implied bias, prejudice, or interest that she or he should not be a juror in a case.

D. Establishing Rapport. Voir dire questions should be used to establish a favorable rapport between the jurors and the attorney and client.

E. Other Uses of Jury Voir Dire. Some attorneys attempt to use voir dire to educate the jury about the case; to obtain commitment to vote a certain way, to instruct the jury, or to argue the case. Using voir dire for such purposes is now specifically prohibited in criminal cases. C.C.P. § 223(d). One should anticipate that judges in civil trials may not allow an attorney to use voir dire for these purposes even though not specifically prohibited in civil trials. This should be addressed in the pre-trial conference.

7.3 PROCEDURE FOR OBTAINING A JURY TRIAL

While the right to a jury trial is guaranteed by the California Constitution (Article 1 Sec. 16), counsel must follow strict procedural requirements or the right to a trial by jury will be waived by operation of law. C.C.P. § 631.

In order to assure a trial by jury counsel must:

A. Indicate in the at-issue memorandum or counter at-issue memorandum that a jury trial is requested. Cal.Rules of Court 507(b)(4) C.C.P. § 631. Local Rules should also be consulted for other local court procedural requirements.

B. Within 25 days prior to the date set for trial, deposit with the clerk of the court a sum equal to the amount of one day's jury fees. C.C.P. § 631(a)(5). Check local rules for amount.

C. On the second and each succeeding day's session of the jury trial the party requesting the jury trial must deposit a sum equal to one day's jury fees plus mileage. C.C.P. § 631(a)(6).

The court has the discretion to allow a trial by jury even though the above requirements have not been met. C.C.P. § 631(d)(8). Counsel should follow the statutory requirements to the letter. Failure to do so may inadvertently waive your client's right to a jury trial and would be grounds for a malpractice suit.

7.4 PREPARATION AND INVESTIGATION

A. Advance Investigation. Trial jurors are chosen from a group of randomly selected people in the community. C.C.P. § 197. At any given time a particular court has a set number of people sitting as the jury panel for that court. The jurors are randomly assigned to courtrooms for a particular trial. There is really no practical way to do advance investigation of each member of the jury panel, unless the jury panel is very small (e.g., Trinity County).

Most larger jurisdictions do have a "Jury Book" service. This is a service provided by local entrepreneurs who gather as much information as possible regarding the present members of the jury panel. This information may include: previous jury service and votes, occupation, educational background, family, community connections and other data regarding possible bias or inclination.

Some attorneys use investigators and law clerks to obtain information about the prospective jurors once their identity is known. This may include such things as locating a juror's parked car to check out bumper stickers for political affiliation, employment or strongly felt sentiments (e.g., "My gun will only be taken out of my cold, stiff hands"; "Save the Whales", or "Nuke the Whales"). However, one must always be careful to respect a juror's privacy.

B. Develop a Theory for Selection. Some lawyers prepare a jury profile in advance and select those jurors who best fit that profile. Other lawyers select jurors based on intuitive feelings developed during the course of voir dire. Theories on how to select a jury are probably as diverse as the number of lawyers who actually pick a jury.

A lawyer may want to consider the following factors whatever the theory used: age, social background, marital status, family status (children), family history (parents, siblings), education, occupation (self, spouse, family), employment history, residence history, personal history, hobbies, activities and experiences relevant to the case. Some theories for jury selection include similarity to parties, ethnic characteristics, work, social class, body language, attitudes, and overall impression.

In the last analysis, the success of the jury selection process depends on the lawyer's ability to relate to the prospective jurors, to use the limited information available, and to make accurate judgments about people. Thus, the jury selection process should be viewed as an art rather than a science, even in cases where social scientific methodology is employed. The more information the lawyer can obtain about each juror, the more trustworthy the art becomes.

C. Selection Considerations. In selecting jurors an attorney should:

1. Consider the type of person the attorney and the client normally appeal to and what type may be aggravated by either the attorney or client.

2. Think about what impact witnesses will have on particular jurors.

3. Consider who will be most receptive to the case, and who will be receptive to the other attorney's case and client.

4. Who will follow the "letter" of the law and who will "bend" the rules.

5. Determine what level of intelligence is required by the case.

6. Try to determine who the foreperson will be.

7. Consider the ethnic, social, and cultural background of each juror.

8. Consider the impact a juror's gender may have on the case.

9. Look at each juror's body language.

10. Note any associations or "cliques" among jurors.

11. Remember that strong-willed or opinionated jurors may deadlock a jury.

12. Note jurors who arrive late, talk during voir dire, or display other questionable conduct which may demonstrate a lack of interest or seriousness.

13. Consider how cohesive the jurors will be together.

14. Determine whether a more harmonious group of jurors will be desirable, or whether jurors who are more individualistic and do not follow a crowd are more desirable.

See Form 7–1 Jury Selection Worksheet.

7.5 JURY SELECTION PROCEDURES

A. Overview. "A trial jury is a body of persons temporarily selected from the citizens of the area served by the court." C.C.P. § 194. "Persons selected for jury service shall be selected at random." C.C.P. § 197(a).

A court maintains a master list of qualified jurors, and chooses the jury panel from that list. The members of the jury panel are present in the courthouse or on call during their period of jury duty. When a case is sent to a courtroom for a trial, some of the members of the jury panel are randomly sent to the courtroom to serve as jurors for that trial.

The jurors are collectively sworn and the judge explains the purpose of the voir dire examination. The judge and the attorneys for the parties then question the prospective jurors for the purpose of determining whether they are qualified, competent and unbiased jurors. The attorneys may challenge for cause or exercise a peremptory challenge.

When a juror is removed the judge will replace him or her with another person from the jury panel. When each attorney completes his voir dire and challenges, the jury selection is complete.

B. Voir Dire Procedures. The general procedure for conducting voir dire is found in California Rules of Court 228 and 516. "The trial judge shall examine the prospective jurors and upon completion of his initial examination the trial judge shall permit counsel for each party who so requests to submit additional questions which he shall put to the jurors. Upon request of counsel, the trial judge shall permit counsel to supplement the judge's examination by oral and direct questioning of any of the prospective jurors." C.C.P. § 228.

The specific procedure to be used and the order of examination should be discussed and agreed upon in the pre-trial chambers conference.

C. Jury Selection Topics to Be Discussed in Pre-trial Conference.

1. Who begins the voir dire questioning, plaintiff or defense?
2. How much time will usually be available?
3. Will questioning of individual prospective jurors be allowed or must the questions be addressed to the entire panel?
4. Is the judge present during voir dire?
5. Is voir dire recorded by a reporter?
6. How are challenges made?
7. Does the jury remain in the room during the challenge process?
8. What grounds must be established for cause?
9. Are the peremptory challenges made after all the questioning is done or one juror at a time? Who goes first?
10. Under what circumstances are the replacement jurors called?
11. What preliminary explanations will the judge make to the jury?
12. Will the jurors be allowed to take notes?

D. Voir Dire by Judge. The judge will usually ask the jury, sitting as a whole, specific questions and inquire into areas using the list found in Cal.Rules of Court, Appendix, Division I. Standards, Sec. 8(c)–(d). Counsel should submit a list of specific questions and areas of inquiry not covered by this list. When the judge finishes his initial questioning, counsel may submit further questions to the judge to be put to the jury. Cal.Rules of Court, Appendix, Div. I Judicial Standards Sec. 8.

E. Voir Dire by Attorney. Attorneys are entitled to voir dire each individual prospective juror. Cal.Rules of Ct. 228. They may ask questions designed to elicit grounds for a challenge for cause or grounds for a peremptory challenge. "The trial judge should permit liberal and probing examinations calculated to discover possible bias or prejudice." Cal.Rules of Ct. Appendix Div. I Sec. 8. However, "The scope of additional questions . . . shall be within reasonable limits." Cal.Rules of Court, Rule 228.

The Jury Selection Process   7–5

While the judge will ask most of his questions to the jury panel as a whole, attorneys should question each juror separately with individual responses to each question. This allows the attorney to form affective reactions and intuitive impressions of the juror and to begin establishing rapport with that juror.

The attorney should individually question all 12 members of the proposed jury. The challenge for cause should usually be made at the time of the discovery of the grounds for cause. In cases where agreements have been made to defer challenges for cause, or where a particular judge prefers to defer such challenges, the challenge for cause may be made at the end of questioning.

The opposing attorney will then examine all jurors. At the end of the questions by both attorneys, the attorneys may then make their deferred challenges for cause and their peremptory challenges. See Sec. 7.8 below.

When the removed jurors are replaced by new prospective jurors, the process starts over with the new jurors. The process continues until the attorneys have either taken all of their peremptory challenge or have passed on further objections and accept the jury as constituted. The jury is then sworn in.

F. Preliminary Instructions. After the jury has been sworn by the clerk and before opening statements, the trial judge will instruct the jurors. These instructions will usually include the following:

1. Refrain from discussing the case among yourselves or with other persons;
2. An explanation of the specific laws applicable to the case;
3. A request to direct any questions or problems to the bailiff; and
4. An order to follow the directions of the bailiff, who is in charge of the jurors, regarding the physical facilities and supplies.

The judge may also provide jurors with instructions regarding:

1. An explanation of important general principles of law applicable to the case, such as the burden of proof or definitions of legal terms;
2. An explanation of the specific laws applicable to the case;
3. The functions of the judge and that the judge will be the source of the law;
4. The responsibilities of the attorneys and that statements and arguments by them should not be considered evidence;
5. A summary of the issues of the case or a reading of the charge or complaint;
6. The identity of the parties and their counsel;
7. Whether note taking is permitted;
8. Any other instructions the attorneys request which the court deems appropriate; and
9. Instructions favored by a particular judge.

7.6 SELECTION PROCESS

A. Generally. The selection process begins as soon as the prospective jurors enter the courtroom. An attorney should observe the jurors as they take their seats and notice their appearance, conduct, and any apparent peculiarities. This first impression and personal intuitive responses may be helpful in later making a final selection. It is helpful to use a seating chart upon which to place the name of the juror and his/her seat in the jury box. This will assist later when jurors are removed and replaced. See Form 7-2 Jury Seating Chart.

B. Notes. Many attorneys take notes concerning the jurors during voir dire. These notes may be written on a chart listing the jurors' names. Once you have the names of the jurors on a seating chart, you can assign them numbers and places on the selection chart. The chart should be designed so there is sufficient room for notes to be taken during voir dire. See Form 7-3 Jury Selection Chart. The notes may include observations by the attorney, responses by the jurors, and other factors which rate the prospective juror as favorable or unfavorable. This information will aid the attorney in determining who to challenge.

C. Addressing the Jurors. Jurors should be addressed by their last names. Women jurors may prefer to be addressed as Mrs., Ms., or Miss. It may be necessary to ask how they prefer to be addressed. Some jurors will be more sensitive to this issue than others, and it is important to correctly address each juror. The attorney could ask their preference, or the attorney could request that the clerk or the judge ask their preference.

D. Areas of Questioning. There are several areas of questions that should be considered with every juror.

    1. Areas the judge should cover:

a) Address;

b) Educational level;

c) Employment status;

d) Marital status;

e) Family status;

f) Relationship with parties, attorneys, and witnesses;

g) Whether jurors have heard about the case or have any information about the case;

h) Previous jury experience;

i) Experience with court system;

j) Experience or education in fields relating to the case; and

k) Whether a juror would suffer any personal hardship as a juror.

Most of these areas will be covered in voir dire by the judge. Keep track of what the judge inquires about and fill in the gaps. (See, Cal.Rules of Court Appendix, Division I, Sec. 8, for areas the Judge is supposed to cover.)

    2. Areas the attorney should probe:

a) Liability issues;

b) Damage issues;

c) Facts;

d) Legal principles;

e) Client;

f) Problems with case;

g) Weaknesses in the case; and

h) Other issues.

There may be some areas that should be avoided during voir dire. Age, religion, and private concerns are examples. There is no need to ask a sensitive question that may offend many jurors. Questions concerning religious beliefs or personal matters when not germane to the case often are embarrassing and uncomfortable. The risk of offending some or all of the jury panel is so high that care must be exercised before questioning in these areas.

E. Selection of Question Areas. Selecting questions may be difficult. The attorney must be sensitive to a juror's position and probable reaction, particularly to personal questions. In some situations, it will be necessary for the attorney to ask sensitive questions because that information is vital to the selection process and in the best interests of the client. In these circumstances the attorney should be as careful as possible to phrase questions in a way that will reduce the chance of any adverse reaction by the jurors.

F. Types and Forms of Questions. There are several types of questions that may be asked during voir dire. These types include:

    1. Specific questions directed to the entire panel which require a yes or no answer and may require follow-up questions;

The Jury Selection Process

2. General questions to the panel which require a explanatory response;

3. Specific questions directed to an individual juror that require a yes or no or short explanation response, and

4. General questions to an individual juror which require a narrative explanatory response.

The form of a question will depend upon its purpose. If the question seeks specific information, the question should be phrased to generate a specific response. The following questions demonstrate examples of such questions:

— Where do you live?

— Do you know the plaintiff, Denise Baker?

— Have you sat as a juror in a previous case? What kind of case was it?

If the question seeks opinions and attitudes of the jurors the question may be phrased either as an open ended or a leading question. Examples include:

— Does the fact that this case involves the death of a child influence you one way or the other in your consideration of the facts?

— This case involves a claim of sex discrimination. How do you feel in general about a woman who claims that a man discriminated against her and hired someone else?

— Will the fact that this case involves a large corporation not influence you one way or the other in reaching a verdict based on the facts?

If the question is designed to provide information to the jurors, the preface to the question may be more important than the question or response. Some examples include:

— The plaintiff in this case is a widow. Did any of you know her deceased husband, Mr. Baker?

— An expert design engineer will testify in this case. Her name is Darlene Cooper. Have any of you seen her on television or read any of her books?

If the question is designed to obtain a commitment or promise from the jurors, the question should seek a yes or no response. Some examples include:

— Will you be able to put aside any feelings of sympathy you may have for the plaintiff and return a verdict based solely on the evidence presented?

— The defendant in this trial is unemployed and has to receive income from welfare payments to provide for her family. You will not allow the fact that she receives welfare to affect your judgment in this case, will you?

Be careful in the use of such questions. The judge may not allow such commitment questions and interrupt your voir dire. This will make a bad impression on the jury.

If the questions are intended to result in an individual juror agreeing to not want to sit as a juror, the questions should be leading and suggestive of the answer. An example is:

— Mr. Morrow, you said your daughter is a doctor. You understand that this case involves medical malpractice by a doctor? Do you agree that the parties in this case may wonder to what degree you may be affected by your relationship with your daughter? Do you agree that you would be more comfortable sitting in another case that did not involve issues that relate so closely to your family interests?

Since the questioning process serves many purposes, the type and form of questions will be mixed and vary depending upon the case plan and the particular goals of the examiner.

The jurors will also need to know how they are expected to respond to questions. The attorney, especially in asking questions of the entire panel, should make clear whether the jurors should respond verbally or by raising their hand.

G. Conduct of Voir Dire. An attorney needs to consider many factors in determining how to conduct jury questioning. These factors include:

1. *First Impressions.* An attorney who makes a good impression during voir dire will benefit from the lasting effect of this impression with the jury.

2. *Sincere, Honest Advocate.* An attorney needs to be viewed by the jurors as a sincere and honest advocate. This attitude needs to be initially projected during voir dire. The attorney must be perceived as a lawyer with integrity. This perception will significantly bolster the credibility and persuasiveness of the attorney throughout the trial.

3. *Rapport.* The attorney should attempt to reduce any anxiety, fear, nervousness, or tension the jurors may feel and begin establishing rapport with them. A respectful attitude, a caring approach, eye contact, attentive listening, and a genuine interest will help establish the proper rapport. The more comfortable and at ease the jurors become with the attorney, the more attention and concentration they can devote to the case.

4. *Scope.* The scope of questioning will depend upon what questions the judge has asked the jurors and what information the attorney feels is necessary to make a decision about a juror. The attorney will need to inquire into those areas the judge did not cover. If an attorney wishes to ask some questions in legally sensitive areas (about insurance) or personal information (hardships), it may be advisable to request that the judge ask these questions.

5. *Planned Questions.* The attorney must appear to be well-prepared and professional. The use of planned questions will help create this appearance. Questions may be written out or the topic of inquiry can be listed on an outline. Unplanned, spontaneous questions may appear to be aimless, rambling, and poorly phrased. A well-structured, thoughtful line of questions will permit the attorney to watch, listen, and appropriately explore unexpected answers.

6. *Avoiding Argument.* A juror may cause problems during voir dire. The juror may disagree with the content or tone of a question or may misunderstand an inquiry. The attorney must remain calm and react in a controlled, professional way. It may be advisable for the attorney to accept the blame for asking an awkward or unclear question and rephrase it rather than imply that the juror is at fault. An admission by a lawyer that a question was inappropriate or that the lawyer was wrong may assist in establishing a sense of humility and rapport between that attorney and the jury.

H. Rehabilitation. After a lawyer completes questioning and has obtained some information that may support a motion to challenge a juror for cause, some judges permit the opposing attorney to ask questions to develop new information and rebut any facts or inferences supporting a challenge. The judge may intervene and ask some rehabilitative questions. This rehabilitation often concludes with a general question such as "You will be able to set aside your attitude and feelings about the matter and be a fair and impartial juror, won't you?" The purpose of rehabilitation is to prevent a challenge for cause and to force the opponent to use one of a limited number of peremptory challenges.

7.7 OBJECTING TO IMPROPER VOIR DIRE QUESTIONS

Attorneys sometimes attempt to use voir dire for purposes other than selection of an impartial jury. Some lawyers see it as a way to argue the case or to present prejudicial information to the jury which would not be admissible at trial; some see it as a way to foster sympathy with a party or to precondition a juror to a particular result. In most cases such tactics are not permissible and must be objected to. Like all objections, failure to make a timely objection to improper voir dire questioning constitutes a waiver of such an objection on appeal.

More importantly, such tactics may severely impair an attorney's ability to win the case, and may subject the offending attorney to mistrial or reversal on appeal.

A. Improper Voir Dire

1. *Presenting Inadmissible and Prejudicial Evidence.* Evid.C. § 352, Cal.Rules of Prof. Cond.Rule 5-200.

2. *Attempting to Predispose and Commit Juror to a Particular Verdict.* Cal.Rules of Court, Appendix Div. I Standards of Judicial Administration Sec. 8(f).

3. *Commenting on the Personal Lives and Families of the Parties or Their Attorneys.* Cal. Rules of Court, Appendix Div. I Standards of Judicial Administration Sec. 8(f).

4. *Questioning Jurors Concerning Pleadings, Applicable Law, or the Comfort of the Jurors.* Cal.Rules of Court Appendix Div. I Sec. 8(f).

5. *Misstatements of Applicable Law.* Cal.Rules of Prof.Cond. Rule 5-200.

6. *Questions or Tactics Designed to Foster Sympathy for One Party or Hostility for Another Party.* (People v. Williams, 29 Cal.3d 392, 408, 174 Cal.Rptr. 317, 325, 628 P.2d 869, 877 (1981)).

7. *Arguing the Case.* (People v. Williams, 29 Cal.3d 392, 408, 174 Cal.Rptr. 317, 325, 628 P.2d 869, 877 (1981)).

When such questions are asked, counsel should make the appropriate objection; request a curative instruction be given to the jury and, where intentional misconduct of counsel is apparent, request the judge to admonish the attorney. If the prejudice is severe, counsel may request a mistrial.

7.8 THE FINAL SELECTION PROCESS

A. Challenge for Cause C.C.P. § 225(a)

1. *Lack of General Qualifications.* C.C.P. § 203. These include: under 18, not a U.S. citizen, not domiciled in California, not a resident of the judicial district, not in possession of natural faculties, lacking in ordinary intelligence, insufficient knowledge of English, commission of a felony, currently serving as a grand juror, and subject of a conservatorship. C.C.P. § 225(a).

The general qualifications of jurors will usually be screened by the Jury Commissioner, and it will seldom be necessary to challenge for lack of general qualification.

2. *For Implied Bias.* C.C.P. § 229. A challenge for cause for implied bias is appropriate when facts indicate:

   a) familial relationship of witness or party;
   b) business or legal relationship to party, or witness;
   c) grand or trial juror in same or previous case with same parties;
   d) having an interest in the action;
   e) unqualified opinion or belief as to merits of case;
   f) state of mind showing enmity or bias. C.C.P. § 229.

3. *For Actual Bias.* The juror demonstrates the existence of a state of mind which will prevent him or her from acting with entire impartiality. C.C.P. § 225(c).

The most common grounds for challenge for cause usually are:

1. "Having an unqualified opinion or belief as to the merits of the action founded upon knowledge of its material facts or some of them." C.C.P. § 229(e).

2. "The existence of a state of mind in the juror evincing enmity against or bias to either party." C.C.P. § 229(f).

In order to prevail on a challenge for cause based on C.C.P. § 229(e) or (f) one must establish either: Admission of knowledge of facts upon which an unqualified opinion or belief regarding the merits of case law has been formed; or admission of bias, or formed opinion that affects his or her ability to be impartial.

Admissions of bias, or prejudice are hard to obtain. If the attorney suspects such bias or prejudice, it is much better to appeal to the juror's sense of fairness in a very nonconfrontational way and attempt to have the juror admit to the possibility of some bias that may lead to unfairness.

If this does not work one might attempt to have the juror admit he or she is reluctant to serve for hardship or inconvenience reasons. The juror may want to find a way out of jury duty in this case without admitting bias or prejudice. The attorney should try to supply a reason for the juror to request not to serve. Judges are more likely to grant such a request.

4. *Making Challenges for Cause.* There is no limit to the number of challenges for cause. C.C.P. § 230. A challenge for cause should be exercised before any peremptory challenges. Challenges for cause should be made soon after the responses to the questions which raise the grounds so that the basis for the objection will still be fresh in the judge's mind. Challenges for cause are taken first by the defendant. C.C.P. § 226(d). The challenge should be made as discretely as possible, preferably at side bar conference so as not to alienate the other jurors or the challenged juror if the challenge for cause is not granted.

In making the challenge, the attorney should state the statutory basis for the challenge, e.g., C.C.P. § 229(f). "The existence of a state of mind in the juror evincing enmity against or bias." This should be coupled with a summary of the evidence supporting the challenge.

Not unlike challenging a judge for cause, one runs the risk of alienating the juror by the challenge. If the challenge is not granted, the attorney may have to use a peremptory challenge to remove that juror.

As a general rule if an attorney does not have a clear-cut, uncontradicted admission by the juror of grounds for removal for cause, he or she should not challenge for cause unless a peremptory challenge is still available to remove that juror.

B. Peremptory Challenges

1. *When Made.* Peremptory challenges are not made until all the prospective jurors (usually 12) are placed in the jury box and voir dire of all 12 jurors by the judge and attorneys for all parties has been completed. C.C.P. § 231. (Note: In civil cases there may be less than 12 jurors if all parties so stipulate. C.C.P. § 220.)

2. *Number Allowed.* In a civil case if there are only two parties, each party shall be entitled to six peremptory challenges. "If there are more than two parties, the court shall . . . divide the parties into two or more sides according to their respective interests in the issues. Each side shall be entitled to eight peremptory challenges." C.C.P. § 231(c).

3. *In What Sequence are They Made?* The challenges are taken or passed consecutively beginning with the Plaintiff. When each side passes consecutively, the jury selection is complete and the jury is sworn. The passing of a peremptory challenge does not decrease the number of peremptory challenges a party has. C.C.P. § 231(c).

If an attorney makes a tactical decision to pass hoping that the other side uses one of its challenges on a juror with the hope of saving a challenge, and the other side passes, the opportunity to challenge further is gone.

4. *Use of Challenges.* Much planning and consideration must go into decisions regarding who to challenge and how. Challenges for cause are often denied and may cause hostility in the juror challenged. Unless the grounds for a challenge for cause are clear, it is best to use a peremptory challenge to remove a juror.

Some lawyers simply go on intuition or affective reactions. Some hire psychologists to prepare profiles of desirable jurors and undesirable jurors. Whatever method is used the attorney should have a good idea going into voir dire of what he wants in a juror and what he does not want.

In addition to a review of the information gained from the questions and an appraisal of the attorney's affective reaction to the particular juror the attorney may want to consult a local "Jury Book" where available. These books contain information about each juror including name, birthdate, marital status, education, occupation and a summary of each case on which that juror has sat and that juror's vote as well as the vote of the rest of the jury.

Using all of this information the attorney should make a peremptory challenge list. He should list jurors in order of least preference. See Form 7-4 Jury Challenge Worksheet.

Usually the attorney will seriously consider challenging the top 2 or 3. Some may be marginal, some will be preferred. Much depends on the makeup of the rest of the jury panel, and tactical considerations.

An attorney does not need to challenge any juror or use any peremptory challenges. There should be a reason for every challenge. The attorney should be mindful of the replacement jurors particularly when there are only one or two challenges left. The replacement juror may be worse than the excused juror.

If you have done your voir dire well and have made a list of the jurors you would remove in order of preference based on all available information, your decisions to remove jurors will be the best you can hope to make.

C. Use of Client. Some attorneys consider their client's feelings about a juror in making a decision about whom to strike from a panel. Other attorneys never consult with the client and prefer to use their own judgment. In deciding whether to use the client as a resource, an attorney should consider the relationship with the client, the attorney's independence in the case, the jurors' perceptions concerning the relationship, the ability of the client, and the attorney's preference.

D. Alternative Jurors. Most lengthy or complex trials have alternate jurors in addition to the regular jurors. An alternate juror will replace a regular juror if that regular juror becomes ill or unable to attend the trial. The selection process for alternates is identical to the procedure used for the other jurors. Typically, two or three alternate jurors will be selected for a 12 person jury.

E. Making the Challenge. Simply stand up and say as politely as possible, "Your honor, with your permission we would like to thank and excuse Mr./Mrs./Ms. _____."

F. Keeping Track of Challenges. Use Form 7-2, Jury Seating Chart to keep track of challenges. As challenges are made, list the name of the removed juror next to the party that made the challenge in the appropriate space on the bottom of Form. As jurors are removed mark off the name on the Seating Chart and put the name of the new juror in the seat vacated by the removed juror. When all challenges are used or passed, you will have your Final Seating Chart. You should update the jury selection chart so you will have accurate information about the jury as finally selected.

JURY SELECTION WORKSHEET

Case _____   File _____

What kind of person could probably best identify with me, my client, the case, or witnesses in the case?

_____
_____
_____
_____
_____
_____
_____

What kind of person would probably be least likely to identify with me, my client, the case, or witnesses in the case?

_____
_____
_____
_____
_____
_____
_____

Specific questions and outline for special points of inquiry to be asked of the prospective jurors (The jury selection chart which follows may be helpful to you for your consideration as to the kinds of specific questions you might want to ask.):

_____
_____
_____
_____
_____
_____
_____

Form 7-1

JURY SEATING CHART

Plaintiff _____ Atty. _____ vs. _____ Atty. _____

CASE NUMBER: _____ Atty. _____

| 1 | 2 | 3 | 4 | 5 | 6 | ALTERNATE #1 |
| 7 | 8 | 9 | 10 | 11 | 12 | ALTERNATE #2 |

CHALLENGES / PLAINTIFF /
1. _____   7. _____
2. _____   8. _____
3. _____   9. _____
4. _____   10. _____
5. _____   11. _____
6. _____   12. _____

CHALLENGES / DEFENDANT /
1. _____   7. _____
2. _____   8. _____
3. _____   9. _____
4. _____   10. _____
5. _____   11. _____
6. _____   12. _____

CHALLENGES BY COURT
1. _____   7. _____
2. _____   8. _____
3. _____   9. _____
4. _____   10. _____
5. _____   11. _____
6. _____   12. _____

Form 7–2

JURY SELECTION CHART

Case _____   File _____

Juror Background Front Row	Juror 1	Juror 2	Juror 3
Name			
Address			
Approximate age/ demeanor/dress			
Occupation/Employer			
Education			
Marital Status			
Spouse's occupation/ Employer			
Children			
Knowledge of case			
Knowledge of parties/ witnesses			
Past claims/lawsuits			
Similar case experience			
Past/present jury duty			
Opinions about issues			
Attitudes toward case			
Will juror identify with me, client, case, witnesses?			
Do I like juror?			
Overall rating 0–10			

Form 7-3

JURY SELECTION CHART

Case _____   File _____

Juror Background Front Row	Juror 4	Juror 5	Juror 6
Name			
Address			
Approximate age/ demeanor/dress			
Occupation/Employer			
Education			
Marital Status			
Spouse's occupation/ Employer			
Children			
Knowledge of case			
Knowledge of parties/ witnesses			
Past claims/lawsuits			
Similar case experience			
Past/present jury duty			
Opinions about issues			
Attitudes toward case			
Will juror identify with me, client, case, witnesses?			
Do I like juror?			
Overall rating 0–10			

Form 7–3 (continued)

JURY SELECTION CHART

Case _____   File _____

Juror Background Back Row	Juror 7	Juror 8	Juror 9
Name			
Address			
Approximate age/demeanor/dress			
Occupation/Employer			
Education			
Marital Status			
Spouse's occupation/Employer			
Children			
Knowledge of case			
Knowledge of parties/witnesses			
Past claims/lawsuits			
Similar case experience			
Past/present jury duty			
Opinions about issues			
Attitudes toward case			
Will juror identify with me, client, case, witnesses?			
Do I like juror?			
Overall rating 0–10			

Form 7-3 (continued)

JURY SELECTION CHART

Case _____   File _____

Juror Background Back Row	Juror 10	Juror 11	Juror 12
Name			
Address			
Approximate age/ demeanor/dress			
Occupation/Employer			
Education			
Marital Status			
Spouse's occupation/ Employer			
Children			
Knowledge of case			
Knowledge of parties/ witnesses			
Past claims/lawsuits			
Similar case experience			
Past/present jury duty			
Opinions about issues			
Attitudes toward case			
Will juror identify with me, client, case, witnesses?			
Do I like juror?			
Overall rating 0–10			

Form 7–3 (continued)

JURY CHALLENGE WORKSHEET

A. *Challenges for Cause*

Juror Number _____

Name _____

Authority _____

Based on what information _____

_____

_____

Challenges for Cause

Juror Number _____

Name _____

Authority _____

Based on what information _____

_____

_____

B. *Peremptory challenges*

List of Jurors in order of least preference

1. Juror No. _____ Reason: _____

2. Juror No. _____ Reason: _____

3. Juror No. _____ Reason: _____

4. Juror No. _____ Reason: _____

5. Juror No. _____ Reason: _____

6. Juror No. _____ Reason: _____

7. Juror No. _____ Reason: _____

8. Juror No. _____ Reason: _____

   Alternate No. _____ Reason: _____

   Alternate No. _____ Reason: _____

Form 7–4

Chapter 8
OPENING STATEMENT

Table of Sections

Sec.
8.1 Purposes.
8.2 What Can Be Presented.
    A. Facts.
    B. Argument.
    C. Law.
    D. A Fact Test.
8.3 Preparation and Organization.
    A. Knowing the Case.
    B. Developing Issues and Themes.
    C. Opening Statement Based on Closing Argument.
    D. Anticipating Opposition's Positions.
    E. Pretrial Rulings.
    F. Selecting Visual Aids.
    G. Order of Presentation.
    H. When to Present or Reserve Opening Statement.
    I. Written Outline or Detailed Script.
    J. Practice.
    K. Local Requirements.
8.4 Structure of an Opening Statement.
    A. Introduction.
    B. Personalizing the Client.
    C. Preliminary Remarks.
    D. The Story.
    E. The Scene and the Characters.
    F. Conclusion.
    G. Length.
    H. An Opening Statement Test.
8.5 Content of Opening Statement.
    A. Detailed Information.
    B. The Use of Exhibits.
    C. References to the Law.
    D. Case Weaknesses.
    E. Qualifying Remarks.
    F. Request for Verdict.
    G. Understatement.
    H. Overstatement.
    I. Promises.
    J. Improper Comments.
8.6 Presentation and Delivery.
    A. Manner.
    B. Word Choice.
    C. Drama.

Sec.
8.6 Presentation and Delivery—Continued
    D. A Positive, Assertive Position.
    E. Developing Style.
    F. Observing the Jurors' Reaction.
8.7 Objections and Motions.
    A. Objections.
    B. Motions on the Opening Statement.
Forms
8-1 Opening Statement Worksheet.

8.1 PURPOSES

The opening statement is the first oral presentation by an attorney at trial directly addressing the facts and issues to be presented at trial. There are two main purposes of the opening statement:

1. To acquaint the jury with the case and the party's positions. This should include a description of the parties, the scene, and the events.

2. To persuade the jury of the merits of the case. The value of a first impression is immeasurable. You will appear more credible throughout the trial if the opening statement is effective.

The opening statement may also be used to achieve several other objectives. It is an opportunity to make effective use of the principle of "primacy". That is, that the jury remembers best that which they hear, see, or experience first. It is an opportunity to introduce and emphasize your theory of the case, humanize your client, and attempt to make the jury want to decide the case in your favor. It is also an opportunity to build on the rapport you have established with the jury during voir dire and to demonstrate your sincere belief in your case.

8.2 WHAT CAN BE PRESENTED

A. Facts. Facts, even those in dispute, may be described and explained, so long as they can be proved during trial. The attorney might even discuss important facts which will be developed by opposing counsel. The facts to be presented should, at a minimum, include the major facts of the case. The term "facts" includes all facts and any lay or expert opinions admissible in a case.

B. Argument. An attorney is not permitted to present arguments, draw inferences, propose conclusions, or otherwise comment on the evidence. LaFrenz v. Stoddard, 50 Cal.App.2d 1 (1942). Closing argument provides the opportunity to present arguments and conclusions. However, an attorney may be able to present the issues or theories of a case by simply stating the evidence that he knows will be admitted in such a way that the members of the jury can begin to make their own inferences.

C. Law. The judge explains the law to the jury. Generally, the opening statement is not for purposes of discussing law. Williams v. Goodman, 214 Cal.App.2d 856, 29 Cal.Rptr. 877 (1963). There are situations in which an attorney may make short, accurate references to the law during opening to help the jury understand the case. It may be necessary for the attorney to describe the legal elements of the case and the burden of proof and show how the facts will prove the elements and meet the burden of proof. Always get approval of the judge before presenting law to the jury.

D. A Fact Test. One method to determine whether a statement may be included during opening is to determine whether a witness, a document, or some other form of evidence will provide the information. If the answer is yes, the statement may be referred to during opening; if no, it is inappropriate and objectionable. Some judges and opposing lawyers will allow more latitude in an opening statement.

Opening Statement 8-3

8.3 PREPARATION AND ORGANIZATION

A. Knowing the Case. Become familiar with every fact, inference, and aspect of the case. This knowledge will be necessary to analyze and select the theories of the case, establish the overall themes, plan the trial presentation, and determine which facts need to be proved in the case and presented in the opening statement.

B. Developing Issues and Themes. The issues and central theme of a case should be chosen, thought out, and organized before the trial begins.

1. *The Issues.* The issues are the key or pivotal questions of fact raised by the contentions of the parties. After deciding what issues exist, the attorney should select the issues to be stressed to the jury. The early presentation of these issues may provide a framework for the trial, focus attention on these issues, and minimize the opponent's case.

2. *The Theme and Theories of the Case.* The theme of the case is the central unifying concept. It is used to put the whole case together so that it is understandable, believable, and appeals to the sense of justice of the jurors. Some refer to it as "the hook". The ultimate goal is to lure and "hook" the jurors with your opening statement. The theories of a case are both legal and factual. See Sections 1.7 and 1.8. The opening statement is the time to present the factual theme and theories in a comprehensive way. The jury may have some idea about the case based upon the judge's preliminary instructions, statements, and questions during jury selection. In opening statement, the attorney explains how the various parts of the trial will fit together.

Select words that reflect and reinforce the theme of the case. These theme words should be used during the opening statement as the attorney describes the story. Theme words should be used throughout the trial to reinforce the theories and issues of the case.

C. Opening Statement Based on Closing Argument. The opening statement should be based on what will be said in closing argument. The closing argument is the part of the trial towards which everything else must point. If a fact, issue, or position is not a part of the closing argument, it should not be a part of the opening statement. The opening statement must be consistent with the theme of the case, the factual and legal theories, the evidence, and the positions to be presented in the closing argument.

D. Anticipating Opposition's Positions. Review the case from the opposition's perspective and take this into account when preparing an opening statement. Anticipate the other side's position in an attempt to negate the position. The more you anticipate the opponent's theories, arguments, and positions, the more complete and effective the opening statement will be.

E. Pretrial Rulings. When selecting the facts that will be presented during opening statement, ascertain whether an in limine ruling regarding certain categories of evidence is necessary. The opening statement may not refer to evidence that will not be admissible during trial. Evidence of questionable admissibility may create a problem. The attorney may not want to refer to this evidence and risk an objection. Pretrial evidentiary rulings permit the attorney to plan the opening statement knowing exactly what information will be available during trial.

F. Selecting Visual Aids. Consider whether to use visual aids or trial exhibits during the opening statement. Consideration should be given to the impact a visual aid may have on the jury and whether the attorney is capable of comfortably and effectively using it. Visual aids may consist of a prepared outline of the opening statement on foam core board, poster board, or overhead transparency, a chart, or diagram, or the use of a blackboard. Trial exhibits, which include real and demonstrative evidence, may sometimes be used during the opening statement. If visual aids or exhibits will be used during the opening statement, inform the court and opposing counsel prior to trial in order to obtain permission for their use and resolve any objections.

G. Order of Presentation. Unless the court finds "special reasons" to change the sequence, the plaintiff is to make the first opening statement. C.C.P. § 6070(1) The most significant "special reason" that justifies a change in the sequence is usually the determination by the judge of which party has the burden of proof.

In cases where the plaintiff's allegations in the complaint are admitted or a summary judgment has been entered in favor of the plaintiff's allegations and where the only remaining factual issues are affirmative defenses raised by the defendant, it would be proper to change the order since the defendant clearly has the burden of proof.

H. When to Present or Reserve Opening Statement. Except in the simplest of bench trials or extreme cases, both plaintiff and defendant should present an opening statement. A defendant may choose to make an opening statement immediately after the plaintiff's opening statement "or wait until after plaintiff has produced his evidence", C.C.P. § 607(2).

The preferred practice is for the defense to present opening statement immediately after the plaintiff presents opening statement. Some attorneys argue the theory of a "primacy" compels it, except in the most extreme cases.

The theory of "primacy" is simply that jurors remember and form firm opinions from that which they hear or see first. Many attorneys feel that it can be almost fatal to allow the plaintiff to capitalize on "primacy" and the defendant must make an opening statement immediately after the plaintiff to negate the plaintiff's first impression on the jury, and to make a good first impression for the defendant.

Examples of extreme caes which justify not making an opening statement are:

1. Where the plaintiff has not engaged in discovery and the defendant may want to keep the plaintiff in the dark regarding theories, defenses, or witnesses.

2. When the defendant expects a protracted trial, the defense may rely on the theory of "finality". That is, in a very long trial, the jury may better remember and be impressed by that which is presented last. This is a judgment call.

Generally speaking, it is better for the defense to present opening statement at the outset of the trial. It is not necessary to present all of the defendant's yet undiscovered theories or defenses. It is very important to cast doubt on the plaintiff's case and make it clear that the defense will be presenting a case and that the jurors should keep an open mind and should await all of the evidence before forming any firm opinions or conclusions.

I. Written Outline or Detailed Script. Organize the opening statement into an outline format. The outline will include the introduction, the body, and the conclusion. Using an outline helps organize the facts and theme of the case into an easily usable and readily accessible format.

Some attorneys find it advantageous to write or dictate a complete opening statement. This draft may then be reviewed and improved. With this format, the attorney knows what the final script of the opening statement contains. The drawback of using a script during an opening statement is the temptation to read the opening statement. Reading a script will appear dry and impersonal to the jury. A better approach for the attorney who wishes to use a script is to prepare a key word outline of the script. After becoming completely familiar with the script, the attorney should be able to present the opening statement using only the key word outline. When notes or outlines are used, they should be used in a candid, forthright fashion.

J. Practice. Practice and rehearsal are necessary to adequately prepare for the presentation. Practicing the opening statement several times prior to trial will be time well spent. The attorney may want to think through the opening statement silently and then practice verbally, concentrating on its content. As the content of the opening statement is mastered, work on stylistic improvements. Practicing and rehearsing the opening statement to an audience of colleagues or others, in front of a mirror, or on videotape for later review and critique is helpful.

K. Local Requirements. Determine before trial whether the trial judge has any special requirements or limitations regarding the opening statement. This will avoid having the opening statement interrupted by the trial judge and reduce the chances of opposing counsel making objections. Local practice and procedures may restrict how an opening statement can be presented.

8.4 STRUCTURE OF AN OPENING STATEMENT

Any reasonable structure is appropriate as long as it is simple and understandable. Most opening statements may be effectively presented as a story in chronological order. Other structures will be appropriate depending upon the circumstances. For example, present the facts in the order in which the witnesses will testify; employ a flashback technique by first explaining the end of the story and then flashing back to earlier events (this approach permits an attorney to first describe the damages in a civil case, and then the events surrounding liability); or present the facts in a topical sequence.

A. Introduction. Begin with an introduction that draws the jurors and their attention to the presentation of the case. The jury's attention level is usually high at the beginning of the opening statement, and full advantage should be taken of this opportunity. Begin in an interesting and dramatic way to pique the jury's interest. The beginning of an opening will depend in part upon what has occurred during the jury selection process and what introductory remarks and instructions the judge may have given.

B. Personalizing the Client. The opening statement should be used to personalize the client. Tell the jury about the person in a way that leads the jury to identify or empathize with your client. This could include talking about family, military service, occupation, or something special about the client. Try to get the jury to like your client. An attorney who wishes to begin an opening statement in a certain way may request that the judge make certain preliminary remarks concerning the identity of the client, attorneys, or the purpose of an opening statement.

C. Preliminary Remarks. Many attorneys begin an opening with an explanation of who they are, who they represent, and the purposes of an opening statement.

The advantage of preliminary remarks is that the jurors may better understand the purpose of the opening statement. The disadvantage of these remarks is that they may not be the most effective way to begin the presentation of the story to the jury. An audience generally remembers best what it hears first and last. The attorney should consider what the jury must remember. Since this preliminary introductory information is most likely not a part of the theme or theory of the case, it may be better placed in the body of the presentation or left out entirely.

D. The Story. The attorney should assume that the fact finder knows nothing about the case. The presentation should explain each fact and element of the case in understandable terms. The lawyer's knowledge of the case will be extensive and may cause obvious facts to be overlooked or avoided. The attorney must keep in mind that the fact finder will be hearing the full case for the first time.

A factual story will constitute much of the content of the opening statement. It should parallel the substance of the trial evidence and the description that will be given in the closing argument. The opening statement may include a description of what did not happen, as well as what did happen. It may be necessary for an attorney, particularly a defense counsel, to explain to the jury what the evidence will not show, as well as what the evidence will show.

The story should be told in simple language, in as dramatic a fashion as appropriate, and with a persuasive style. The things that make a story interesting and believable in great works of literature, art, and theater are the same things that often make an opening statement effective.

E. The Scene and the Characters. The opening statement must include a description of the scene of the event and the persons who will testify as witnesses in the case. Some attorneys attempt to personalize their witnesses and depersonalize the opposing party's witnesses. Depersonalization may be achieved by impersonal references made about those characters, including identification by their last name, as the plaintiff, or as the defendant.

F. Conclusion. Conclude with a strong ending. This effect may be achieved with a concise summary of the vital facts, a compelling statement justifying a verdict, or a dramatic summary of the major theme of the case. The jurors are more likely to remember what is said at the end of the opening statement than what is said in the middle. Take advantage of this during concluding remarks. The style and delivery should be consistent with the entire presentation. A strong presentation can be ruined by an apologetic or weak conclusion.

G. Length. The opening statement should be long enough to cover the essential aspects of the case, yet short enough to maintain the jurors' attention. The optimum length of an opening statement depends upon the circumstances and complexity of the case and the speaking pace and ability of the attorney. Some opening statements may last five minutes; others will extend for more than an hour. Many opening statements last between 10 and 30 minutes. The longer an opening statement is, the more the attorney must be concerned with maintaining the jurors' interest. One should always use visual aids with a long opening statement.

H. An Opening Statement Test. Questions that may assist in determining whether an opening statement has been properly constructed include:

1. Does the opening statement tell the jury what happened?
2. Does the opening statement tell the jury why to find for the client?
3. Does the opening statement make the jury want to find for the client?
4. Does the opening statement tell the jury how to find for the client?
5. Does the opening statement have a structure that is clear and simple?
6. Is the opening statement consistent with what will be proved and with what will be argued in final argument?

8.5 CONTENT OF OPENING STATEMENT

The content of an opening depends upon the facts and circumstances of each case.

A. Detailed Information. The facts presented during an opening statement should be as detailed as necessary. A detailed story is usually perceived as more credible and persuasive. However, presenting detailed specific facts increases the risk that evidence will not be presented with the specificity suggested in the opening statement. Detail that provides necessary information for a full understanding or that explains sources of corroboration or credibility will usually bolster the essential aspects of the case.

B. The Use of Exhibits. Make every effort to make effective use of exhibits, demonstrative evidence and visual aids in the opening statement. Most people better understand and retain information transmitted visually rather than orally. The judge has discretion to allow the use of such visual aids to assist counsel in presenting the opening statement.

Obtain stipulations from opposing counsel regarding the use of such exhibits and visual aids. If stipulations cannot be obtained, ask the judge during the pre-trial conference to allow such use. Be prepared to show that such evidence meets all standards of admissibility, and be prepared to counter arguments that the evidence is unduly prejudicial. Local rules should be consulted for the policy regarding use of exhibits.

The design, placement, and use in the presentation are as important as the exhibits themselves. The impact of words and colors on a visual aid, the importance of an exhibit in the trial, the location in the room for clear viewing and easy access, the placement in the order of the presentation, and the style of the lawyer in the use of and reference to an exhibit are important considerations in determining whether an exhibit will aid in or interfere with the opening statement presentation.

C. References to the Law. Opening statement is not the place for frequent or substantial references to the law. Lengthy explanations of the law are reserved to the judge and to the attorney during closing argument. Some reference to the law may be appropriate. Know the local rule regarding how much law can be discussed in the opening statement. The jury needs a framework relating the facts to the elements and burden of proof. While the attorney may briefly tell the jury what the appropriate law is for the case, the jurors may have already been informed of this by the judge during voir dire. Any reference to the law in opening statement should be approved in advance by the judge.

D. Case Weaknesses. Consider whether to describe weaknesses in a case. The better practice is to present those weaknesses in a candid and forthright manner. The weak points of the case may have been mentioned during voir dire and may require less attention in the opening statement. Weaknesses in a case which have not been explained to the jurors and which will be brought out by the opposition should be addressed during opening statement. An open and candid disclosure of this information increases the credibility of the attorney and often reduces the impact of the opposition's tactics.

E. Qualifying Remarks. During opening statement an attorney may use as a preface the phrase: "The evidence will show." Some judges may require an attorney to employ this or a similar phrase periodically during an opening to prevent the presentation from sounding like argument. Many attorneys prefer not to use this phrase because they believe it reduces the impact of the story. Some attorneys prefer not to remind the audience that what is being said has yet to be proved.

A qualifying introduction such as "the evidence will show" used as a preface to the presentation of a theme or argument may be an effective tactic for preventing an objection. If this tactic is overused and it becomes apparent that it is being used to argue or introduce otherwise inappropriate information into the opening statement, objections will be sustained and the attorney will lose credibility. The better tactic is to simply state a summary of the evidence that will be presented and admitted. If put together properly, the jury will begin to draw their own conclusions. Simply state the evidence as fact without diluting its impact.

Some attorneys advise the jurors that what an attorney says during opening does not constitute evidence and that the jurors must determine the facts only after hearing the evidence. Comments like this may reduce the intended impact of the opening statement. Defense counsel may use this type of comment to reduce the effectiveness of the plaintiff's opening statement and remind the jurors that they must weigh the evidence as it is introduced during trial. Comments such as this should be avoided unless the opposing side has made an extremely persuasive opening statement.

F. Request for Verdict. An opening statement should contain an explanation of the verdict. This explanation should be clear and distinct so the jury understands what it is that they are being asked to do. Some attorneys will say that "the client is entitled to" or "has a right" to such a verdict. Better practice is to explain that the jurors have an opportunity, and even a duty, to return a verdict based upon the facts of the case.

An attorney for a plaintiff seeking damages may or may not want to request a specific amount of damages. This tactical judgment should be based on a consideration of whether it is better for the jury to first hear specific amounts of damages during the trial or to suggest an amount of damages in opening statement to predispose the jury towards that amount during trial. When plaintiff is seeking punitive damages, defense counsel should prevent plaintiff from mentioning a punitive damages amount until plaintiff has produced evidence of liability for punitive damage under C.C.P. § 3294. This can be done through a motion in limine.

G. Understatement. Understatement can be a useful credibility-building device for an opening statement. The presentation of the evidence at the trial will surpass the jurors' expectations, enhancing the credibility of the case and the attorney. However, the use of understatement may reduce the attorney's ability to explain the facts in a persuasive way. Jurors may perceive an understated case to be weaker than the attorney intended.

H. Overstatement. Avoid overstatement during opening statement. The jury may be initially impressed, but this impression will not last once the jury realizes the evidence presented during trial did not match the attorney's opening statement. Opposing counsel may comment during closing argument about the absence of the exaggerated evidence.

I. Promises. An opening can be presented effectively if an attorney "promises" the jury that certain evidence will prove a certain fact and can fulfill that promise. Often a promise cannot be kept, causing the jury to disbelieve the facts of the case as well. A promise is a tactical approach that must be employed carefully. If a lawyer makes promises or otherwise asserts that certain evidence will be forthcoming, the opposing lawyer should record all these statements and mention all unkept promises during closing argument.

J. Improper Comments. An attorney may not comment about the quality of evidence, the credibility of the witnesses, or assert personal opinions. Nor may an attorney denounce or attack the opposing party or attorney.

8.6 PRESENTATION AND DELIVERY

A. Manner. The manner in which the attorney delivers the opening statement will affect the jurors' understanding of the facts of the case, significantly influence their initial impression of the attorney and the strengths and weaknesses of the case, and shape their perspective of the entire trial. The more effective and persuasive the attorney can be in presenting an opening statement, the greater the chance of a favorable verdict. The following factors affect the quality of the opening presentation and parallel most of the considerations discussed in Section 10.4 regarding final argument.

1. *Confidence.* Be confident, in control, and have a command of the case. Be forceful yet tactful, candid yet not confessional, and positive yet realistic.

2. *Sincerity.* A sincere belief in the merits of your client's cause will impress the jury.

3. *Integrity.* Be fair in the eyes of the jury. A jury will not trust an attorney who appears sneaky or underhanded or who overstates the case.

4. *Attitude.* Approach and treat the jurors with respect at all times.

5. *Positioning.* It will usually be more effective for an attorney to stand in front of the jury box and not behind a lectern or table. This stance will usually hold the juror's attention more than if the attorney hides behind a lectern. Move about the courtroom to use exhibits and visual aids and to make the presentation more interesting. (Check local rules and the judge's preference.)

6. *Proper Distance.* The attorney must maintain an appropriate distance from the jurors. This distance should neither be too far away so that personal contact is lost, nor too close so that the jurors feel uncomfortable. The exact distance will depend upon the number of jurors, the size, energy, and presence of the attorney, the size, shape, and acoustics of the courtroom, and the content of the statement being made. A distance of between eight and twelve feet can be used as an appropriate guide, but the distance should be flexible and vary in different circumstances. An attorney can approach closer or stand further away to make a point more effectively.

7. *Posture.* Body language must match what is being said. Good posture is essential for an advocate. Good posture does not require that the attorney stand stock still and straight as a rod during opening. A comfortable non-slouching posture should be appropriate.

Some movement and gestures are useful, particularly if the opening is long. Movement, stance, pacing, and timing should be orchestrated so as not to be distracting. An attorney may use movement as a transition or to make a point more effectively and should avoid movement that appears purposeless.

8. *Dress.* An attorney who is tastefully dressed and well groomed will appear more professional and credible to the jury.

9. *Gestures.* Establish eye contact with jurors to help create a sincere and courteous relationship with the jury. Looking jurors in the eye while talking will substantially increase the impact of what is being said. However, staring at a juror will undoubtedly make the juror uncomfortable and adversely affect the attorney's rapport with that juror. It is vital for the attorney to periodically make eye contact with each individual juror.

10. *Voice Control and Pace.* Use varied tone, volume, modulation, and pace in delivery. A dull, monotone presentation is as ineffective as ranting and raving. A balanced and well-modulated approach will usually be most effective.

B. Word Choice

1. *Simple Language.* Clarity of expression is important. Simple and clear language is preferable to complex legalese. Large words used just to show off vocabulary skills are not effective. Overly simplistic words may give the jury the impression of being talked down to. Balance the need for simple language against the danger of appearing condescending.

2. *Factual Words.* Use factual, rather than conclusory words. These words will more accurately reflect the content of the evidence and reduce the opportunity for opposing counsel to object.

3. *Impact Phrases.* Descriptive words will be useful in emphasizing the important facts of the case, will create a more vivid image of the events for the jury, and will be remembered by the jurors. Impact language includes those words that more graphically describe a situation. ("Smashed" instead of "hit," "huge" instead of "large," and "shrieked" instead of "yelled".) These words may be used as long as they accurately reflect what happened. Impact words may be obtained from a thesaurus, a dictionary and from works of literature and drama.

4. *Silence.* Sometimes the best thing an attorney can say is nothing. Silence can be an effective way to highlight a point, gain attention, or make a transition. An attorney must be aware of the power of silence and use it constructively.

5. *Transitions.* Employ transitions in the presentation. Prefatory remarks, silence, a louder voice, a softer voice, movement, and gestures can signal a transition.

C. Drama.
Present the opening in a serious, dramatic manner. Take full advantage of the theatre of the courtroom.

Some cases permit an attorney to create suspense as well. If the attorney understates some facts, the natural curiosity of the jury may cause them to pay close attention when the complete facts are introduced at trial. For example, during opening, the attorney can tell the jury about the substance of a conversation, but leave the exact words for the witness.

D. A Positive, Assertive Position.
Assert positive positions. Avoid an opening statement that merely responds to or anticipates an opponent's facts and theories. Counter punching has its place in boxing, but in opening statement the object is to take control of the collective minds and emotions of the jury.

E. Developing Style.
Deliver the opening in a style that reflects that attorney's abilities. Avoid copying and mimicking another lawyer's style. However, be open to adapting and reworking what someone else has done if it appears effective.

F. Observing the Jurors' Reaction.
Observe the jurors' reactions during the opening statement and adjust the presentation accordingly. The reactions displayed by a jury may also be useful in determining how the evidence is later presented and what might be an approach to an effective closing argument. Some jurors may express a reaction during the opening statement and may not display reactions as the trial progresses.

Determining what a person is thinking just by watching them is difficult. Care must be taken not to overreact, or to completely change an approach because of a perceived reaction. Avoid focusing on one or two jurors because they seem to be responding positively.

Revise a presentation depending upon the location of the trial and the types of individual jurors. An aggressive, hard driving style may be effective in urban areas, but may be inappropriate in a rural area.

8.7 OBJECTIONS AND MOTIONS

A. Objections.
Grounds for objection to opening statement include the following:

1. *Arguing the Case.* The attorney should limit the opening statement to a preview of what will be presented. Making arguments regarding the inferences, deductions and conclusions which should be drawn from the evidence are objectionable and should be avoided. LaFrenz v. Stoddard, 50 Cal.App.2d 1 (1942).

2. *Referring to Irrelevant Material.* Evid.C. § 350. Facts which may be true but are logically or legally irrelevant should not be brought up. They may be successfully objected to which will disrupt the opening statement and make the attorney look bad in the eyes of the jury at the very time the attorney must form a good impression.

3. *Referring to Inadmissible Evidence.* Evid.C. § 352. Referring to inadmissible evidence is subject to objection and causes problems when the evidence alluded to is not admitted. See Section 6–8C for further objections on opening.

Tactically, an attorney may not want to object, but rather write down what was said and use it in closing argument. Most attorneys will not object during opening statement unless the opponent is saying or doing something that is clearly improper. In these situations, an objection and request for a curative instruction may be necessary to preserve the issue for appeal. Many attorneys extend a courtesy to each other so that opening statements are uninterrupted and zealous.

B. Motions on the Opening Statement. At the completion of the plaintiff's opening statement, the defendant may move for a Judgment of Nonsuit, if it clearly appears that the evidence to be presented is not sufficient to entitle the plaintiff to relief under any applicable theory. C.C.P. § 581c.

A judgment of nonsuit may be granted only when it clearly appears from all the facts and all inferences that can be drawn from the fact stated in the opening statement that no cause of action exists. It is equivalent to a demurrer to the evidence. Darr v. Lone Star Industries, Inc., 94 Cal.App.3d 895, 157 Cal.Rptr. 90 (1979). See sec. 4.8.

It is critical for an attorney, in preparing the opening statement, to assure that the opening statement refers to evidence which will be presented to support each contested element of each cause of action. The attorney should prepare a checklist of each contested element of each cause of action and note the evidence to be presented to prove up each contested element of the causes of action. See form 8–1 Opening Statement Worksheet.

A judgment of nonsuit operates as an adjudication upon the merits. In order for a nonsuit to be granted, it must be apparent that the plaintiff does not have any case.

OPENING STATEMENT WORKSHEET

Case _____   File _____

1. Introduction of attorney and establishing rapport with jury.

   _____
   _____
   _____
   _____
   _____

2. Introduction and personalization of client.

   _____
   _____
   _____
   _____
   _____

3. Factual contentions at issue in the case.

   _____
   _____
   _____
   _____
   _____

4. Theme and theories of the case and theme phrases.

   _____
   _____
   _____
   _____
   _____

Form 8–1

5. Summary of facts in chronological order including ultimate facts which will be proven for each contested element of each cause of action.

1st cause of action: _____
_____
_____

2nd cause of action: _____
_____
_____

3rd cause of action: _____
_____
_____

1st affirmative defense: _____
_____
_____

2nd affirmative defense: _____
_____
_____

6. Introduction of witnesses who will testify and what they will testify to.
_____
_____
_____
_____

7. Visual aids to be used for what purpose.
_____
_____
_____
_____

Form 8–1 (continued)

8. Discussion of case weaknesses.

_____
_____
_____
_____

9. Request for verdict/justification for damages claimed.

_____
_____
_____

10. Conclusion.

_____
_____
_____
_____

11. List promises made to jury during opening.

_____
_____
_____
_____

Form 8-1 (continued)

Chapter 9
DIRECT EXAMINATION

Table of Sections

Sec.
9.1 Purpose.
9.2 The Order of Direct Examination.
9.3 Preparation and Organization.
  A. Considerations in Preparation.
  B. Witness Selection and Preparation.
  C. Order of Questions.
  D. Exhibit Management.
9.4 Presentation and Delivery.
  A. Portraying a Story.
  B. Parts of Direct Examination.
  C. Conduct of the Attorney.
  D. Enhancing the Credibility of the Witness.
  E. The Questions.
  F. Questions to Avoid.
  G. Order of Witnesses.
9.5 Types of Direct Examination.
  A. Adverse Examinations and Hostile Witnesses.
  B. Deposition Transcripts or Videotaped Depositions.
9.6 Redirect Examination.
  A. Question Format.
  B. Limited Scope.
  C. Reserving the Introduction of Evidence.
  D. Refreshing the Witness' Recollection.
  E. Foregoing Redirect.
9.7 Avoiding Mistrials and Reversals.
  A. Never Facilitate the Presentation of Perjured Testimony.
  B. Do Not Willfully Conceal Evidence.
  C. Prepare the Witness.
  D. Instruct Witnesses to Avoid Contact With Jurors.
  E. Do Not Allow Any Witness Under Your Control to Knowingly Testify Falsely.
  F. Do Not Intentionally Mis-state or Cite the Law.
  G. Do Not Assert Personal Knowledge of the Facts at Issue Unless Called as Witness.

Forms
9–1 Witness List.
9–2 Direct Examination Outline.

9.1 PURPOSE

By asking questions on direct examination, the attorney attempts to communicate relevant information to the fact finder through a witness. By answering questions on direct examination, a witness attempts to describe or explain all or part of an incident in a persuasive, credible manner. Direct examination constitutes the most common device for presenting evidence.

The trial lawyer must recreate through the testimony of the witness an historical event in the courtroom. Generally, the focus of attention will be on the witness and not on the lawyer. The evidence should appear to come naturally, and almost spontaneously from the witness. It should not appear to come from the attorney. The most marvelously presented direct examination will seldom be credited to the attorney but rather to the witness. The attorney's job on direct examination is to make the witness look good.

Direct examination should:

1. Present evidence that is legally sufficient to support a prima facie case that will overcome a motion for non-suit or a directed verdict.

2. Convince the fact finder of the integrity of the evidence and the credibility of the story.

3. Counter or contradict evidence submitted by the opposition.

4. Present the evidence in a clear and understandable manner.

9.2 THE ORDER OF DIRECT EXAMINATION

The court has the discretion to regulate the order of proof and presentation of witnesses.

The order of presentation of witnesses is based on which side has the burden of proof. C.C.P. § 607, Evid.C. § 320. The usual order of presentation of evidence is:

1. The plaintiff presents evidence.

2. The defendant presents evidence.

3. Plaintiff offers rebuttal evidence.

4. Defendant offers surrebuttal evidence. C.C.P. § 607.

9.3 PREPARATION AND ORGANIZATION

A. Considerations in Preparation

1. *Rules of Evidence.* The applicable provisions of the California Evidence Code must be reviewed to determine how to admit the evidence. Local or individual courts may relax or expand the rules of evidence to limit or broaden the presentation of evidence. Different opponents may have theories or tactics which increase or limit their objections. See Chapter 6.

2. *Professional Responsibility.* The California Rules of Professional Conduct § 5–200 and rules of decorum, along with local court rules and practices, have a profound effect on the way in which the witness testifies, the lawyer behaves, and the evidence is presented.

3. *Witness Ability.* Each witness will have different capabilities. Explore and evaluate the witness' strengths and weaknesses in order to make the witness as effective as possible.

4. *The Facts.* The facts in a case include the objective information as well as the emotions and feelings involved and will affect the extent and quality of the examination.

5. *The Law.* The burden of proof, the elements of the cause of action and the defenses will affect the amount of permissible testimony.

B. Witness Selection and Preparation

1. *Which Witnesses to Call.* Decide which facts are necessary to support the case and which witnesses are most capable of presenting those facts. Consider which witnesses can make the most effective presentation; which witnesses will be persuasive; which will be the most cooperative; who are less inconvenienced; and who need not testify. Consider which

witnesses can corroborate information. Remember that too much corroboration may be boring and confusing.

  2. *Special Needs of Witnesses.* A witness may have special value to the case or need particular attention due to physical or mental problems, difficulty in communication, nervousness, stubbornness, hostility, anger or indifference.

  3. *Sequence of Witnesses.* Decide whether a witness should be called at the beginning, middle, or end of the case, and when during the day a witness should testify. The primacy/recency effect suggests that a strong witness is the most effective when called first or last. Often a strong witness will be called immediately before a recess. However, consider whether the recess is for minutes, the evening, or for the weekend. Witnesses will often be called in an order that supports a chronological presentation of the case. Another order may be used, however, depending on the circumstances of the trial. Sometimes, the order of witnesses can be arranged so that a strong witness will follow a weak witness to bolster the testimony of the weak witness.

C. Order of Questions. The order of questions and the techniques used should help the witness communicate effectively. The lawyer should consider which kind of questions are best suited to each witness—narrative, specific, or a combination of each. Some questions should be avoided with some witnesses. See Form 9-1 Witness List.

D. Exhibit Management. After deciding which exhibits are necessary, including real and demonstrative evidence, determine how the exhibit is to be prepared and presented and which witness will be used to present it. All the witnesses should understand the exhibit and the foundation necessary for its admission. If any witness does not agree with its accuracy, resolve the inconsistencies. See Form 9-2 Direct Examination Outline.

9.4 PRESENTATION AND DELIVERY

See Form 9-2 Direct Examination Outline.

A. Portraying a Story. Generally, assume that the judge and jury know nothing about the case. The direct examination should start at the beginning and tell everything. The courtroom is a theater and the story is more than a still picture. It includes the sounds, smells, touches, and emotions of the case. The trial is like a play—the lawyer is the director and the witnesses are the characters. The lines must be persuasive, interesting, compelling, and clear. The script and action must be prepared before "going on."

  1. *A Simple Play.* The story should be told simply. People have only a limited ability to absorb and retain oral information. Because most of what is learned comes through senses other than hearing, the words should be chosen carefully. People do not understand "lawyer talk," jargon, technical descriptions, or expert terms.

  2. *The Audience.* Pay careful attention to the audience in order to present the case effectively. Watch the jurors and make sure that they can see and hear what is going on. Stand where the jury can observe the questioning. The audience must be able to hear. Both the attorney and witness must project their voices, but neither should need to yell to be heard.

  3. *The Scene, Then the Events.* Describing the parties and the scene before describing the action may be the most appropriate direct examination sequence. Action testimony is generally most effective and dramatic when presented in an uninterrupted manner. Flowing descriptions allow the jury to visualize the action.

  4. *Chronological Presentation.* Chronological presentation is generally the easiest to present and understand. However, any logical order of presentation may be appropriate. In some cases, for example, the witness might give the most dramatic or important testimony early when the jury is most alert. Sometimes, too, a witness is not available or an expert must be worked in around the expert's schedule.

  5. *Detail and Repetition.* A witness who describes an event in vivid detail will be more persuasive and credible than a witness who testifies using general descriptions. Too much

detail, however, particularly concerning minor events, may confuse the fact finder. Excessive repetition may also become boring.

B. Parts of Direct Examination

1. *The Question.* Questions govern the structure of the direct examination. The attorney needs to consider how a question is asked—its wording, tone, and pacing. The attorney should also consider when the question will be asked and the likely response.

2. *The Answer.* The witness' answer should be honest, concise, accurate, complete, and responsive. The answer should not be evasive, speculative, argumentative, or vague. An answer should not express an opinion unless the witness is an expert or the question involves an area in which a nonexpert can give an opinion.

C. Conduct of the Attorney

1. *Appear Interested.* If the attorney does not appear to be interested in what is going on, the judge and jury probably will not be interested either. Look at the witness during the examination. The attorney's posture will indicate how important the witness or testimony is.

2. *Tempo, Rhythm, Pacing, Timing, and Modulation.* Like music, a feeling can be developed through rhythm, tempo, and modulation, short or long questions, fast or slow questions, pauses between questions, or raised or lowered voices. The speed or words may also indicate intensity. Generally, effective direct examinations move quickly through general information and more slowly through the specifics of critical action.

3. *Listen.* Listen to the witness' answers and react as if they were being heard for the first time. Be aware of the jury's and judge's responses to the witness' answers. Follow-up questions may be tailored to the witness' answers to create smooth flowing testimony.

4. *Relationship to the Witness.* Do not appear too "chummy" with any of the witnesses. The attorney's credibility is enhanced by maintaining an interested and concerned, yet professional, profile during direct examination.

D. Enhancing the Credibility of the Witness

1. *Humanize the Witness.* The jury is more likely to believe the witness if they view the witness as a likeable, nice person. How does the witness fit into the community? What is the witness' background? Does the witness have a family?

A witness may also be humanized by using the witness' first name if permitted by local rule or by the judge. (Ask permission first.) A progression of names from formal to personal may be used by referring to a witness first by full name, then by surname, and then by first name. This progressive familiarity may help the fact finder gradually become more comfortable with the witness.

2. *Background Information.* Initial questioning typically includes background questions to personalize the witness. Background information should be selected which may serve other purposes including:

   a) Allowing the witness to answer simple questions to relieve some of the initial anxiety.

   b) Identifying similarities the witness may have with the background of the jurors.

   c) Displaying the sincerity of a witness.

   d) Offering background traits or job experience which buttress the inferences of a case and the credibility of the witness.

3. *Demonstrate the Credibility of the Witness.* The credibility of the witness may be enhanced by eliciting certain details that corroborate the testimony, that the witness had a good opportunity to observe the incident, that the witness reported the incident and that the witness is a careful, caring person.

The witness' credibility is also enhanced by letting the witness tell the story in a way that appears natural. Do not interrupt unless necessary; i.e., when the witness is off track, rambling, or acting improperly. If inconsistencies arise, they should be explained.

E. The Questions. Questions should be prepared in advance in outlines or notes. Prepared questions should not be read unless they are technical and must be exact.

1. *Language.* Simple and brief language using everyday conversational words is generally the most effective, unless it is snobbish, technical, or vulgar. "After" should be used instead of "subsequent"; "how far" instead of "would you indicate the distance"; "did you" instead of "did you have occasion to"; "on April 1st" instead of "calling your attention to the date of April 1"; "car" instead of "motor vehicle." The lawyer should also avoid talking down to the jury or using double negatives. Matters that do not make sense should be clarified and technical or unclear terms defined.

Statutory language may be used in order to fulfill the exact requirements of the burden of proof. Otherwise, legalese is to be avoided.

2. *Impact Words.* The use of impact words such as "blown apart" rather than "fell apart" or "shot in the back" rather than "wounded" may be effective. The use of words that may influence the answer such as "how fast" rather than "how slow" may favorably affect the judge or jury.

3. *Respect the Jury.* The witness should explain to "us" and avoid talking down to the jury. The jurors should not be embarrassed or demeaned. Avoid any "tricks." The attorney is most persuasive when polite and courteous.

4. *Use Chronological Order.* Design the direct examination to allow the witness to tell his or her version of the facts in chronological order. It is natural for a witness to tell a story in chronological order and the jurors are used to hearing stories told in chronological order. This also makes it easy for the examiner to control the questioning by directing the witness to a certain time and place, and interrupting where appropriate with a simple "and what happened next".

Make sure that all cause and effect questions are resolved by asking direct questions designed to elicit specific information. Make extensive use of why and how questions on direct to elicit cause and effect answers.

5. *Be Concise.* Specific, short questions make it easier for the lawyer to control the flow of evidence and result in more precise information. These questions do, however, tend to minimize the witness' role and may break the rhythm or prevent a good witness from testifying well.

6. *Double Direct.* An attorney will be able to emphasize testimony by repeating key words of a previous response in a preface to a follow-up question.

7. *Refreshing Recollection.* A witness who exhibits a memory lapse on the stand may be refreshed by providing the witness with a previous statement or any other thing that assists the witness to recall the answer.

How to refresh recollection:

a) Establish that witness has no present recollection to testify as to a matter.

b) Ask whether something would help the person remember (e.g., "Would looking at a copy of your deposition help you to remember?")

c) Identify and mark the object.

d) Authenticate the object (e.g., "Do you remember having your deposition taken on _____?" "Was your memory regarding the matter fresh at the time of the deposition?" "Is this a copy of your deposition?" "Is this your signature on the deposition?"

e) Ask the witness to examine the object or read the deposition (e.g., "I direct your attention to page ___ line ___; would you read that portion to yourself.")

6. Establish that the witness' recollection has been refreshed (e.g., "Is your recollection refreshed as to _____?")

7. Take the object back and have the witness testify. Counsel on Direct, may ask leading questions to lay the foundation. Evid.C. § 767. The cross-examiner will have access to the statement or thing used to refresh recollection. Evid.C. § 771.

8. *Handling Weaknesses.* Weaknesses in the witness' testimony may need to be presented during the direct examination to minimize the impact of the weakness and enhance the credibility of the witness and the attorney. Weaknesses that are exposed later during cross-examination by opposing counsel can be very damaging. The decision to admit weaknesses in the case is a major strategic decision. If a flaw or weakness cannot be protected by the rules of evidence or procedure and the cross-examiner will bring out the weakness or flaw, it should be exposed on direct examination. Weaknesses may be left for re-direct if the witness has an effective response for cross-examination inquiries.

F. Questions to Avoid

1. *Leading Questions.*

a. What is a leading question?

A leading question is a question that suggests to the witness the answer that the examining party desires. Evid.C. § 764. Evid.C. § 767(1), specifically prohibits a leading question of a witness on direct or redirect information.

Generally, but not always, questions that can be answered with a simple yes or no are leading questions. But a question can be leading if it calls for more than a yes or no answer. If the answer to the question is fully contained in the question itself, it is usually a leading question. e.g., Tell the jury how defendant's car did not have its turn signal on when it made the left hand turn. (Note: this statement may also assume facts not in evidence.)

b. Why avoid leading questions?

Besides being specifically prohibited, leading questions will often be objected to and the objection may be sustained by the judge. This interrupts the flow of the testimony and tends to diminish its impact. It also tends to make the attorney look less than competent in the eyes of the jury and the judge. Leading questions also diminish the impact of the witness' testimony because the evidence appears to be presented by the attorney, not the witness. Important testimony should come directly from a witness, not the attorney.

c. When are leading questions allowed?

The judge has discretion to allow leading questions on direct examination "under special circumstances." C.C.P. § 767. These include:

i. In preliminary matters which do not bear directly on the material issues in the case. Evid.C. § 767, Comm. Comments.

ii. To examine some expert witnesses. People v. Campbell, 233 Cal.App.2d 38, 43 Cal.Rptr. 237 (1965).

iii. In examining children and handicapped witnesses. Evid.C. § 767b and Law Revision Commission Comments.

iv. To examine a hostile witness or a witness predisposed to the case. Evid.C. § 767a.

v. To refresh recollection. People v. Jones, 221 Cal.App.2d 619, 34 Cal.Rptr. 618 (1963).

vi. To lay foundation where the use of leading questions is necessary to establish the preliminary facts for admission of relevant evidence. Evid.C. § 767 (Commission Comments).

2. *Narrative Questions.*—Evid.C. § 765. A narrative question is an open-ended question which asks the witness to relate a series of events in an unstructured, uninterrupted way, and which has the propensity to result in a lengthy, rambling response which may contain irrelevant and inadmissible matters.

The court has discretion to either exclude or allow questions calling for narrative answers. Evid.C. § 765(a).

Open-ended narrative questions can be used effectively to allow the witness to tell his story and establish rapport with the jury. Use of such questions should be rehearsed with the witness to avoid improper, irrelevant, or rambling and boring responses.

In general, unstructured, unrehearsed narrative questions should be avoided, but planned and well prepared narrative questions can be most helpful.

3. *Vague, Ambiguous, or Unintelligible Questions.*—Evid.C. § 765. Besides being subject to objections, avoid such questions because they usually result in vague, ambiguous, and unintelligible answers, and because they may confuse the witness, the judge, and the jury. The major problem is that they add nothing to the case that can be used later on final argument or appeal.

4. *Compound Questions.*—Evid.C. § 765. A compound question is one which combines two or more distinct questions into one question. Such questions make it difficult for a juror to determine which question is being answered. It may also compound a proper question with an improper question, and make it difficult for the witness to respond because the answer may not be consistent.

Such questions are subject to objection and should be avoided.

5. *Argumentive or Harassing Questions.*—Evid.C. § 765. Questions which are not designed to elicit information, but rather to argue with, harass, or embarrass a witness are improper, objectionable, and should be avoided. e.g., How can you say such a thing? These questions make the attorney who asks this kind of question to his own witness look bad in the eyes of the jury. It makes the case look worse.

6. *Assuming Facts Not in Evidence.*—Evid.C. § 765. A question that assumes facts not in evidence is one that contains in the question itself a statement of fact or an implication of a fact that has not yet been admitted into evidence, or assumes, as proven, an issue in dispute that is still subject to dispute.

Both of these are illustrated by the following question which is asked of a percipient witness when first questioned about an accident at an intersection, "When the defendant negligently went through the traffic light at a high rate of speed, what did you see?"

Besides being leading, this question assumes facts not in evidence and states as true the ultimate issue to be decided. Such a question is improper because it presents to the jury facts or propositions which have not been and may not be proven by admissible evidence.

G. Order of Witnesses. When a witness testifies will generally be determined by where that witness' testimony fits into the presentation of the case. See Form 9–1 Witness List.

1. *First and Last Witnesses.* The first and last witnesses and those with the strongest personality characteristics should be scheduled to have greatest impact. The jury is more likely to remember what is heard first and last. Effective use of first and last witnesses requires daily preparation, review, and flexibility by the lawyer. The lawyer must try to anticipate recesses and adjournments and end on a high point.

2. *Differing Testimony.* Every witness is an individual whose perceptions will not be identical to those of other witnesses. Sometimes the differences in witnesses' testimony are great enough to require explanation. The attorney must decide whether to call the witness at all, whether to elicit testimony concerning those differences, and anticipate how opposing counsel will use the differing testimony.

3. *Weak or Boring Witnesses.* Weak or boring witnesses can damage the case because they cause the jury to disbelieve their testimony by their demeanor, or they simply put the jury to sleep. The order of witnesses should be adjusted so that weak or boring witnesses are not presented consecutively.

4. *Rebuttal Witnesses.* Although the last witness is the most likely to be remembered, it is generally not a good idea to save a witness for rebuttal. The attorney may not get the opportunity to call the witness. Moreover, jurors may view "sandbagging" as unfair or "sly."

5. *Strong Finish.* The final witness should be a strong witness. The witness should present important aspects of the case, have good style, and be able to withstand cross-examination.

9.5 TYPES OF DIRECT EXAMINATION

A. Adverse Examinations and Hostile Witnesses. A case may require that a witness who has an interest adverse or hostile to the attorney's client be called during the case in chief. Direct examination of this type of witness may be conducted by using leading questions as if the examination were a cross-examination. See Evid.C. § 767a and Law Rev.Comm.Comm.

B. Deposition Transcripts or Videotaped Depositions. A deposition transcript may be used as direct testimony at trial "so far as admissable under the rules of evidence." C.C.P. § 2016(d). The deposition of a party may be used against a party who had notice or was present or represented at it for any purpose. The deposition of a non-party witness may be used if (1) the witness is unavailable as defined by Evid.C. § 240, or (2) exceptional circumstances exist to make it desirable to introduce the deposition as direct testimony. C.C.P. § 2016(d).

The deposition may be read to the jury but cannot be taken into the jury room. C.C.P. § 612. If deposition testimony is to be read it must be offered and received into evidence. Before being offered into evidence it should be edited to remove objectionable material and to determine the most compelling and interesting testimony. The portions to be read should be given to opposing attorney and to the judge for the purpose of raising objections to its content.

When reading the transcript it is best to have a person play the part of the witness so that the questions and answers are more interesting to the jury. A videotaped deposition may also be used to present the testimony of the witness providing proper notice is given under C.C.P. § 2019(c).

9.6 REDIRECT EXAMINATION

Redirect examination is the examination of a witness after the opposing attorney has finished cross-examining the witness. The purpose of redirect examination is to clarify any issues raised during the cross-examination. This includes clarifying and explaining contradictions, dismissing fallacies, and correcting any other problems created by the cross-examination.

A. Question Format. The rules of evidence applicable to direct examinations apply to redirect examination. Leading questions are not allowed on redirect examination, however many judges will allow a greater use within the scope of the redirect examination. Because the witness has testified on direct and cross, an attorney may legitimately refer to previous answers by the witnesses.

B. Limited Scope. The scope of the redirect examination is limited to new matters covered during the cross-examination. Redirect examination may not be used to repeat matters covered on direct examination. Evid.C. § 774.

C. Reserving the Introduction of Evidence. The entire case should be presented during the direct examination and not saved for redirect examination. An attorney who preserves some evidence runs the risk of not being able to present an important or essential element of the case because the opposing attorney may not cover that area during the cross-examination. A strict judge could prevent that area from being covered during redirect examination. The same could be true if the opposing attorney decides not to conduct a cross-examination. Individual judges may be more or less willing to allow the attorney to cover new areas during the redirect examination. Some judges may allow the attorney to reopen the direct examination or allow the witness to be called again.

There may be an occasion when delaying the introduction of evidence for redirect is worth the risk. If the information to be "sandbagged" will have a significant impact on redirect, and the attorney knows or structures the case so that the opposing attorney *must* delve into that area during the cross-examination, "sandbagging" may be appropriate.

D. Refreshing the Witness' Recollection. Redirect examination may be used to refresh the witness' recollection if the witness has misstated or forgotten information during the cross-examination. See Evid.C. § 771.

E. Foregoing Redirect. A well-prepared case and a good direct examination will often make redirect examination unnecessary. In making the decision whether to conduct a redirect examination, consider:

1. Having the last word is not necessarily that important.

2. Continuing with redirect examination may bore the jury, bother the court, or accomplish very little.

3. Closing argument may be a better time to repeat the best parts of the case.

4. Cases can be lost be asking too many questions.

9.7 AVOIDING MISTRIALS AND REVERSALS

A. Never Facilitate the Presentation of Perjured Testimony. The California Rules of Professional Conduct prohibits the knowing use of fraudulent, false, or perjured testimony. An attorney has a duty to prevent the mispresentation of testimony. Business and Professions Code Section 6068; Cal.Rules of Professional Conduct (1988) § 5–200(A)B.

If an attorney knows that a client or a witness is going to testify falsely, he cannot call that witness to knowingly testify falsely. The California Rules of Professional Conduct provides that an attorney "shall not seek to mislead the judge, judicial officer or jury by an artifice or false statement of fact or law." § 5–200(B).

If an attorney knows that a client or witness has testified falsely. The attorney must try to convince the witness (in private) to retract the testimony. If the witness is the client and the client refuses to retract the testimony, the attorney may have to withdraw from the case. See California Rules of Professional Conduct § 3–700B.2.

B. Do Not Willfully Conceal Evidence. It is misconduct and reversible error to conceal relevant evidence from the court or jury. California Rules of Professional Conduct § 5–220. Los Angeles v. Decker, 18 Cal.3d 860, 135 Cal.Rptr. 647, 558 P.2d 545 (1977).

C. Prepare the Witness. The inadvertent blurting out of inadmissible evidence by a witness can result in a mistrial or reversal. Control a witness through preparation prior to trial. Inadmissible evidence may be sometimes "cured" by an admonition from the presiding judge to the jury to disregard any improper statements or to forget what they heard. The adequacy of the curative admonition may become a question on appeal. However, a ruling upon an objection will seldom be disturbed, unless a clear abuse of judicial discretion occurs.

D. Instruct Witnesses to Avoid Contact With Jurors. Any unauthorized communication with a juror, whether intentional or inadvertent, may give rise to a mistrial. C.C.P. §§ 611, 613.

E. Do Not Allow Any Witness Under Your Control to Knowingly Testify Falsely. If an attorney knows that a client or a witness is going to KNOWINGLY testify falsely, he cannot call that witness to testify. Under Bus. & Prof.C. § 6068(d) an attorney has an obligation to "never . . . seek to mislead the judge . . . by an artiface or false statement of fact or law." The ABA Code of Professional Responsibility provides that an attorney is subject to discipline if the attorney "knowingly participates in the introduction of "fraudulent, false or perjured testimony."

If an attorney knows that a client or witness has testified falsely, the attorney must try to convince the witness (in private) to retract the testimony. If the witness is the client and the client refused to retract the testimony, the attorney may have to withdraw from the case. See Cal.Rules of Prof.Cond. 2–111 B2. See California Civil Procedure Before Trial Vol. 1 § 9.58 CAL CEB 1982.

F. Do Not Intentionally Mis-state or Cite the Law. Cal.Rules of Prof.Cond. Rule § 5–200(c)C.

G. Do Not Assert Personal Knowledge of the Facts at Issue Unless Called as Witness. Cal.Rules of Prof.Cond. Rule § 5–200(E).

WITNESS LIST

Case _____   File _____

In Order of Presentation:
Name   Address/Phone

1. _____

   _____

Purpose: _____

_____

_____

_____

_____

Name   Address/Phone

2. _____

   _____

Purpose: _____

_____

_____

_____

_____

Name   Address/Phone

3. _____

   _____

Purpose: _____

_____

_____

_____

_____

Form 9–1

Name   Address/Phone

4. _____

   _____

Purpose: _____

_____

_____

_____

_____

Name   Address/Phone

5. _____

   _____

Purpose: _____

_____

_____

_____

_____

Name   Address/Phone

6. _____

   _____

Purpose: _____

_____

_____

_____

_____

Form 9–1 (continued)

DIRECT EXAMINATION OUTLINE

Case _____   File _____

Name of Witness: _____ (See Form ___ for background information)

A. Key facts to be proved by witness: _____
_____
_____
_____
_____
_____

B. Trigger words to give to elicit testimony:

FACT 1: _____
_____
_____
_____

FACT 2: _____
_____
_____
_____

FACT 3: _____
_____
_____
_____

C. Key words of witness factual theme testimony: _____
_____
_____
_____
_____

D. Exhibits to Be Introduced by Witness   E. Foundation Needed

1. _____   _____
2. _____   _____
3. _____   _____

Form 9-2

Chapter 10
CROSS-EXAMINATION

Table of Sections

Sec.
10.1 Purposes.
10.2 Preparation and Organization.
    A. Background.
    B. Anticipation.
    C. Scope of Cross-Examination.
    D. Credibility.
    E. Should There Be a Cross-Examination?
    F. Prepare Written Questions in Advance.
    G. Structure.
    H. Attention.
10.3 Presentation and Delivery.
    A. Be Confident.
    B. Do Not Repeat Direct Examination.
    C. Lead the Witness.
    D. Ask Simple, Short Questions.
    E. Ask Factual Questions.
    F. Control the Witness.
    G. Maintain Composure.
    H. Adopt an Appropriate Approach.
    I. Stop When Finished.
10.4 Expert Witnesses.
10.5 Impeachment.
    A. Sources of Impeachment.
    B. Extrinsic Evidence of Prior Inconsistent Statement.
    C. Cross-Examination of Character Witness.
10.6 The Ten Commandments.
10.7 Avoiding Mistrials and Reversals.
    A. Do Not Ask Insinuating Questions or Use Innuendo.
    B. Do Not Make Derogatory Remarks to the Witness.

Forms
10-1 Cross-Examination Outline.
10-2 Cross-Examination Planning Worksheet.
10-3 Impeachment by Prior Inconsistent Statement Worksheet.

10.1 PURPOSES

Cross-examination is the process of questioning an adverse party or witness. Cross-examination questions should be limited to those which reveal information necessary to support statements made in the closing argument. Cross-examination usually consists of narrow, leading questions calling for "yes or no" or specific answers. There are exceptions to this generalization which are most likely to occur during supportive cross-examination. Careful consideration must be given, however, before open-ended questions are asked on cross-examination.

Cross-examination serves two primary purposes:

Destructive Cross. Cross-examination is used to discredit the testifying witness or another witness. This may be accomplished in several ways including attacking the credibility of the witness or testimony. Most of the questions asked on cross-examination will be designed to reduce the credibility or persuasive value of the opposition's evidence.

Supportive Cross. Cross-examination can be used to bolster evidence that supports the cross-examiner's theory of the case. Cross-examination may be used to independently develop favorable aspects of the case not developed on direct examination.

10.2 PREPARATION AND ORGANIZATION

A. Background. Full preparation, including knowledge of the facts, evidence, law, opponent, and witness will facilitate cross-examination. All available discovery and investigation techniques should be used to learn everything about the case.

B. Anticipation. Anticipate the opponent's side of the case. Consider what all the witnesses will testify to, how the other side will try the case, how both sides of the case can be attacked, and what evidence can be kept out under the rules. Determine key areas of cross-examination and sources of cross exam. See cross-examination outline Form 10–1.

C. Scope of Cross–Examination. The scope of cross-examination is limited to questions involving the subject matter of the direct examination or the credibility of a witness. Most judges provide the cross-examiner reasonable latitude to explore relevant areas affecting the case or the credibility of a witness. The outside limits of cross-examination fall within the discretion of the trial judge.

If an area of inquiry extends beyond the scope of direct and does not involve credibility, the cross-examiner can request the judge to permit a broader inquiry, or can call the witness to testify as an adverse or hostile witness during the presentation of the case in chief or during rebuttal.

An attorney cannot ask a question on cross unless the attorney has proof of the underlying facts. An attorney cannot fabricate innuendos or inferences on cross-examination. The attorney must have a good faith basis which includes some proof of such facts.

D. Credibility. Factors involved in evaluating and attacking the credibility of a witness include bias, interest, association with the other side, motive, experience, accuracy, memory, demeanor, candor, style, manner of speaking, background, and intelligence.

When weighing the credibility of the testimony consider:

1. Is the testimony consistent with common sense?
2. Is the testimony consistent within itself?
3. Is the testimony consistent with other testimony?
4. Is the testimony consistent with prior statements made by this witness?
5. Is the testimony consistent with the established facts?

E. Should There Be a Cross–Examination? Consider:

1. Has the witness hurt the case?
2. Is the witness important to the other side?
3. Will the jury expect cross-examination? Will it affect the case if there is no cross-examination?
4. Was the witness credible?
5. Did the witness leave something out on direct examination that might get in if there is a cross-examination? Was the omission intentionally set up as a trap for the inexperienced cross-examiner?

6. Will cross-examination unavoidably bring out information that is harmful to the case?

7. Are cross-examination questions being asked only for the sake of asking questions?

8. Does the witness know more than the attorney about the case or the subject matter of the cross-examination?

9. Will the witness be difficult to control?

10. Has the witness been deposed or given statements?

11. Is there a reasonable likelihood of impeaching the witness?

F. Prepare Written Questions in Advance. Cross-examination is most effective when questions are prepared in advance. Most prepared questions will not be significantly altered during the trial, but an attorney must retain flexibility to adapt to new material or inconsistencies as they arise.

G. Structure. Structure the areas selected for cross in a way that clearly shows their purpose and helps the fact finder remember that point. Begin and end the cross with strong points.

H. Attention. Close attention to the witnesses on direct examination may reveal signs of deception, lack of assurance, or bluffing that can be explored on cross-examination. The attention shown by the jury or judge may also be a clue.

10.3 PRESENTATION AND DELIVERY

A. Be Confident. A confident attitude will assist in making the cross-examination effective and persuasive.

B. Do Not Repeat Direct Examination. Generally, repetition of the direct examination only emphasizes the opponent's case. Repetition of any part of the direct that is supportive of the cross-examiner's case, however, may be effective and justify the use of an open-ended question.

C. Lead the Witness. Questions that suggest or contain the answer should be asked on cross. Questions that require "yes," "no," or short, anticipated answers help control the witness so the testimony develops as anticipated. The question "why" and questions requiring explanations should be avoided because they call for uncontrolled open-ended answers.

D. Ask Simple, Short Questions. Short, straightforward questions in simple, understandable language are most effective. Broad or confused questions create problems of understanding for witnesses, attorneys, the jury, and the judge. They also lead to confusing answers or answers with explanations.

E. Ask Factual Questions. Questions that seek an opinion or conclusory response may allow the witness to balk or explain an answer. Questions which include fact words and accurate information force the witness to admit the accuracy of the question.

F. Control the Witness. The most effective way to control a witness is to ask short factual questions. Some witnesses must be politely directed to respond; some witnesses may require the intervention and control of the judge.

G. Maintain Composure. An attorney who displays a temper or argues with a witness may irritate the court and the jury, causing them to side with the witness or the opponent and may draw objections.

H. Adopt an Appropriate Approach. Some witnesses may require righteous indignation, others may be attacked, but most need to be carefully and courteously led. A cross-examiner can be very effective by being politely assertive and persistent without having to attack a witness.

Certain witnesses require special consideration in both the formulation and delivery of questions. These witnesses include children, relatives, spouses, experienced witnesses, investigators, experts, the aged, the handicapped, and those with communication problems. Outside resources may be used to assist in developing tactics to deal with special witnesses.

I. Stop When Finished. When the planned questions are asked and the desired information is obtained, the attorney should stop. The case may be harmed more by asking too many questions than by not asking enough.

10.4 EXPERT WITNESSES

Areas for cross-examination of experts parallel areas for lay witnesses and permit additional areas of inquiry regarding:

1. Their fees.
2. Whether they routinely testify for the plaintiff or defendant.
3. The number of times they have testified before.
4. Their failure to conduct all possible tests.
5. The biased source of their information.
6. Their lack of information.
7. The existence of other possible causes or opinions.
8. The use of a treatise to impeach.

Develop a command of the expert's field before examining the expert in a specific area. A well constructed concise hypothetical question may be effective if it elicits an opinion contrary to the testimony on direct examination. This requires intense study and analysis.

10.5 IMPEACHMENT

Impeachment discredits the witness or the testimony. To evaluate whether impeachment is appropriate, the following should be considered:

1. How unfavorable is the testimony and how much did it hurt the case?
2. Will impeachment be successful?
3. Is there a sound basis for impeachment and can it be accomplished?
4. Is the impeachment material relevant to the facts or the credibility of the witness?
5. Is the impeachment material within the court's discretion and not too remote or collateral?

See Form 10-2 Cross-Examination Planning Worksheet.

A. Sources of Impeachment. The credibility of a witness may be attacked in any number of ways. Many witnesses, however, will not have obvious or apparent weaknesses in their testimony. The following factors represent the more common and frequent matters employed to reduce the credibility of a witness.

1. *Misunderstanding of Oath.* The witness may not understand the oath or know the difference between telling the truth and telling a lie. This situation rarely arises.

2. *Lack of Personal Knowledge or Perception.* The witness may not have actually observed the event, or the witness may have perceived something through the senses (sight, taste, hearing, smell, or touch) and it can be shown that conditions were not favorable to that perception. Evid.C. § 780(c), (d).

3. *Lack of Memory.* The witness may not have a sound, independent memory of what was observed. Evid.C. § 780(c).

4. *Lack of Communication.* The witness may be unable to adequately communicate what was perceived. Evid.C. § 780(d).

5. *Bias, Prejudice, or Interest.* The witness may have a personal, financial, philosophical, or emotional stake in the trial. Evid.C. § 780(f).

6. *Prior Criminal Record.* The witness may have a prior felony conviction which may be admissible. Evid.C. § 788. Evid.C. § 352 requires weighing the probative value of the felony conviction.

7. *Character Evidence.* A witness may be impeached by a character witness who is familiar with the reputation of the witness for truth and veracity or who has an opinion regarding the truthfulness of the witness. Evid.C. §§ 780(e), 1324. (Caveat: This may also open the door to testimony regarding good reputation.)

8. *Prior Inconsistent Statements or Omissions.* The witness may have made former contradictory or inconsistent oral statements or may have omitted some facts during previous testimony or in a prior statement. If the witness denies these prior statements a copy of the statement or another witness may be needed to prove them. Evid.C. § 780(g) and § 1202. See Impeachment by Prior Inconsistent Statement Worksheet Form 10–3.

B. Extrinsic Evidence of Prior Inconsistent Statement. An attorney may be able to introduce extrinsic evidence of a prior inconsistent statement if a witness denies a cross-examination impeachment question. However, a prior inconsistent statement cannot be used without either confronting the witness with the statement, or providing the witness with an opportunity to explain it. Evid.C. § 770. The extrinsic evidence of a prior inconsistent statement may be admitted if the witness has not been excused from giving further testimony in the action and is subject to recall. Evid.C. § 770(b).

To introduce prior inconsistent statement or omissions lay the following foundation.

1. Commit the witness to, or have the witness repeat the direct examination testimony;

2. Lead the witness through a series of questions describing the circumstances and the setting of the prior inconsistent statement. For example, if the prior inconsistent statement was made in the course of a deposition, the attorney may refer to that deposition and ask questions regarding the taking of the depositions; and

3. Once the cross-examiner has established a foundation for the introduction of the prior inconsistent statement (such as the witness signed the deposition under penalty of perjury while the facts of the matter were fresh in her mind), the prior inconsistent statement may be used to impeach the witness. This may be done in several ways. The attorney may read from the prior statement or have the witness read it. If the witness admits the prior inconsistent statement, the impeachment process is complete. If the witness denies the prior statement, the exhibit should be marked, identified and offered into evidence. Proper foundation must be laid for its admission.

Opposing counsel has the right to read to the jury other deposition testimony which will correct any misimpression or provide proper context. Evid.C. § 356. This can be done immediately after the impeachment, or opposing counsel may wait to explain or clarify any discrepancy or rehabilitate the witness with the prior inconsistent statement if available.

C. Cross–Examination of Character Witness. Character witnesses may be impeached like any other witness. They may also be cross-examined regarding their knowledge of specific instances of bad conduct by the person whose character they praised. See Evid.C. § 1324.

10.6 THE TEN COMMANDMENTS

Irving Younger's Ten Commandments for cross-examination are worth remembering:

1. Be brief.

2. Ask short questions and use plain words.

3. Never ask anything but a leading question.

4. Ask only questions to which you already know the answers.

5. Listen to the answer.

6. Do not quarrel with the witness.

7. Do not permit a witness on cross-examination to simply repeat what the witness said on direct examination.

8. Never permit the witness to explain anything.

9. Avoid one question too many.
10. Save it for summation.

10.7 AVOIDING MISTRIALS AND REVERSALS

A. Do Not Ask Insinuating Questions or Use Innuendo. Avoid asking questions using words such as "Isn't it true that. . . ." for the purpose of presenting prejudicial matters not in evidence. Such tactics have been held to be misconduct and grounds for a new trial. Love v. Wolf, 226 Cal.App.2d 378, 38 Cal.Rptr. 183 (1964).

B. Do Not Make Derogatory Remarks to the Witness. It is misconduct for counsel to personally attack the character or motives of witnesses on cross-examination. Such conduct as name-calling or asking accusatory questions without clear relevance to the case can cause a mistrial. Garden Grove School Dist. v. Hendler, 63 Cal.2d 141, 45 Cal.Rptr. 313, 403 P.2d 721 (1965), Simmons v. Southern Pac. Transp. Co., 63 Cal.App.3d 341, 351, 133 Cal.Rptr. 42, 47 (1976).

CROSS–EXAMINATION OUTLINE

Case _____ Witness _____ File _____

Key Facts of Anticipated Direct Examination	Key Areas for Cross-Examination	Source of Information

Form 10–1

CROSS–EXAMINATION PLANNING WORKSHEET

Case _____ Witness _____ File _____

A. Destructive Cross: Sources of Impeachment

   1. Poor Perception _____
_____

     Basis _____
_____

   2. Poor Memory _____
_____

     Basis _____
_____

   3. Poor Communication _____
_____

     Basis _____
_____

   4. Testimony inconsistent with common sense _____
_____

     Basis _____
_____

   5. Testimony inconsistent with other facts _____
_____

     Basis _____
_____

   6. Bias/Prejudice/Interest _____
_____

Form 10–2

Basis _____

_____

7. Prior Criminal Record _____

_____

Basis _____

_____

8. Bad Reputation/Bad Acts _____

_____

Basis _____

_____

9. Character Evidence _____

_____

Basis _____

_____

10. Prior Inconsistent Statements (See Form 10–3)

B. Supportive Cross Exam: Supportive Fact to Elicit on Cross

1. _____

_____

    a. Prior statement relied upon _____

_____

    b. Location _____

_____

2. _____

_____

    a. Prior statement relied upon _____

_____

Form 10–2 (continued)

b. Location _____

_____

3. _____

_____

    a. Prior statement relied upon _____

_____

    b. Location _____

_____

C. Other Areas for Cross: _____

_____

_____

_____

_____

_____

Form 10–2 (continued)

IMPEACHMENT BY PRIOR INCONSISTENT STATEMENT WORKSHEET

Case _____   Witness _____   File _____

Previous Statements Made:

A. *Deposition* (Significant prior statements)

   Date of Deposition _____

   Date of Signing _____

   1. Summary of Statement _____
   _____
   _____
   _____

Page ___   Line # ___

   2. Summary of Statement _____
   _____
   _____
   _____

Page ___   Line # ___

   3. Summary of Statement _____
   _____
   _____
   _____

Page ___   Line # ___

   4. Summary of Statement _____
   _____
   _____
   _____

Page ___   Line # ___

Form 10–3

B. *Interrogatories*

    1. Summary of Answer _____
_____
_____
_____

Question # ____

    2. Summary of Answer _____
_____
_____
_____

Question # ____

    3. Summary of Answer _____
_____
_____
_____

Question # ____

    4. Summary of Answer _____
_____
_____
_____

Question # ____

C. *Request for Admissions*

    Date of Response or Default:

    Admission # ____   _____

    Admission # ____   _____

    Admission # ____   _____

Form 10–3 (continued)

D. *Statements to Law Enforcement Officers:*

_____
_____
_____
_____
_____

E. *Other Sworn Statements*

_____
_____
_____
_____
_____

Form 10–3 (continued)

Chapter 11

JURY INSTRUCTION AND CLOSING ARGUMENT

Table of Sections

Sec.
11.1 Jury Instructions.
  A. Understandable Jury Instructions.
  B. Party's Right to Instructions.
  C. Necessity to Submit Instructions.
  D. Time for Submission.
  E. Formal Requirements.
  F. How to Prepare and Submit Jury Instructions.
  G. Selection of Jury Instructions.
11.2 Closing Argument.
  A. Purposes.
  B. Right to Closing Argument and Order of Argument.
  C. What Can Be Argued.
11.3 Preparation and Organization of Closing Argument.
  A. Early Preparation.
  B. Refining the Issues and Theme for the Case.
  C. Jury Instructions.
  D. Anticipate the Opponent's Position.
  E. Select Visual Aids and Exhibits.
  F. Written Outline or Detailed Script.
  G. Practice.
  H. Local Requirements.
11.4 Structure of a Closing Argument.
  A. Introduction.
  B. Explanation of Purpose.
  C. Argument.
  D. Explanation of the Evidence.
  E. Explanation of Law.
  F. Conclusion.
  G. Jury Participation.
  H. Length.
  I. A Final Argument Test.
11.5 Content of Closing Argument.
  A. Analogies/Anecdotes.
  B. Credibility of Witnesses.
  C. Contradictions.
  D. The Use of Exhibits and Visual Aids.
  E. Burden of Proof.
  F. Liability and Damages—Which to Argue First.
  G. Case Weaknesses.

Sec.
11.5 Content of Closing Argument—Continued
　　H.　Attacking Opposition's Positions.
　　I.　Broken Promises.
　　J.　Non-facts.
　　K.　Lie v. Mistake.
　　L.　Rhetorical Questions.
　　M.　Emotion v. Logic.
　　N.　Avoiding Improper Comments.
　　O.　Rebuttal.
　　P.　Request for Verdict and Damages.
11.6 Presentation and Delivery.
11.7 Objections.
Forms
11-1 Request for Jury Instructions.
11-2 Jury Instruction Worksheet.
11-3 Closing Argument Worksheet.

11.1 JURY INSTRUCTIONS

The jury instructions explain the law to the jury and provide the elements of law that need to be proved. Serious trial preparation should begin with the preparation of jury instructions, and they must be used in the preparation of the closing argument.

A. Understandable Jury Instructions. Jury instructions should be clear, understandable, and legally correct. All terms of art, and words and phrases that have a specific legal meaning must be defined in plain English. The jury must be able to understand the instructions. This is as important as ensuring that the instructions reflect the proper law.

B. Party's Right to Instructions. The judge has a duty to instruct or charge the jury, and each party has a right to have the jury instructed on all theories of the party's case, provided they are supported in the pleadings and the evidence. If there is any substantial evidence on an issue and a party has submitted appropriate proposed jury instructions regarding that issue, it is error for the court to refuse to instruct on it. Phillips v. G.L. Truman Excavation Company, 55 Cal.2d 801, 806, 13 Cal.Rptr. 401, 403, 362 P.2d 33, 35 (1961).

C. Necessity to Submit Instructions. A party cannot claim error on appeal of a judge's failure to give an instruction regarding a issue if the party has not submitted an instruction regarding that particular issue. Each party has the responsibility to compose complete and comprehensive instructions consistent with that party's theory of the case. Carbaugh v. White Bus Line, 51 Cal.App. 1, 195 P. 1066 (1921).

D. Time for Submission. Before the first witness is sworn, counsel must deliver to the trial judge and serve on opposing counsel, "all proposed instructions to the jury covering the law as disclosed by the pleadings." C.C.P. § 607a. Also, "before the commencement of the [closing] argument, counsel may deliver and serve "additional proposed instructions to the jury on questions of law developed by the evidence and not disclosed by the pleadings." C.C.P. § 607a.

Judges preferences vary. Some judges prefer to have a complete set of jury instructions before opening statement so that the judge may decide on the appropriate pre-instructions to give the jury prior to opening statement, and so that counsel may comment on the law in opening statement. In practice, counsel should have jury instructions prepared at the time of the pretrial conference and should discuss with the judge and opposing counsel the exact time to submit the complete set of jury instructions. Check Local Rules of Court for specific requirements.

E. Formal Requirements. Except for instructions requested by number reference to California Jury Instructions, Civil (commonly referred to as BAJI Instructions), each proposed jury instruction must be in the form and format specified by California Rules of Court § 201(c) (Superior Court) or 501(b) (Municipal and Justice Courts), and must indicate the party on

Jury Instruction and Closing Argument

whose behalf it is requested. Cal. Rules of Court §§ 229(b), 501(b) 517(b). At the bottom of each instruction must be a citation of authority supporting the statement of law it contains. California Rules of Court 229(a).

Special instructions prepared by counsel must be type written, each on a separate sheet, and must be numbered consecutively, but not firmly bound together. Cal. Rules of Court § 517(b).

F. How to Prepare and Submit Jury Instructions. Counsel will normally be called upon to submit three different kinds of jury instructions. They are: (1) California Jury Instructions, Civil, (BAJI instructions) with no changes or modifications; (2) BAJI instructions with modifications; and (3) specially prepared instructions proposed by counsel.

1. *BAJI Instructions.* The Book of Approved Jury Instructions–Civil (commonly known as BAJI) contains jury instructions that have been prepared by the Committee on Standard Jury Instructions of the Superior Court of Los Angeles County. The California Rules of Court Appendix Division 1 Section 5 recommends that the court use the BAJI instructions wherever applicable. Some Local Court Rules require that BAJI instructions be used whenever applicable.

BAJI does not cover all possible areas. For questions of law not covered by BAJI, one must submit specially prepared jury instructions. Generally, BAJI instructions have been upheld on appeal, and if the BAJI instruction applies, it should be used.

Procedure for requesting BAJI instructions. The request should be on the usual pleading paper with the name of the court, cause, and number. Cal. Rules of Court § 501. The document should be entitled "Instructions Requested by _____". The contents should read "Plaintiff/Defendant request the following numbered BAJI instructions be given:" (The numbers for the requested BAJI instructions should then be listed serially). See Form 11-1 Request for Jury Instructions.

Copies of BAJI instructions are usually available in the trial clerk's office. And, if the BAJI instructions requested are available and not modified, one can simply list the BAJI number on the request. Again, check Local Court Rules for practice in the particular court.

2. *BAJI Instructions as Modified.* Some BAJI instructions require modification prior to submission to the court. The prime example of this is BAJI 2.60, which sets forth which party has the burden of proof, regarding which issues. BAJI 2.60 requires the attorney to state the ultimate facts that the plaintiff has to prove by a preponderance of the evidence to prevail and the ultimate facts that the defendant has to prove in order to prevail on any affirmative defenses. The modified BAJI instructions are submitted by including the BAJI number on the proposed jury instruction request form with a notation in parentheses ("as modified"). A party who submits a modified BAJI instruction should indicate on the instruction with a parentheses or other appropriate means, what part has been modified. Cal. Rules of Court Appendix Division 1 Section 5.

3. *Specially Prepared Jury Instructions.* When BAJI does not contain a jury instruction needed in a particular case, counsel must prepare special jury instructions. The primary sources of law on which special jury instructions are based are statute or court opinions. When counsel relies on either a statute or a court opinion for a special jury instruction, the wording of the instruction should match the wording of the statute or the court opinion as closely as possible, and be applicable to both the party involved and the facts of the case. Each special instruction must contain, at the bottom, a citation of authorities supporting the statement of law therein. California Rules of Court 229a, 517(a). See Form 11-2 Jury Instruction Worksheet.

G. Selection of Jury Instructions. Sometime prior to the closing argument a judge will hold a Chambers Conference and decide which jury instructions to give.

Under C.C.P. § 607a, the court must do the following on request of counsel prior to closing argument:

1. Decide which proposed instructions to give, refuse, or modify;

2. Decide which instructions the court will give on its own motion;

3. Advise counsel of all instructions that will be given.

The judge will hear formal argument from both sides and rule on any objections to and offers of proposed jury instructions. The judge will also rule on the materials that can go with the jury to the deliberation room. The court, usually, will also determine which verdict and special finding forms, if any, will be submitted to the jury. See *California Judges Bench Book; Civil Trials,* § 13.19. Check Local Rules of Court for detailed description of Chambers Conference regarding jury instructions.

After the court has made its final determination of which instruction to give, refuse, or modify, it will indicate its disposition on each individual instruction and sign or initial it. Upon request, the court will indicate the reasons for refusing the instruction and should indicate on the refused instruction the reason for the refusal. California Rules of Court 229c, 519c.

While C.C.P. § 647 provides that an objection to a refused instruction is automatic, it is better practice for counsel to make a specific objection to specific instructions which counsel believes to be erroneous, excluded, or included. Counsel should be wary of agreeing to, or stipulating to the jury instructions. If there are any reservations about the correctness or appropriateness of any jury instructions review and discuss them with the judge or opposing counsel.

11.2 CLOSING ARGUMENT

A. Purposes. Following the presentation of evidence, the closing argument is made to either a judge sitting without a jury or to a jury. During closing argument, the attorney attempts to convince the judge or jury that the evidence presented requires certain conclusions that necessitate a particular verdict or decision in light of the applicable law. Lawsuits are won by what happens during an entire trial. Rarely will an attorney be able to convince the judge or jury of the legitimacy of the attorney's cause in summation if the attorney was not able to do so during the presentation of the evidence.

The value of closing argument, however, should not be minimized. It is important for several reasons.

1. The closing argument, prepared in advance of trial, provides the focus, structure, and themes for the entire trial. The entire case points to the final argument and should be prepared and presented to be consistent with the closing. The focus, structure, and themes of the final argument will be those used in preparation, voir dire, opening, direct, and cross examination.

2. Closing argument is the attorney's last opportunity to summarize for the fact finder what the evidence has shown.

3. Summation is the most effective occasion to explain the significance of the evidence.

4. The closing is the time when the creative trial lawyer can draw inferences, argue conclusions, comment on credibility, refer to common sense, and explain implications which the fact finder may not perceive.

5. Closing argument is the only chance the attorney will have to explain and comment on the judge's jury instructions and to weave the facts and law together.

6. Summation is the attorney's last opportunity to urge the fact finder to take a specific course of action.

B. Right to Closing Argument and Order of Argument

1. *Right to Argument.* In a jury trial both Plaintiff and Defendant have an absolute right to make closing argument to the jury. Either or both may waive that right. C.C.P. § 607(7), (8). There is no such absolute right in a case tried to a judge without a jury, Kenny v. Trust Oil Co., 215 Cal.App.2d 305, 307, 29 Cal.Rptr. 909, 910 (1963). Most judges allow closing argument. Failure to allow closing argument has been held to be reversible error in some cases. Gillette v. Gillette, 180 Cal.App.2d 777, 4 Cal.Rptr. 700 (1960).

2. *Order of Argument.* C.C.P. § 607 provides that unless "special reason" exists the Plaintiff "must commence and may conclude the argument." C.C.P. § 607(7).

If the defendant has the burden of proof in the case, the judge may allow the defendant to open and close final argument.

The last opportunity to argue may be a significant advantage. If an attorney does not have the last opportunity to argue it is permissible and advisable to tell the jury that the law does not allow an opportunity to rebut what opposing counsel will say in the closing final argument and that failure to rebut does not mean agreements.

C. What Can Be Argued

1. *Facts.* Facts and opinions presented by any side of the case which are a part of the record, even those in dispute, may be part of the closing argument and may be persuasively woven into the presentation.

2. *Inferences.* Inferences are reasonable conclusions drawn from the evidence presented. Generally, the attorney may draw all permissible inferences from any of the facts on the record so long as the inferences are logically related to the evidence presented.

3. *No Requirement to Discuss All Facts.* The attorney is not required to summarize or comment upon any facts whether supportive or contrary to the theories of the case. Closing argument should, however, summarize and emphasize the major points the attorney attempted to establish throughout the trial. A failure to comment on or refute a credible position developed by the opposing counsel may prove fatal. A decision not to address an issue, theory, or particular fact should be based on an analysis of the importance of that item and the opponent's ability to present the point persuasively.

4. *Urging a Result.* Closing argument is the time to convince the jury that the facts and the law support a verdict in favor of the client, that the verdict will result in justice being done and that the jury will have met their responsibility as jurors. In a court trial, summation is used to persuade the judge that certain findings of fact and conclusions of law have been established.

5. *Closing Limited to Rebuttal.* The scope of Plaintiff's (or Defendant with burden of proof) closing final argument is limited to rebuttal. That is, Plaintiff is limited to answering arguments raised by the defendant during the defendant's argument. California Judge's Benchbook Civil Trials § 12.19 (CAL CJER 1981).

11.3 PREPARATION AND ORGANIZATION OF CLOSING ARGUMENT

See Form 11–3 Closing Argument Worksheet

A. Early Preparation. The preparation of a case for trial should include the planning of the closing argument. The closing argument provides the focus for the entire case. Throughout all facets of the trial, the attorney should be preparing the jury or judge for what will be heard during the closing argument. A closing argument should reemphasize the central theme and major points repeatedly presented to the jury in voir dire, opening statement, and case presentation. The factual and legal foundation that supports the closing argument must be laid throughout the entire case presentation. The preparation of a closing argument will resemble preparation efforts for an opening statement. See Chapter 8, Opening Statement.

B. Refining the Issues and Theme for the Case. The issues, theme and theories of case preparation provide a framework for the closing argument. These concepts may need to be refined or expanded depending on how the evidence was developed during the trial.

C. Jury Instructions. Prior to the closing argument the judge will inform the attorneys of the exact instructions of law to be provided to the jury. See Sections 11.1 and 11.2. Review these final instructions to make certain that the evidence explained in summation supports the elements of law as explained by the judge.

Any statement of the law by the attorney must be accurate. Know what the judge will say and define the law exactly as the judge does. The judge will tell the jury that if the attorney has defined the law differently the jury must ignore the attorney's statement. If there is a misstatement of the law the attorney will lose credibility and diminish the impact of an otherwise good closing.

D. Anticipate the Opponent's Position. The preparation of the case requires an attorney to anticipate the various issues, themes, and theories of the opposing lawyer. By the close of the evidence, know what the opposing attorney will argue in closing argument.

E. Select Visual Aids and Exhibits. Decide whether to use any visual aids or trial exhibits during the closing argument. Give consideration to the impact the visual aid or exhibit may have on the jury, the importance of the exhibit in the trial, and whether the attorney is capable of effectively using these tools.

Real evidence, demonstrative evidence, deposition transcripts, witness statements, discovery responses, and any other exhibit that has been introduced may be used during closing argument. Visual aids may be used if they accurately depict evidence that has already been presented or otherwise help the jurors decide the case within the confines of the evidence.

Most trial judges allow the use of visual aids that have not been received in evidence provided that the material to be displayed by the visual aid is in evidence. This includes blowup of documents such as contracts and important jury instructions, using posters, photographic enlargements or overhead projection of transparencies. California Judges Benchbook: Civil Trial § 12.23 (CAL CJER 1981).

F. Written Outline or Detailed Script. The final argument outline that was prepared during trial preparation usually needs to be revised to reflect all the evidence presented during trial. Some lawyers prefer to write or dictate a complete closing argument. This approach may help finalize the contents of the closing argument and determine whether some matter has been omitted. A script should not, however, be used during the presentation of the closing argument to the jury. Reading a script will quickly bore the jurors and significantly diminish the persuasive power of the presentation. Reading will appear dry and impersonal. Instead, prepare a key word outline from the script. With practice and preparation, the outline should be all that is needed during final argument.

G. Practice. Rehearse the argument before presentation to the jury. Verbally practicing the closing argument will help improve both its content and the style of delivery. Rehearse the closing argument before colleagues or others, in front of a mirror, or on videotape for later review and critique.

H. Local Requirements. Ascertain before summation whether the trial judge has any special requirements or limitations regarding the argument. This determination will avoid having the closing argument interrupted by the trial judge or opposing counsel. Local rules and procedures, such as the prohibition of the use of some trial exhibits during closing argument, may limit what can be done during summation.

11.4 STRUCTURE OF A CLOSING ARGUMENT

A closing argument must be presented in a structured, ordered fashion. Plan and shape it to conform to the theory, facts, themes, and circumstances of the case. Any structure is appropriate provided it is simple and clear. While a chronological story is one effective way of structuring a closing argument, other structures can be equally effective depending on the circumstances. The facts can be presented in the order in which the witnesses testified. The evidence could be explained by describing the undisputed facts first and then summarizing the disputed facts. A flashback technique can be used by explaining the end of the story and flashing back to earlier events. Injuries and damages could be described first and then the facts surrounding liability could be described. The story can be presented in topical or emotional clusters.

An effective technique to determine the most effective structure is to review the initial outline of the proposed closing argument and then move the segments around experimenting with different presentation patterns keeping an open mind until the most clear and persuasive structure appears.

A. Introduction. Summation should begin with an introduction that draws the jury's attention and interest to the case. The jury's attention level will often be high during summation because they realize the trial is nearing a conclusion. The introduction should highlight the information, facts, and themes the jury should remember.

Some attorneys begin summation by indicating that the trial is almost over and thanking the jurors. This courteous explanation, if done with sincerity, may be effective. On the other hand, it can be stated at a later stage of summation, preserving the introduction for more important purposes. One should consider using a more dramatic or aggressive approach that piques the jury's attention to what will follow.

Consider the following techniques:

1. Focus on some dramatic or compelling testimony that strongly reinforces the theme of the case. Use it to highlight your theme of the case.

2. Focus on your client's strong points to engender sympathy or empathy. Use this to make the jury want to find for your client so that they will listen to your argument to find reasons to find for your client.

3. Focus on the obvious wrongs of the opponent so that the jury listens for reasons to find against your opponent.

B. Explanation of Purpose. Some attorneys begin a closing argument with an explanation of the purpose of summation. The advantage of these preliminary remarks is that the jurors may better understand the value and import of the closing arguments. The disadvantage of these remarks is that they may not be the most persuasive way to begin summation.

Introductory "boiler plate" remarks are often used because the attorney needs something comfortable to say to reduce nervousness, is unprepared, does not know how to structure a final argument, or has heard someone else say the same thing and has never thought through about the need to begin the presentation in a more persuasive way.

C. Argument. The closing argument allows an attorney to say almost anything that falls within the broad definition of argument. An attorney may:

1. Draw reasonable inferences from direct or circumstantial evidence,

2. Suggest that certain evidence implies a reasonable conclusion,

3. Present conclusions based upon the circumstances of the case,

4. Use analogies and metaphors to explain the import of certain situations,

5. Suggest that the jurors apply their common sense and life experiences in determining a fact, and

6. Comment on the credibility of witnesses.

The primary tasks in closing argument are to be creative, innovative, and explain to the jury the significance of inferences to the jury. The direct and circumstantial evidence may lead jurors to clear and obvious conclusions. Explain the less obvious conclusions to the jurors. Highlight the subtleties and nuances of the facts presented.

D. Explanation of the Evidence. Much of a closing argument consists of the attorney summarizing and explaining the evidence. Descriptions should be consistent with the facts described in the opening statement and with the evidence produced during the trial. Be careful not to exaggerate the nature of the evidence presented during the trial. Jurors will easily recognize overstatements and will lose faith in the credibility of the attorney. Some attorneys will take closing argument to an extreme arguing that certain evidence has more value than a reasonable juror would give to that evidence. This approach generally fails because the jury understands that they are the finders of fact and not the attorney.

1. *The Story.* The explanation of the facts may be told in a story form which includes descriptions of the scene, the characters, and the event. The goal is to summarize such facts in a way that is reasonable and consistent with the recollection and memory of the jurors. Keep in mind that the jurors have heard the evidence and need to be accurately reminded of the facts and not misled by inaccurate argument.

2. *Reference to Actual Testimony.* Employ the words used by the witnesses or supported by the contents of documents. Neither overstate the facts nor understate them. Quoting testimony of a witness and mixing the quote with a factual summary may be an effective approach. Reading testimony from a transcript (not usually available) of the case is also permissible.

3. *Detail and Corroboration.* The amount of detailed facts included in a closing argument depends upon the circumstances of the case. A very detailed factual explanation has the advantage of refreshing the recollection of the jury and explaining evidentiary relationships that may not have been obvious during the trial. A detailed presentation has the disadvantage that the jury's memory of the evidence may differ from the attorney's explanation. A detailed explanation will be more effective if the attorney accurately and consistently summarizes the details.

E. Explanation of Law. The judge will usually give final jury instructions after closing argument to the jurors. The judge may give some before closing argument. The attorney may believe that some instructions do not adequately or clearly explain the law. In these situations, comment on the instructions and provide an expanded description of an instruction or its meaning provided it is not at variance with instructions that the court has or will give.

In either case, the attorney will know what Jury Instructions will be given. The attorney may refer to some, read some or even use blow ups of especially important ones as visual aids.

The attorney must not deviate from the Jury Instructions selected by the judge or explain them in a way that is misleading or inaccurate.

F. Conclusion. Conclude with a climactic ending. Review the facts, the themes, and the law to create a conclusion that leaves the jury believing that the requested verdict is the only fair and just verdict. The final remarks of a presentation are likely to be remembered by the audience. Even if there have been some problems in the argument and the attorney gets flustered or lost, a strong conclusion helps offset these problems. The conclusion of the argument should be well thought out, well prepared, and make clear what is being requested of the jury. Remember the principle of "primacy" and "recency" that is, jurors remember and form opinions based on that which they hear first and that which they hear *last*.

The conclusion will also be an opportunity for an attorney to politely and sincerely thank the jurors for their time and attention. Most jurors will appreciate this courtesy if done appropriately.

G. Jury Participation. Design the closing argument to actively involve the jurors in the presentation. The conclusions the attorney suggests during closing argument should not be the attorney's position but rather should be a position that the jurors have reached and adopted as their own. Most of the statements an attorney makes during summation should reaffirm conclusions and deductions the jurors have already adopted having listened to the voir dire, opening statement, and presentation of the evidence. The inferences the attorney explains during summation should parallel many of the inferences the jurors have already made.

The more the jurors mentally participate in the trial the stronger their conviction will be during deliberation. Do not approach summation with the idea that all the jurors need to be persuaded by all of the arguments. Many jurors will have already made decisions regarding certain facts, inferences, and arguments. Recognize this phenomenon and employ techniques that take advantage of it. One technique is to advise the jurors that much of what will be said during closing argument will only reaffirm what they have been thinking already.

H. Length. Summation should be long enough to cover the essential arguments of the case, yet short enough to maintain the jurors' attention. The optimum length for a closing argument varies depending upon the circumstances and complexity of the case and the attorney's speaking ability. Many closing arguments last between twenty and forty minutes. The longer a closing argument is the more difficult maintaining the interest of the jurors will be and the more need there will be for visual aids.

Jury Instruction and Closing Argument 11–9

I. A Final Argument Test. After constructing the closing argument, the attorney can reflect on the following test to determine if the argument is adequate:

1. Does the closing argument tell the jury why to find for the client?
2. Does the closing argument make the jury want to find for the client?
3. Does the closing argument tell the jury how to find for the client?
4. Does the closing argument have a structure that is clear and simple?
5. Is the closing argument reasonable and consistent with the opening statement, the facts, and the law?
6. Does the closing argument give a basis or a reason to award each element of monetary damages claimed.

11.5 CONTENT OF CLOSING ARGUMENT

A. Analogies/Anecdotes. The jury will base their verdict upon common sense and life experiences in addition to the facts and law presented during trial. Concrete images described through an analogy or anecdote can assist the jury in understanding a point of law or application of fact to law. An effective story will command the jurors' attention and will provide them with a comparison to determine the appropriateness of a point made during argument.

While a carefully drawn, common sense anecdote or analogy may assist the jury in understanding a concept, give careful consideration before one is used. If the analogy or anecdote is too simple or does not make sense, there will be no impact. If there is an opportunity to argue following the presentation of an analogy or anecdote, the opponent could use the analogy or anecdote as a part of the opponent's case or may make the analogy or anecdote appear foolish or simplistic by carrying it out to its logical or illogical extreme. Consider whether they need to be employed, whether they are reasonable and convincing, and whether an opponent could turn them around or make the argument look silly.

B. Credibility of Witnesses. An attorney may comment on the credibility of a witness, may demonstrate how an observation or statement is inaccurate, or may attempt to show a witness is biased or prejudiced. Impeachment techniques may be used during the trial to establish facts that reduce a witness' credibility. During closing the attorney can summarize different facts and inferences that have been established and argue that a witness should not be believed or that a witness' perceptions are unlikely or improbable. The attorney may also refer to the instruction on credibility that the judge will provide. See BAJI 2.20, 2.22, 2.24, 2.26.

C. Contradictions. It will be obvious to the jury that a dispute exists between the parties. However, the specific factual contradictions that exist in the case will not always be obvious. Many cases do not involve major factual differences, but rather involve contrary inferences and conclusions. Highlight the inconsistencies between witnesses, point out the contradictions in testimony, and make certain the jury understands the issues in dispute.

D. The Use of Exhibits and Visual Aids. The design, placement, and use of exhibits and visual aids in the presentation are as important as the visual aid or exhibit itself. The impact words and colors on visual aids, the importance of the exhibit in the trial, the location in the room for clear viewing and easy access, the placement in the order of the presentation, and the lawyer's use and reference of the exhibit are important considerations in determining whether the exhibit will aid or interfere with the final argument.

E. Burden of Proof. Consideration must be given regarding whether the judge's instructions defining preponderance of the evidence are sufficient. In most cases the requirements of the term "by a preponderance of the evidence" must be repeated, emphasized, explained, and related to the facts. Many jurors confuse the burden of proof in a civil case and think that the phrase "beyond a reasonable doubt" which they have heard countless times in movies, books, and television should apply.

F. Liability and Damages—Which to Argue First. A plaintiff may prefer to argue damages after explaining the basis for liability. This tactic may leave the jurors at an emotional peak with a lasting impression of the damages the plaintiff has suffered. A defense attorney may prefer to argue initially against damages and then argue lack of liability. This approach may reduce the awkwardness of having to explain the possibility of damages after arguing the plaintiff has no right to recover.

G. Case Weaknesses. Every case will have some weak points that must be addressed in closing argument. If an attorney can think of a reasonable interpretation that reduces the obvious weakness of a point, that explanation should be provided the jury. If the attorney cannot think of any mitigating explanation, the weakness should be conceded in a candid and forthright manner. This disclosure may enhance the credibility of the attorney and reduce the impact of the opposition's focus on that weakness.

H. Attacking Opposition's Positions. An effective technique may be to attack the logic and reasonableness of the opponent's contentions. Select one or more specific arguments of the opponent, demonstrate the weakness of the evidence or contentions, and explain how this information must be reconciled in favor of the attorney's client.

Using major portions of the closing argument to respond to an opponent's issues, positions and argument is inadvisable. Arguments which attack the opponent's case must be balanced with arguments that support your case. The defendant must usually spend more time attacking plaintiff's case because the defendant does not have rebuttal as does plaintiff.

I. Broken Promises. During opening statement the opposition may have described alleged facts to the jury for which no evidence has been introduced during the trial or may have made some promises to the jury which have not been met. Review statements made during the opening and inform the jury that opposing counsel has failed to do what was described or promised.

J. Non-facts. An attorney may comment on the facts that have not been introduced as well as the facts that have been introduced in the case. If the opposition has failed to have a witness testify; if a witness fails to attend a trial and testify, or if a witness is unable to recall certain important points, an attorney may comment on the significance of that non-evidence. Evid.C. § 412. Commenting on the lack of certain evidence if that information is protected by a privilege may be improper. Evid.C. § 913(a).

K. Lie v. Mistake. Every trial involves contradictory evidence pitting one witness against another. Few witnesses will deserve to be called a liar. Describing a witness as being mistaken about a fact rather than denigrating that individual by suggesting that perjury was committed will usually be more effective. It may be sufficient to point out that everyone sees an event from different perspectives and how the witness has perceived an event may be a mistaken observation based on an incorrect initial perspective. There are some instances in which it is absolutely clear that a witness lied. If so, say so.

L. Rhetorical Questions. Rhetorical questions can be an effective tool of persuasion because they involve the jurors in the presentation. The essential aspect of a rhetorical question is that, after the question has been asked, the answer should be obvious. Never answer the rhetorical question. The jurors should answer it silently to themselves. When a juror has answered a rhetorical question, the thought becomes that of the juror and not just another part of the closing.

Rhetorical questions may, however, diminish the positive force of summation. The jurors may not answer the rhetorical question in the same way the attorney will, and there is no way to know for sure. They and you may have missed a point.

M. Emotion v. Logic. In some cases, presenting a rational, logical explanation of the evidence and the law will be effective. In other cases, relying on the emotions and feelings created by the facts will be more effective. Often a mixture of both approaches is required. Carefully balance the use of emotion in a case. An attorney may more dramatically present an argument by relying upon its emotional aspects, but one should be cautious and not overly play to the the passion and prejudice of the jurors.

Jury Instruction and Closing Argument 11-11

N. Avoiding Improper Comments. Section 9.8 describes in detail types of comments that will be inappropriate during closing argument. Some comments may not fall within the category of unethical or legally improper statements but may offend the jury. Comments that denounce the opposing counsel, party, or witnesses may damage the attorney's image unless evidence has been produced during the trial to support these comments.

O. Rebuttal. The party who has the burden of proof and the opportunity to begin the closing argument may also conclude summation with a rebuttal. It may be necessary to reserve time for rebuttal by requesting permission from the judge. The points made during a rebuttal should be limited to rebutting points made by the opposition during that closing argument. Cortez v. Macias, 110 Cal.App.3d 640, 167 Cal.Rptr. 905 (1980). Plan the rebuttal in advance and coordinate it with the initial closing. Revisions and additions can be made during and after the opposition's summation.

P. Request for Verdict and Damages. The closing argument must include an explanation of the verdict requested and in a case for damages should include a list of the damages claimed and the amount if the amount can be specified.

In a personal injury case, for example, the attorney should make and display a visual aid setting forth the damages requested, e.g.:

Medical Expenses:	Amount	$_____
Lost earnings (to date):	Amount	$_____
Future lost earnings:	Amount	$_____
Cost of retraining:	Amount	$_____
Physical pain and suffering:	Suggested Range	$_____-_____
Mental pain and anguish:	Suggested Range	$_____-_____

11.6 PRESENTATION AND DELIVERY

The manner in which the attorney delivers a closing argument will affect the jurors' understanding of the evidence, significantly influence many of their conclusions about the case, and shape their deliberations and verdict. The more effective and persuasive an attorney can be in presenting a closing argument the greater the chance that a favorable verdict will be reached by a jury. If the evidence presented in a case is weak, the attorney will have little or no chance to convince the jury in closing argument. If the evidence presented during trial was strong, statements made by the attorney during summation will most likely match the conclusions the jury has already reached. If, however, the evidence presented by both sides is balanced, then the closing argument becomes vitally important and may determine which verdict the jury returns.

Many of the same factors that influence the manner and presentation of an opening statement affect summation. Before presenting a closing argument, review the factors in § 8.6 regarding Presentation and Delivery of the Opening Statement. In addition to the consideration listed in § 8.6, consider the following in making your closing argument:

1. *Rapport With the Jury.* At this point of the trial the attorney should know intuitively how the jury feels about the attorney and the client. Look for body language clues, and proceed accordingly. If the jury is very receptive, go very close; if hesitant, watch for signs to approach; if standoffish—standoff and look for an opening.

Do not rush in like a fool where wise men fear to tread.

2. *Sincerity/Integrity.* The jury has probably formed some opinions of these traits by this phase of the trial. Be aware of this. Is there some arrogance or haughtiness by the attorney that must be dispelled? Can this be resolved or abated by appearing genuinely humble and sincere on closing? Did the client appear less than sincere and truthful? What can be done to negate this impression?

3. *Overall Manner of Delivery.* After all the evidence is in, and the jury instructions have been approved, and the attorney has had the chance to assess the judge and the jury, it comes down to the subjective opinion of the attorney arguing the case.

Be yourself! If you are emotional—be emotional. If you are analytical, be analytic. If you are a story teller—tell stories. If you are humorous, be humorous. But be yourself, at your best and tell the jury why your side should prevail.

11.7 OBJECTIONS

Section 6.8 lists common objections that may be asserted during closing argument. If an attorney has an opportunity for a closing argument or rebuttal after the opposition, that attorney may prefer not to object but later comment on the inappropriate statement made by the opposing lawyer. If an attorney has no further summation, then an objection and a curative instruction may be necessary to repair any damage. Moreover, an objection and a request for a curative instruction may be necessary to preserve a matter for appeal.

Most attorneys will not object during final argument unless the opponent is saying or doing something that is clearly improper and damaging to the case. Attorneys usually extend a courtesy to each other so that the final arguments are uninterrupted. The court may interrupt an attorney on final argument on its own motion if the law is misstated or stated incompletely, and to curb misconduct. California Judges Bench Book, Civil Trials § 12.24 (CAL CJER 1981).

REQUEST FOR JURY INSTRUCTIONS

CHARLES W. ABLE
1234 Main Street
San Diego, CA 92123
(619) 234-5678
Attorney for Plaintiff
MICHAEL GARBER

SUPERIOR COURT OF THE STATE OF CALIFORNIA
FOR THE COUNTY OF SAN DIEGO

MICHAEL GARBER
                                    Plaintiff,
v.
JAMES DOE,
                                   Defendant.

CASE NO. _____
PLAINTIFF/DEFENDANT _____
PROPOSED JURY INSTRUCTIONS

    Plaintiff/Defendant (insert name) requests that the following BAJI instructions be given (here list numbers of BAJI instructions to be given: e.g., BAJI 1.01, 1.02).

    The following BAJI instructions are requested to be given with modifications (e.g., 2.60).

    In addition Plaintiff/Defendant requests that the court give the attached special instructions and other instructions that may be required based on the evidence.

Dated: _____   _____
                                                                 Attorney for Plaintiff/Defendant

Form 11-1

JURY INSTRUCTIONS WORKSHEET

A. BAJI instructions (unmodified) list by BAJI number: _____
_____
_____
_____

B. BAJI instructions, as modified: _____
_____
_____
_____

C. BAJI 2.60 as modified:

    1. Facts which plaintiff must prove by a preponderance of the evidence:

    1st cause of action (list facts to prove each contested element). _____
_____
_____

    2nd cause of action. _____
_____
_____

    3rd cause of action. _____
_____
_____

    2. Facts defendant must prove by a preponderance of the evidence:

    1st affirmative defense. _____
_____
_____

    2nd affirmative defense. _____
_____
_____

Form 11-2

D. Special jury instructions needed:

1. Special instruction No. 1. _____
_____
_____

Authority. _____

Special Instruction No. 2. _____
_____
_____

Authority. _____

Special Instruction No. 3. _____
_____
_____

Authority. _____

Special Instruction No. 4. _____
_____
_____

Authority. _____

Special Instruction No. 5. _____
_____
_____

Authority. _____

Special Instruction No. 6. _____
_____
_____

Authority. _____

Form 11-2 (continued)

CLOSING ARGUMENT WORKSHEET

Case _____   File _____

Themes/Theories _____
_____
_____
_____
_____
_____
_____

Introduction _____
_____
_____
_____
_____

Facts _____
_____
_____
_____
_____
_____

Inferences _____
_____
_____
_____
_____
_____

Credibility of Witnesses _____
_____
_____
_____
_____

Form 11-3

Analogies/Anecdotes _____
_____
_____
_____
_____

Exhibits/Visual Aids _____
_____
_____
_____
_____

Case Weaknesses _____
_____
_____
_____
_____
_____

Opposing Argument _____
_____
_____
_____
_____
_____

Facts Not Proved/Promises Not Kept _____
_____
_____
_____
_____
_____

Form 11-3 (continued)

Jury Instructions _____

Damages _____

Conclusion _____

Form 11-3 (continued)

Chapter 12
VERDICT AND POST VERDICT MOTIONS

Table of Sections

Sec.
12.1 Jury Deliberation Procedures.
12.2 The Verdict.
    A. General Verdict.
    B. Special Verdict.
    C. Reading of Verdict.
    D. Entry of Verdict.
12.3 Post Trial Motions.
    A. Motion for Judgment Notwithstanding the Verdict.
    B. Motion for a New Trial.
    C. Motion to Vacate Judgment.

Forms
12-1 Post Trial Motion Worksheet.

12.1 JURY DELIBERATION PROCEDURES

After the judge has instructed the jury, the jurors will be sworn to render a true verdict, and will be placed under the bailiff's charge to start secret deliberations. When the jury retires for deliberation, it may take the following:

1. All papers that have been received in evidence, except depositions. C.C.P. § 612.

2. Any exhibits the court considers proper. C.C.P. § 612.

3. Any notes the jurors have personally taken of the testimony or proceedings. C.C.P. § 612.

4. In the court's discretion, the written jury instructions given. C.C.P. § 612.5.

The jury may also ask for certain testimony to be reread. See Hutton v. Brookside Hospital, 213 Cal.App.2d 350, 353, 28 Cal.Rptr. 774, 776 (1963). The jury may also request a rereading of the jury instructions Asplund v. Driskell, 225 Cal.App.2d 705, 712, 37 Cal.Rptr. 652, 655 (1964). If the original jury instructions are faulty or inadequate, the trial court may give proper additional instructions where the jury's questions indicate confusion or need for clarification. Bartosh v. Banning, 25 Cal.App.2d 378, 387, 59 Cal.Rptr. 382, 388 (1967).

12.2 THE VERDICT

The jury's verdict can be either general or special. In either case, a vote of at least three-fourths (¾) of the jury is necessary to render a verdict. C.C.P. § 624. California Constitution Article I § 16; C.C.P. § 618.

A. General Verdict. "A general verdict is that by which they pronounce generally upon all or any of the issues, either in favor of the plaintiff or defendant". C.C.P. § 624: A general verdict is a finding in favor of the prevailing party on every fact essential to the support of his action or defense. Price v. Beacons Van and Storage Company, 179 Cal. 326, 328, 176 P. 452 (1918).

B. Special Verdict. "A special verdict is one in which the jury finds the facts only leaving the judgment to the court. It "must present the conclusions of fact as established by the evidence, and those conclusions of fact must be so presented as nothing shall remain to the court, but to draw from them conclusions of law." C.C.P. § 624. The special verdict generally consists of a series of questions for the jury to answer. Once these questions of ultimate fact are resolved by the jury, the judge then can make a decision as a matter of law which constitutes the judgment in the case. See Estate of Keithley, 134 Cal. 9, 66 P. 5 (1901).

C. Reading of Verdict. Verdict forms are usually given to the jury to fill in with the names of the parties for and against whom the verdict is found, the amount of damages awarded and any other conclusions to be reached. The verdict forms should be worded in such a way that the jury may use them for any of the possible conclusions to which they may arrive. See e.g. BAJI Forms 16.00–16.90.

When the jury has agreed on a verdict, they are led into the courtroom by the bailiff, and the written verdict signed by the foreman is read to the jury by the clerk, and they are asked whether it is their verdict. Either party may have the jury polled, and if the inquiry discloses a disagreement by more than one-fourth (¼) of the jury, they may be sent out again to correct the verdict. If no discrepancy is noted, "the verdict is complete and the jury discharged from the case". C.C.P. § 618.

D. Entry of Verdict. Upon the completion of the verdict, a minute entry is made specifying the time of trial, names of the jurors and witnesses, and setting out the verdict. C.C.P. § 628. Where a special verdict is found, it is filed with the clerk and entered in the minutes, and the minute entry will later be used to set forth the judgment rendered on the basis of the special verdict. C.C.P. §§ 625–628. See California Judge's Bench Book, Civil Trials, Chapters 14 and 15 for complete discussion of jury deliberation and verdict.

12.3 POST TRIAL MOTIONS

After a verdict, one or both parties may submit post trial motions requesting the court to review the verdict. These motions will often be required in order to preserve the right to appeal. See Form 12–1 Post Trial Motion Worksheet.

A. Motion for Judgment Notwithstanding the Verdict. A motion for Judgment Notwithstanding the Verdict (Judgment N.O.V.) may be made after the verdict has been returned by the jury. The basis for determining whether to grant or deny this motion is identical to a motion for directed verdict. If the trial court determines that there is no substantial evidence to support the verdict, the court may grant a judgment notwithstanding the verdict under C.C.P. § 629. The motion may be made by either party, or the court may act on its own motion after five (5) days notice to the parties. This motion does not address adequacy or inadequacy of damages. Rather, the sole issue is whether there is a substantial conflict in the evidence. It can only be sustained on appeal, where, as a matter of law, no other reasonable conclusion can legally be deduced from the evidence, and any other holding would be so lacking in evidentiary support that the reviewing court would be compelled to reverse it. Moore v. San Francisco, 5 Cal.App.3d 728, 733, 85 Cal.Rptr. 281, 283 (1970). The time limit for a party moving for a Judgment N.O.V. is the same as a motion for a new trial C.C.P. §§ 629, 659.

B. Motion for a New Trial. A new trial is defined by C.C.P. § 656 as a re-examination of an issue of fact in the same court, after a trial and decision by a jury court or referee. A party may seek a new trial if some irregularity regarding the law, facts, rules, or procedure occurred during the first trial. The grounds for a new trial are wholly statutory, and are found in C.C.P. § 657.

Verdict and Post Verdict Motions

1. *Grounds.* The causes for which a new trial may be granted in whole or in part are:

a) Irregularity in the proceedings of the court, the jury, or the adverse party. C.C.P. § 657(1).

b) Any court order or abuse of discretion that prevented either party from having a fair trial. C.C.P. § 657(1).

c) Jury misconduct. C.C.P. § 657(2).

d) Accident or a surprise against which prudence could not have guarded. C.C.P. § 657(3).

e) Newly discovered evidence that is material for the party making the application and that party could not have discovered with reasonable diligence and produced at the trial. C.C.P. § 657(4).

f) Excessive damages. C.C.P. § 657(5).

g) Inadequate damages. C.C.P. § 657(5).

h) Insufficiency of the evidence. C.C.P. § 657(6).

i) Verdict or other decision is contrary to law. C.C.P. § 657(6).

j) Error in law, occurring at the trial and excepted to by the party moving for a new trial. C.C.P. § 657(7).

2. *Time for Filing.* The Notice of Motion for a new trial must be filed and served either before judgment is entered, or after judgment is entered and within the earliest of the following times:

a) Fifteen (15) days after the court clerk mailed Notice of Entry of Judgment under C.C.P. § 664.5;

b) Fifteen (15) days after any party served a written Notice of Entry of Judgment on the moving party; or,

c) One Hundred and Eighty (180) days after judgment is entered. C.C.P. § 659.

3. *Requirements for Motion.* A party seeking a new trial must file with court clerk and serve on the opposing party a Notice of Intention to Move for a New Trial, stating the grounds with specificity, designating whether the motion will be made on affidavits, declarations, or on the court minutes, or both. C.C.P. § 659.

An application for a new trial must be made on affidavits (or declarations under C.C.P. § 2015.5) if it is based on any of the following grounds:

1. Irregularity in the proceedings of the court, jury, or adverse party;

2. Any court order or abuse of discretion that prevented either party from having a fair trial;

3. Jury misconduct;

4. Accident or surprise that ordinary prudence could not have guarded against;

5. Newly discovered evidence. C.C.P. § 658.

See California Judge's Bench Book, Civil Trials, Chapter 17; Witkin, California Procedure, 3rd Ed., Sections 18 through 137.

C. Motion to Vacate Judgment. Under C.C.P. § 663, a judgment that is based upon a court's findings of fact or the special verdict of a jury may be set aside and vacated for the following reasons, which materially affected the substantial rights of the party and entitle the party to a different judgment:

1. Incorrect or erroneous legal basis for the decision, not consistent with or not support by the facts;

2. A judgment or decree not consistent with or not supported by the special verdict. C.C.P. § 663.

This motion is designed to permit the trial court to correct its own judicial error. The aggrieved party may simply point out the error to the judge, rather than going through the time and expense of obtaining a reversal on appeal. He may move the trial court to correct its own erroneous judgment by amending the judgment to conform to the findings of fact or special verdict.

A motion to vacate judgment must be filed, noticed, and served either (1) before the entry of judgment, (2) within fifteen (15) days after notice of entry of judgment is mailed by the clerk or served by a party, or (3) if no such notice is given within 180 days after entry of judgment. C.C.P. § 663a.

POST TRIAL MOTION WORKSHEET

Case _____   File _____

A. Motion for Judgment Notwithstanding the Verdict. C.C.P. § 629:

   How is verdict unsupported by any substantial evidence?_____
   _____
   _____
   _____
   _____

B. Motion for New Trial Grounds:

   1. Irregularity in proceedings by court, referee, jury, or prevailing party. C.C.P. § 657(1).
   _____
   _____
   _____
   _____

   2. Irregularity in order or abuse of discretion resulting in deprivation of fair trial. C.C.P. § 657(1). _____
   _____
   _____
   _____

   3. Misconduct of jury. C.C.P. § 657(2). _____
   _____
   _____
   _____

   4. Accident or surprise. C.C.P. § 657(3). _____
   _____
   _____
   _____

Form 12-1

5. Newly discovered material evidence. _____

_____

_____

6. Excessive or insufficient damages. C.C.P. § 657(5). _____

_____

_____

7. Errors of law. C.C.P. § 657(7). _____

_____

_____

8. Verdict not justified by evidence or contrary to law. C.C.P. § 657(6). _____

_____

_____

C. Motion to Vacate Judgment Grounds. C.C.P. § 663:

   1. Erroneous legal basis for the decision not consistent or not supported by the facts.

_____

_____

_____

   2. Judgment not supported or inconsistent with the special verdict. _____

_____

_____

_____

†

Form 12-1 (continued)